Praise for *The Career Chase*

"In *The Career Chase*, Helen Harkness does a [   ] job of providing guidelines for the career-minded individual. Cognizant of the constant changes going on in the workplace, Harkness uses her expertise to teach the reader how to evaluate his or her skills, learn what new skills need to be acquired, and how to go on to success from there."

> Edward Cornish
> President
> World Future Society

"Her insights and unique assessment process have literally changed people's lives for the better. Dr. Harkness blends visionary career wisdom and an extensive personality assessment process to bring her clients in touch with what many people scarcely believe possible . . . a job and career that they love."

> Laura Lawrence, M.D.

"Thanks to Dr. Harkness, I have the courage to unlock and peek behind whatever unknown doors challenge me."

> Gene Murray
> Composer in Residence
> Amarillo Opera Inc.

"*The Career Chase* enabled me to transition myself from the fears and unknowns involved in becoming self-employed into a successful, confident entrepreneur."

> Ed Bamberger
> Editing Express!

"If career success is a journey, then Dr. Harkness is an excellent guide. She addresses the key element to successfully changing careers: the psychological component. Her approach will prove invaluable to anyone engaged in this search."

> Alex Roman
> Roman Management Services

"Dr. Harkness is a visionary and a catalyst for guiding adults through these uncertain and chaotic times in the workplace. . . . With Dr. Harkness' business strategies and resources, I launched a consulting firm capitalizing on all my past experiences and knowledge. This book provides the insight into this career redirection process."

> John A. Bell
> Bell & Associates
> Educational Civil Rights and Management Consultants

"Helen Harkness helped to integrate my past business experiences and educational training from several creative fields. My new career allows the opportunity for the 'dailiness' of running a company, while at the same time nourishing my soul in an area of my 'passion.'"

> Sandra C. Goodloe
> The Cuisinary Fine Foods

"Her understanding of what it takes to be a successful entrepreneur helped me to see clearly what was holding me back from success and what was needed to overcome my self-imposed limitations."

> Kathy Maixner
> Owner
> Communicate for Success

"Her incredible intuition, creativity, and inspiration have facilitated powerful changes in people's professional lives . . . her clients also experience powerful changes in their personal lives. I cannot recommend Dr. Harkness highly enough."

> Susan Abrahamson
> President
> Searchcom Inc.

"Helen Harkness: this woman turned my life around. She made me realize I had entrepreneurial talents and should start my own company. Ten years later, I have the satisfaction of owning a growing company."

> Glenn J. Straus
> CMI Straus and Company

"*The Career Chase* is essential for anyone seeking their highest and best calling."

> Madeline Johnson
> President
> Communications and Advocacy

THE CAREER
CHASE

THE CAREER CHASE

TAKING CREATIVE CONTROL IN A CHAOTIC AGE

Helen Harkness

Davies-Black Publishing
Palo Alto, California

Published by Davies-Black Publishing, an imprint of Consulting Psychologists Press, Inc., 3803 East Bayshore Road, Palo Alto, CA 94303; 1-800-624-1765.

Special discounts on bulk quantities of Davies-Black books are available to corporations, professional associations, and other organizations. For details, contact the Director of Book Sales at Davies-Black Publishing, an imprint of Consulting Psychologists Press, Inc., 3803 East Bayshore Road, Palo Alto, CA 94303; 415-691-9123; Fax 415-988-0673.

Cover: Images © 1996 PhotoDisc, Inc.

01 00 99 98 97   10 9 8 7 6 5 4 3 2 1
Printed in the United States of America

Library of Congress Cataloging-in-Publication Data
Harkness, Helen Leslie
    The career chase : taking creative control in a chaotic
age / Helen Leslie Harkness.
        p.   cm.
    Includes bibliographical references and index
    ISBN 0-89106-098-7
    1. Career changes.   2. Vocational guidance.   I. Title.
HF5384.H37   1997
    650.1′4—dc20   96—43661
                                                           CIP

FIRST EDITION
First printing 1997

Contents

Preface   ix

Glossary   xv

**PART I   THE NECESSITY OF CHANGE:
             CAREERS IN COLLISION**

Chapter 1   Career Shock as the Epidemic of Our Age 3

Chapter 2   Careers Caught Between Two Ages 15

Chapter 3   New Skills for a New Age 21

**PART II   THE PAIN OF CHANGE:
             DARK NIGHT OF THE SOUL**

Chapter 4   The Challenge of Change 45

Chapter 5   Career Unrest and Dissatisfaction 55

Chapter 6   Discovering the Sources of Career Unrest 69

Chapter 7   Who Changes Careers and Why? 95

Chapter 8   The Dozen Deadly Myths Defeating
             Contemporary Careers 111

Chapter 9   The Dark Night of the Soul 133

Chapter 10   Facing and Solving the Career Problem 145

**PART III   THE POWER OF CHANGE:
MOVING FROM PAIN TO PERSONAL POWER**

Chapter 11   Overview of the Career Change Process 157

Chapter 12   Self-Assessment 161

Chapter 13   Career Exploration 173

Chapter 14   Future Direction and Focus 181

Chapter 15   Strategic Action Plan 189

Chapter 16   Peak Psychological Points for Change 197

References 209

About the Author 217

Index 219

Preface

"If we have no options, we are slaves."

—Albert Camus

This book is for all adults exploring or interested in career change, whether forced or voluntary. Since successful and lasting personal and career changes start internally, my purpose particularly is to provide insight into the internal factors, those emotional and psychological issues creating both the pleasure and pain of changing careers. These emotional and psychological shifts that occur when we change careers are a very major part of the process and are the least anticipated and understood. Once we move through these internal issues, we are then free to deal more effectively with the very real external barriers and obstacles, as well as identify the opportunities and challenges of changing careers.

If you are seriously considering changing your career, understanding and integrating internal and external realities for a satisfying and potentially profitable future will be one of the most creative challenges in your life.

This book focuses on the process of change as it relates directly to our contemporary careers. It is not a "how to" book focusing on techniques and quick-fix action steps; there are countless other resources that provide these. The focus is on what to expect as you work through all the complex issues involved in a successful career change.

The book is divided into three major parts. Part I: "The Necessity of Change: Careers in Collision," introduces the problems of change and the resulting career shock syndrome—a painful splinter of future shock. It explores the effect of careers caught in a kind of "twilight zone," of being neither here nor there, between the former Industrial Age and our Age of Runaway Technology.

Part I also emphasizes the necessity for us to develop a new personality for the future: Type CC Chaos Chaser, far different from the compulsive, driven Type A or the laid-back, more passive Type B. I coined this term to describe this new personality type, designed to thrive on the edge of chaos, to look at complexity straight on, and to search out the opportunity and the underlying order in the center of our current storm. The Type CC Chaos Chaser is a resilient and resourceful pathfinder, a pioneering spirit, an overcomer, and a lifelong learner and skillbuilder. Such types can embrace change and face the future with confidence and freedom from fear.

Part II: "The Pain of Change: Dark Night of the Soul," identifies the issues and levels of career unrest, assessing and pinpointing its sources and understanding its documented negative effects on our physical and mental health. The twelve deadly myths instrumental in blocking and delaying a career change are discussed briefly to help readers understand our frequently unconscious rules or "half-truths" that defeat and stall our career success.

This part also examines the details and the emotional issues of the falling apart of the former career identity and the growth of the new. This transition is bridged by a "dark night of the soul," following the theme of St. John of the Cross, which is that supreme joy and meaning can only be experienced after venturing through a "dark night" of adversity.

A specific model, the Chaos of Change, is presented next. It traces the emotional and psychological process of career change, a two-step process of falling apart and renewal, a "letting go and taking hold." Delaying tactics are frequently used, but to change careers successfully, we inevitably reach a moment of truth—a time when we decide to face squarely the reality of our career problem and choose to change.

Part III: "The Power of Change: Moving from Pain to Personal Power," focuses on the strength we gain from taking charge of our career. This moving from pain to personal power is the payoff for making a successful career change. This part also outlines the specific steps in a successful career change process:

Step I: *Self-Assessment,* identifying our own DNA fingerprint, our particularly unique success criteria that is our bedrock and will remain constant though perhaps shift in priority throughout our life

Step II: *Career Exploration,* discovering what's out there in the work environment besides our current position and tracking future trends to identify opportunities that match our success criteria

Step III: *Future Direction and Focus,* deciding our future image based on the success criteria developed in the self-assessment step, and the realities discovered in the Career Exploration step

Step IV: *Strategic Action Plan,* designing, implementing, and taking the action steps to gain the new direction identified as our future image

Although this book concentrates primarily on changing careers, many of the principles can be applied to other areas where change plays a key role—and there are no places in our world today that are "change proof."

I wrote this book because I am a teacher, and my payoff comes from seeing people in career pain and paralysis move to their personal power by designing and activating a plan to develop their potential, take creative control, grow, and provide value to our world.

I know that sometimes, in the midst of difficulty and disorder, we can only dimly perceive where we are, what is happening to us, and what actions to take. In the early 1970s, when I was questioning and searching for answers and insight on my own personal and career chaos, reading Alvin Toffler's *Future Shock* was a key experience, a moment of truth providing a missing piece of the pattern that helped me to understand that my problems were not due to some unnamed "failure" on my part. Later, after reading about Prigogine's 1978 Nobel Prize-winning *Theory of Dissipative Structures,* and later applying the chaos theory to our human condition in constant change, I began to value the possibilities of renewal that can come from apparent random disorder.

I could have been more effective in managing my life and career had I read a book outlining in more detail what was happening to the world in which I lived and worked. If only someone had explained, "You are in a painful but potentially positive and profitable process of change. Let me teach you the predictable steps in what seems your negative and totally random chaos, and here are strategies you can use to move through this." With awareness and direction, I could have made more conscious and well-informed choices and avoided wasted time, psychic energy, and financial resources in gaining my eventual career direction and personal power.

Adults today face two realities: First, whether we like it or not, *major change is affecting us all and will continue to do so with even greater impact as we move through the early decades of the twenty-first century.* The sooner we accept the notion that we can *choose to change,* to actually revive and renew ourselves in spite of the continuing chaos and our inexperience in maneuvering through it, the sooner we accept, embrace, and capitalize on change itself, then the better we can channel its positive power into our work and personal lives.

The second reality we are facing is that true change initially can be painful, extremely foreign, and frightening for most of us, particularly when it's unexpected and perceived as uncontrollable, as is most change today. In the glitter of technological possibilities that confront us, we tend to ignore these natural reactions. Consequently, the very real human fear of change is not being addressed directly in our society. The greatest need that adults have currently is to understand the change and its resulting chaos in today's world and to build the skills, personality traits, confidence, and courage to take creative control and to thrive successfully.

In summary, a major purpose of this book is to:

- Introduce the necessity for, but also the problems of, change, especially as it focuses on our work life

- Provide insights into the barriers and outdated half-truths that block career change

- Introduce a chaos of change model for the human elements in the change process

- Describe the basic four steps for making a creative career change

- Encourage people to accept responsibility for their careers by teaching them the process and providing essential information and strategies

- Describe the personality traits critical for career success in the future

As we succeed in taking creative control of our careers, we will develop the personality traits that allow us to understand that we can choose to be creative thrivers in today's chaotic sea of change, that we have options, and that releases a very real, lasting surge of freedom and personal power. We become educated and calculated risktakers rather than victims caught in the twilight zone of former career expectations, disappointments, and achievements.

It is important to realize that getting what we want is not the major problem for most of us: The real issue is knowing what it is! Once we have an image of what we will do in the future, most of us can move toward it with confidence, courage, and the strategies to make it happen. It's the "knowing," not the "getting," that's the major problem of a career change.

My own commitment, experience, and expertise began when I developed the resources to solve my own career problem. I switched from a rather mindless pursuit of a doctorate in English to higher education, and for my dissertation researched everyone I could locate in the United States in any setting doing any work on career and job-related issues. From the scattered resources and my experience as a director of continuing adult eduction and academic dean of a small college, I developed a comprehensive model for what I believed adults in a career crisis needed. I was awarded two Labor Department grants to establish a one-stop pilot career counseling and community referral center in our public library. After training eight paraprofessional counselors in eighteen months, we directly served a total of three thousand adults in career-related activities, plus an additional three thousand by phone in the human service area.

In 1978, I founded Career Design Associates, Inc., and since then, have worked with thousands of adults from all career, economic, professional, educational, and age levels. This is a comprehensive, time-intensive career program, taking people from the very earliest stages to the completion of the career change process, when they are fully focused and actually working successfully in their new career.

"Freedom is knowing your options" has been my motto from the beginning. After you read this book, it is my hope that you will feel the freedom of having options, that you will understand our changing age and see yourself as a pioneer and pathfinder in using to your advantage the "winds of change." My goal is for you to develop the awareness, resources, strategies, attitude, career skills, and indeed the courage to make the transition to a new career that will allow you to take creative control of your life in a chaotic age.

ACKNOWLEDGMENTS

This book is dedicated first to my many clients over the years who, as pathfinders, have taken creative control of their careers, thus demonstrating that we do have options in spite of, or perhaps because of, the changing and chaotic world. We have kept in touch and communicated, and I have watched and learned much from their growth.

I am especially strengthened by and grateful for their willingness to keep in contact, thus creating a community to share information, ideas, and insight to help other clients traveling through the "dark night" of moving from pain to their own personal power in their worklives. Making a public commitment to my clients to complete this writing after long delays and procrastination was frequently the only motivation for keeping at it—a kind of "promise made is a debt unpaid."

A special acknowledgment is due to my parents, John and Ivery Leslie, both independent entrepreneurs and thinkers whose spiritual lessons were actively and daily demonstrated by resourceful and practical help to others. My father took honor and integrity to the highest level, and my mother sang, told stories, ran successful businesses, and made the superwoman role seem deceptively simple until I tried it! I want to formally thank my longtime friends and my children, John, Ann, and Jane, their families and my grandchildren who have been patient with my benign neglect of birthdays and family outings. I thank my sister, Madolyn Stewart, and my business associate, Dr. John A. Bell, whose encouragement kept me focused. I especially value my many long-standing friends who have kindly listened to my ideas as I worked through them.

A special appreciation for the skill of my staff editor, Shelley Fleming, in translating my handwriting; Connie May, my assistant, who picked up countless extra administrative responsibilities; Leslie Burkett, who keeps all our technology under control while writing and researching her dissertation in Information Science on how to organize the vast information available today in a useful form; and Scott Hendrie, our Internet expert.

And thanks to my editors and staff at Davies-Black: Lee Langhammer Law, Melinda Adams Merino, Laura Simonds, and Sharon Sforza, whose enthusiastic spirit on the manuscript was especially heartening and affirming when I needed it.

It is highly appropriate for me to acknowledge the professionals from the many diverse fields who as catalysts have strongly influenced my learning and thinking, thus enabling me to develop the Career Design™ process that capitalizes on all my strengths as a teacher and provides my clients with the resources and information to take control of their careers: Roderic Duchemin, Daryl Dunham, William Moore, Alvin Toffler, Marilyn Ferguson, John Holland, Dick Knowdell, Peter Drucker, Ilya Prigogine, and Thomas Kuhn.

The works of countless others impact my thinking as I provide the resources and the strategies for my clients in taking creative career control. These include: Carl Jung, James O'Toole, John Naisbitt, Studs Terkel, Rollo May, Joseph Campbell, Frederic Flach, David Viscott, John Gardner, James Hillman, Tom Peters, William Redford, John Crystle, Richard Bolles, and Roberto Assagioli.

Glossary

Career Collision   our former career expectations for success clashing with the current realities in the workplace.

Career Shock   a painful splinter of future shock. The effect of careers caught in a kind of "twilight zone," of being neither here nor there, between the former Industrial Age and our Age of Runaway Technology.

Career Shock Syndrome   paralysis and pain created by the shocking and sudden realization of the vast gap between your career expectations and aspirations, and your actual achievement.

Career Unrest   fallout from Career Shock created by the collision between our current job and career reality, and our past expectations. More than a "blue funk down day," it can range from occasional dull feelings of incompleteness to prolonged physical, intellectual, and psychological ill health.

CC = P > F   equation indicating that career change takes place only when the pain of the current situation is greater than the fear of the unknown and of the potential new situation.

Chaos of Change Model   a model sketching the emotional/psychological pain and power process of loss and positive change. The falling apart of the old and the birth and renewal of the new, bridged by the "dark night of the soul."

Creative Rate of Recovery   the recognition that an emotional impasse or downturn is beginning and that it is time to consciously activate your safety valve.

Dark Night of the Soul   the necessary but painful and emotional time of adversity bridging the movement or growth from the old identity to the new.

Glass Balls   the top priorities in personal and work life. They demand attention and care and should not be ignored or dropped and broken, for they cannot be repaired.

Future Image   the vision or picture of yourself that guides you and provides direction in your life and career in the years ahead. It's developed by knowing yourself and your success criteria, and matching these to external environmental realities.

Future Shock   coined by Alvin Toffler to name the fear and emotional conditions resulting from being suddenly ejected from the comfort zone of the familiar and forced to travel with an incomplete and inaccurate map through unknown and fearful territory where all the rules are different.

Old Career Paradigm   the former model of expected success up a career ladder in a Womb-to-Tomb environment with a benevolent patriarchal controlling culture promising lifetime tenure.

Power Point   a moment of truth, a blinding glimpse of the obvious, an "Aha! I see!" that shifts your past reality to a new point of view that changes your perceptions.

Proteus Principles   a model for modern people, deeply steeped in wisdom. Proteus, a Greek mythical god, had the skill of creative foresight and the ability and readiness to transform and rapidly change shapes when he sensed danger. Proteus also balanced his life and work with rest and repose.

Rubber Balls   the cluster of issues less important in one's personal and work life. They may bounce around undamaged until it is time to consider or implement them.

Safety Valve   those activities or situations that feed your soul, that revive and refresh you when stressed or on a downturn.

Sisyphus Syndrome   refers to the Greek mythical character who displeased the gods and was sentenced to the outskirts of Hades. A victim with no options, he daily pushed a heavy stone up a steep mountain, only to step aside and watch as it rolled back down again.

Success Criteria   a list of fundamental and unique needs to be filled in order to feel successful in your career.

Type CC Personality/Chaos Chaser   new personality type designed to thrive on chaos, to face complexity, and to find opportunity and order in the center of our current storm. The Type CC Chaos Chaser is a resilient and resourceful pathfinder, a pioneering spirit, an overcomer, and a lifelong learner and skill-builder. The Type CC Chaos Chaser can embrace change and face the future with confidence and freedom from fear.

THE NECESSITY OF CHANGE

Careers in Collision

Career Shock
as the Epidemic
of Our Age

1

"There is no coming to consciousness without pain."

—Carl G. Jung

Let's start with a story of a very successful career change, gained only after great pain and uncertainty. Imagine what humankind would have lost without the insight, creativity, and wisdom released by this career change. Carl G. Jung, one of the most respected psychiatrists influencing our era, changed his career direction at midlife, and he vividly describes the very powerful emotions involved. Jung at that time was fully established and very successful in his academic career, but he withdrew abruptly after eight years of lecturing, suffering from what we today would call burnout. He said that after the publication of his *Psychology of the Unconscious* he couldn't bear to read another scientific book. He labeled this his *fallow period,* since his mind was occupied but not fully seeded with images of the unconscious. He could not keep up with his former prescribed world of the intellect, and more importantly, he could no longer teach what he himself doubted. His self-dialogue about his choices clearly parallels what individuals in career change tell me.

His options, as he saw them, were to continue on the same smooth academic road that was already conveniently laid out for him or to change and follow the "laws of my inner personality, of a higher reason . . . I abandoned my academic career for I felt something great was happening to me . . . I knew it would fill my life, and for the sake of that goal I was ready to take any kind of risk."

Jung's vision, or, as he called it, "this curious task of mine," was his confrontation with the unconscious. A future image such as this is essential to changing careers successfully. However, it bothered Jung greatly to give up his academic career, and he went through a "dark night" before resolving it. In his words, he "stormed at destiny . . . but if we pay heed to what the inner personality desires say, the sting vanishes. . . . These emotions are transitory and do not count" (1963, pp. 193–194).

Jung's experience is a vivid illustration of the twin emotions of the pain and pleasure of making a significant career change. This process, as Jung describes it, can be lonely but ultimately rewarding, and it has changed little since his time. Indeed, the necessity for changing careers as we race into the twenty-first century has only dramatically intensified. His body of work helps to give us a strong base on the emotional issues of change, and I have drawn many ideas and insights on people and change from his theories and direct experience.

For you too, changing careers can be the most rewarding experience of your life. We have all read about people who happen to fall into an ideal career change. They are fortunate, and we envy them—but to deliberately determine to make a career change and to initiate this process is in defiance of tradition and is not necessarily easy or automatic. People change careers only when the pain of their status quo becomes greater than the fear of making the change. The pain has an internal source, as with Jung, or an external source, as when the career opportunities have dried up. Hence my formula for a creative career change: $CC = P > F$. If your current career pain is not intense, a career change may not be to your advantage.

CAREER SHOCK: A PAINFUL SPLINTER OF FUTURE SHOCK

If we are to take creative control of our careers, we must understand our current reality. Millions of Americans are in career shock, a painful splinter of future shock. This is a widespread epidemic resulting from career collision, the collapse of our former career aspirations, dreams, expectations, and plans for success under the current realities of our chaotic work world. Americans of all ages, cultures, economic and education levels, from blue- and white-collar fields, lawyers, bankers, newspaper editors, accountants, academicians, business executives, physicians, engineers, teachers, secretaries, homemakers, factory workers, and computer programmers, indeed, from every career field—all are experiencing unexpected confusion and chaos in their work lives.

"This isn't the way it's supposed to be and certainly not what I ever had in mind" is echoed by adults whose careers are in this direct collision with their former expectations. After years of dedicated, loyal service, well-paying jobs are being lost with little or no warning or are changing so radically that they are unrecognizable and undesirable. Expectations based on automatic and continually rising affluence and opportunity collapsed with the failure of the traditional career success formula. Prospects that flourished throughout the 1950s and peaked in the 1960s and early 1970s ended in the late 1980s and 1990s.

Countless contracts, unwritten but long considered binding, are being broken by corporations and also by our changing culture, and many individuals feel powerless to chart a career direction that is both satisfying and rewarding. The old career paradigm, our former chosen career paths, models, formulas, and skills are simply not working. Millions of adults caught in career shock and career collision are being forced to refocus, to restructure, and to change careers with little real insight, direction, information, or workable strategies. There are few if any reliable coaches, guidebooks, or translation manuals. Our respected traditional institutions and our familiar cultural support systems such as churches, public schools, higher educational institutions, and government agencies, provide little help or insight. Many operate much as they have in the past, easily ten to twenty years behind the reality that we are experiencing. In fact, only recently has there been recognition or acknowledgment that there is a problem! In career shock, we are indeed "strangers in a strange land" traveling with an incomplete map, dealing with surrealistic conditions we never knew existed.

Furthermore, perceptive leadership is conspicuous in its absence. If we assume, as many of us have in the past, that there is a White Knight coming to rescue us, to resolve all these issues, then we are setting ourselves up for failure. Our business and political leaders, with their vested interests in maintaining the status quo, getting reelected, being politically correct, or finding a quick fix for their quarterly bottom line while keeping an eye on Wall Street and their own lucrative jobs, frequently create additional problems rather than insight and solutions to career shock.

Realistically, fifty percent of our country's population lacks the basic skills to move into an economy stressing brainware. Yet under government leadership, millions of dollars are being spent annually training people for jobs with a very limited life span or, even more importantly, for jobs that may only marginally fit the individual's abilities or motivation. Many programs go through the motions, ignoring the real career needs of the individual and the immediate future, trying to solve the complexity of career shock with old remedies, many even dating back to the 1930s, probably with limited value even then. We can ill afford this mindless luxury as we move through the twenty-first century. Career shock is when we are directly experiencing all the problems but see no creative or workable solutions.

Never before in history have people had as much power as the present generation to shape their future, and never before have so many adults needed to make so many urgent and individual decisions about their work lives. Yet in this Age of Information, many highly talented and educated people are stalled, severely limited by the lack of career focus and direction; information on opportunities outside their specialized career field; genuine insight into themselves, their skills, interests, and personality; strategies and direction to take charge and effectively alter their own careers; and courage and resilience to self-direct their work life.

Young college graduates not yet in the workplace, along with their parents, are bewildered to find that after spending a fortune on higher education, perhaps accumulating debt, the readily available entry-level jobs are mainly in the lower-paying service sector—they are, in effect, "MacJobs." Good jobs are being created, but in smaller and moderate-sized young companies, not in large corporations as in the past. However, without structured, careful planning and more reliable information than we've used before, many college graduates will slip into and remain in unrewarding low-level service jobs throughout their career.

FANTASY OF THE '50s: WHERE ARE YOU NOW?

Surviving and thriving in a career in this time of chaos requires skills that many adult Americans simply have not learned. Even more critical, many are only now becoming aware of the need to learn new career/job skills and strategies and unlearn the former conventional ones. But how do we unlearn deeply instilled and perhaps unconsciously learned messages? Can we change our old pattern or model of career success quickly? Our Industrial Age model throughout the decades developed into one that valued security, stability, and loyalty to a passive established order; however that model is not only passé but also highly negative for us today.

In the late 1940s through the 1950s, our expectations for success were high. The message of the 1950s was to work hard, not necessarily to be smart but rather to learn and activate the formula and rules for success, and we would be automatically rewarded with affluence, satisfaction, recognition, or whatever we wanted. For those of us growing up then, life decisions were quite simple. We were to do the right thing and we could count on living happily ever after.

So we carefully and unquestioningly followed the values and direction of our family, society, and the established system. We were expected to achieve more status and material possessions than our parents through more education or through marrying well. For women, it was an orderly, sequential pattern of maintaining virginity, being attractive or smart enough to find the man with the most potential, then falling in love, marrying for life, and assuming all direct responsibility for perfect children and an increasingly larger home in a higher-status neighborhood. The entire success of the marriage and the children rested on the shoulders of the female.

The man in turn became the good family provider, whose work was most important. To succeed in his work, the provider needed to be emotionally detached from the family scene. Corporate men worked loyally for one or perhaps two companies until retirement at sixty-five, by which time they were to have amassed a secure retirement fund. The golden years that followed were to bestow all the rewards for the commitment of playing by the rules. In reality, the average corporate male, if he didn't die of a heart attack before age sixty-five, found himself with little real purpose in life after retiring. Dying approximately fifteen to eighteen years before his wife, he left his widow well-fixed financially. Our social institutions and Hollywood movies fueled our fantasies. All we had to do was follow the established system and if we didn't search too deeply, it worked well for those who fit or bought into the system.

But we eventually found that this model life was a sham, often a disaster, an ordeal we would not want our children to repeat. Yet as parents, we have somehow transferred this pattern of expectations to our children. So it's little wonder our children and grandchildren are experiencing confusion, uncertainty, and lack of direction in their career paths. The confusion of the thirteenth generation—eighty million born after 1960, the generation after the baby boomers—may be a natural response to our earlier unrealistic expectations. This generation is defined by Howe and Strauss (1993, p. 7) as the "only generation born since the Civil War to come of age unlikely to match their parents' economic fortune . . . to grow up personifying not the advance, but the decline of their society's greatness." I recall that Margaret Mead said that the parents of the baby boomers are the first generation that had nothing to teach its children.

FAILURE OF OUR CAREER FORMULA

Our old formula for success was a system that, if followed carefully without question or evaluation, was supposed to take care of us. It should have been a guide to help us, not confine us or define us forever. However, we began to worship this formula, and the established way became the only system for success, so that because we bought into it exclusively and mindlessly, the formula became our prime goal rather than a tool to serve our needs in our work lives. The more we believed in and accepted this paradigm, the more problems and trauma we now experience as it fails us. We neglected to think for ourselves, to realize that this system existed to aid the teachings and the rules for managing our lives and careers in an earlier, far different age.

Today, however, coupled with unbelievably rapid changes in technology and the restructuring of organizations, we are facing the failure of this career formula. Thus we feel abandoned, powerless in our work or lives. We have few former internal belief systems to follow that will work for us in our career today, because our earlier model was built mainly on external factors and rules. As technological advances spur social and organizational change, the failure of our career formula leaves us without control, commitment, challenge, competence, courage, or even common sense, the very traits we need in order to be in creative control of our career today. In our earlier model, we labored under and valued external factors and rules that have now collapsed. For most of us, our current internal belief system has not been refined to take us into the twenty-first century, nor does it provide rules to help us during this time. We must create our own.

Our former simplistic "one size fits all" career formula will not fit our complex age, caught as we are between the death-throes of the Industrial Age and the beginnings of the Information Age. Technology spins off, seemingly unlimited, while change and chaos seem to lead us into a twilight zone. Many of us, the once highly paid production workers as well as those with advanced specialized academic degrees, bought into the assumption of continuing financial success through the accumulation of advanced degrees, corporate stability, and job security. Now we are feeling confused, powerless, and paralyzed. Ill prepared to match the needs of our rapidly changing age, many of us question our ability to maintain a foothold in the middle class. We lack not only the information, strategies, and skills, but even more critically, millions lack the will, the personality, the courage, society's blessing, and the social policies to be able to move with certainty and confidence into the new era.

CAREER SHOCK: ASSESSING WHERE YOU ARE

Earlier in your work life, you may have had the career success formula down to the fine points. You acquired credentials, advanced degrees, special skills, and invaluable experience and coupled all this with dedicated work, ambition, and the expectation that you would not only meet but also far surpass your career and financial goals. You believed in and followed all the rules—no gaps in your résumé since you were five years old! But now you know that something is missing. You feel stale, lost, stalled, anxious, frustrated, and fearful.

Consider these questions:

1. Are you working harder but enjoying it less?

2. Do you live for Friday and suffer from Sunday night/Monday morning blues?

3. Have you lost a well-paying job that you doubt you can ever replace?

4. Are you trapped in a "doomsday job" without focus, direction, or options, on a fast track going nowhere and running low on fuel?

5. Do you have potential but see no opportunity to develop it in your job?

6. Do you daydream frequently about "cashing out," doing something else, but have no idea what it is?

7. Are you chronically insecure and stressed about your financial future?

8. Could your job end tomorrow, without warning?

9. Is your work life causing problems in your personal/family life?

10. Has your corporate ladder collapsed into a "down-only" escalator?

11. Has your "status" career become a job only to pay the bills?

12. Do you see your career as out of your control?

13. Are you caught in "golden handcuffs," rewarded only by money?

14. Would you gladly give up a portion of your salary for more time off?

15. Has your work ceased to provide you with meaning and a sense of mission?

If you answer yes to most of the following questions, you are indeed suffering from *career shock syndrome,* the evident but unrecognized epidemic of our current age. Career shock syndrome affects our lives, physically and psychologically. If not treated, it can be fatal to a productive and fulfilling work life; it can cut short career dreams and hopes.

However, perhaps your career pain is not acute: Your job is going well. Maybe you picked up this book because you are only idly curious about changing careers; it's crossed your mind after some particularly difficult days or weeks at your job. Or perhaps your intuition is telling you that your career field or your entire industry is in a slump and unlikely to improve. You are beginning to feel uneasy, to wonder about future opportunities, perhaps to think about developing a career contingency plan, a backup alternative just in case your current career plans fade out.

On the other hand, you could be near the other extreme: "Take this job and shove it!" You dislike everything about your work: your company, your boss, your co-workers, your work activities and responsibilities, your hours, your pay. There are countless stresses, no challenges, no meaning, no tangible results, no learning curve, no self-expression, growth, creativity, control, or future in your present work and you know it. In the extreme, you may feel like a dinosaur, disconnected from any sense of meaning or mission, a cast-off from the rapidly evolving Age of Information and Technology.

Perhaps for very real internal and/or external reasons, you don't have the option of staying where you are in your current work life. Your career has ended. It isn't even just a question of getting another job; for whatever reason, staying where you are is not a choice. A radical career change, or at least major refocusing, is absolutely imperative and you haven't the slightest idea how to start or where to begin! You are in career shock. In many ways, this is very similar to post-traumatic stress syndrome.

Coping with career shock and career collision is a serious issue because we feel like victims of our economy, squeezed by the pressures of daily living. To be slaves with no options in our work lives does not fit the American psyche. However, just coping is no longer about simple stress management: It is about survival and revival in a world of failed expectations and shattered dreams.

If we are to deal effectively with career collision, it is critical that we understand the forces that are reshaping our lives. The better we understand them and our career shock in relation to them, the better we can maintain some measure of creative control about the way they affect us. True, the map to our future may have huge gaps, but as a real pathfinder knows, better an incomplete map or no map at all than one that is trusted but highly flawed and directs us off target. If alerted that we travel in unknown territory, then we can plan for ambiguity. But we need all the information, insight, creativity, skills, courage, and resilience we can gather to succeed in our unpredictable and rapidly changing era. The days of conventional, passive, and complacent personality traits are over.

SISYPHUS SYNDROME:
FREEDOM IS KNOWING YOUR OPTIONS

Millions wrestling with career shock have a clear choice as we move into the early twenty-first century. We can remain locked into the Sisyphus syndrome. Sisyphus was the Greek mythical character who displeased the gods and was sentenced to the outskirts of Hades where he daily pushed a heavy stone up a steep mountain, only to step aside and watch as it rolled back down again. Sisyphus eternally and hopelessly repeated his meaningless task. He saw no options: only the stone and the mountain.

It's no exaggeration to say that many Americans feel that they lead a Sisyphesian work life, forced into trivial, inane work, with no control, commitment, creativity, hope, or opportunity to change. On our familiar treadmill, we can see and expect only our particular mountain and the stone, oblivious to all our other options.

Many, though feeling trapped, see their labors as necessary to support their family lifestyle and to meet the expectations of our society. In fact, Camus, in his 1942 essay *The Myth of Sisyphus* (Le Mythe de Sisyphe), elevated Sisyphus to the role of martyred hero. Camus was famous for his theory of the absurd, reflecting the philosophy of existentialism, which is that lucid and conscious individuals who yearn to find meaning, to know and understand, confront an unintelligible, silent universe where meaning, insight, and knowledge are impossible. In this way, according to Camus, people are set up for a life without hope, and the tragedy is created by our failure to become properly conscious of this reality or, if we do become conscious of it, to fail to find the alternative human values by which to shape our lives.

Rejecting both despair and suicide, Camus argued that a limited life and creation, such as that of Sisyphus, is possible within the very narrow limits of what people know and can do. Camus proposed that, even with our knowing, we should just keep pushing our stone up the mountain. He believed that there is a certain degree of dignity in honestly facing our solitary condition and trying to find and assert the human values of individual freedom, even love, within the very narrow limitations of that condition. Sisyphus is Camus' hero of the absurd because at least he is aware and accepting of his fate, and the rock and the mountain belong to him. That he is conscious of his futile struggle towards the heights is enough to fill a man's heart and thus make him happy.

However, May in *The Cry For Myth* (1991), counters that the myth of Sisyphus fits a seemingly hopeless situation of repetitive, perpetual, and monotonous toil and sweat. It denies progress and depicts a world without hope, a twilight zone that leads nowhere and that directly contradicts our traditional American Dream and any variations of it.

Even if our work life casts us as Sisyphus, an unwilling hero of the absurd toiling with limited control, meaning, challenge, or hope of options, contrary to Sisyphus and Camus, we do have options and freedom and they are directly connected. We don't have to act on our options, but we should know that we have them. We are far from trapped, regardless of our surrounding chaos. However, we can accept a pointless fate and, as Sisyphus, remain locked forever in a monotonous work pattern. We can live with our hopelessness, keep our expectations low, and do the best we can in our limited circumstances. We can continue to suffer the anxiety and uncertainty of corporate layoffs, cutbacks, downsizing, or whatever newly coined phrase is next used to soft-pedal severe changes and job loss. We can consider ourselves lucky to keep a mindless, dead-end job in a shrinking career field, or one that fails to fit our interests or skills.

However, if this role becomes too painful and we rebel, we do have other options. We can directly confront our despair and use it constructively. We can choose to take creative control of our career, to thrive in a chaotic age, not merely survive.

PROTEUS PRINCIPLES

To continue the mythological metaphor, we have the option of recasting ourselves as the Greek god Proteus, a prophet deeply steeped in wisdom whose principles and personality traits we could well model to thrive in our current career chaos. The Proteus Principles are fundamental to taking creative control in our current work life.

Proteus had creative foresight, the intuitive ability to determine future possibilities. His insights were highly valued by the Greeks going into battle. While making exact predictions into our own future is risky, it is wise and timely to become informed and more keenly aware of current rapidly developing trends and the changes likely to affect our life and our world of work. This thoughtful foresight into our possible future can provide us a critical measure of control in our chaotic age.

Proteus also was willing, able, and ready to transform, to creatively and rapidly change shapes when he sensed danger; it was almost impossible to catch Proteus unaware. Of all the skills necessary for making our transition into the evolving new work world, the ability to change rapidly in order to creatively handle unexpected complexities, shifts, and upsets is the most crucial. However, to make these changes successfully, we must have self-knowledge: our unique bedrock, our DNA fingerprint, our basic core being that remains regardless of all changes we make. Later, we will discuss how to determine our most essential selves.

A third Proteus Principle, while it could seem minor in relationship to the gift of foresight and prophecy and the ability to change shapes, is increasingly essential to contemporary, overworked, stressed-out Americans. In fact, in our increasingly helter-skelter, pressure-laden work life, the development of this third Proteus Principle could well become equal or even superior to the other two. Every afternoon, after carefully tending his sea calves, Proteus took a nap. This wise one balanced his life and work with rest and repose.

Though committed to his work, he was not frantic, fearful of losing a footing on the corporate ladder, as are many today. Stress and burnout have doubled in the workplace since 1985 and are deadly to productivity and to our personal life. One client, a young saleswoman, reported that her manager told her that the organization expected her to "work an eight-day week and a forty-hour day." She said that he wasn't kidding, either!

Toffler, working from a government study on mental health stated that "fully one-fourth of our citizens in the United States suffer from some form of severe emotional illness" (1980, p. 381). The *Trend Letter* (1992), raised this to four out of ten, with 39 percent considering quitting their jobs because of stress. Executives may be anxious over global competition, and workers in the lower ranks are facing automation, newer technologies, and a feeling of isolation and loss of control. Stress-related disability cases have doubled since 1981. "Medical research has found that high levels of stress can cause ulcers, insomnia, headaches, heart attacks, immune system disorders, and drug and alcohol abuse" (p. 6). Sixty-two percent of top managers and business owners feel burned out (*Trend Letter*, 1992). This is costing U.S. companies sixty million annually.

A five-year study released in 1993 by the Families and Work Institute, a non-profit organization in New York (reported in the *Dallas Morning News,* 1993), surveyed a representative sample of 3,000 employees. Based on one hour interviews, they found: 42 percent said they felt "used up at the end of the work day;" and 27 percent said they often feel emotionally drained from work. Equally significant, 99 percent said they remain strongly committed to doing a good job, but are motivated more by personal pride than company loyalty, while 57 percent said they try to do their job well whatever it takes. Forty-two percent surveyed worked for companies that had recently had a cut in their workforce, and 20 percent feared losing their jobs.

As millions of Americans are nearing or are operating under burnout conditions, guaranteed to eradicate initiative, control, creativity, and commitment in work, the balance between work commitment and the rest of our lives will become an increasingly critical issue for our personal and professional spheres.

You may not be caught in this Sisyphus Syndrome, or you may be in it and not object to its limitations. As Camus put it, the awareness and stoic acceptance of your fate may be enough to make you happy. Or you may think the Greek god metaphor is overdramatic and doesn't really apply to you. If so, consider yourself fortunate.

Careers Caught Between Two Ages

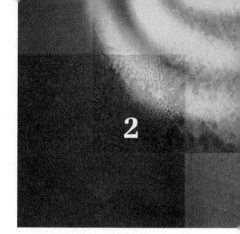

2

"If we would first know where we are and where we are tending, we could then better judge what to do and how to do it."

—Abraham Lincoln

To gain the insight to move effectively from our career shock and to effectively adapt and change, we must view our external world realistically in relation to our careers. We cannot take our formerly narrow, single-focus view or approach to solving a complex problem. This current chaos is evidenced by multiple factors that are becoming increasingly familiar to all Americans: organizational downsizing, merger mania, bankruptcies, burnout, plateaued careers, job dissatisfaction, and permanent career and job loss by long-term employees. These symptoms directly mirror issues and problems on a more fundamental and complex level.

Since our careers are a major part of our lives and identity, they are directly affected by all of the conditions in our society and our world as a whole. So before we can acquire any real insight into our own individual career shock, we must gain a much broader viewpoint. We must approach our career problems and issues as a direct reflection of our current changing complex world.

Our work world as we have known it in past decades is breaking apart, a metamorphosis that we individually and as a society are unprepared to understand and deal with. This chaos in our personal and career paradigm is a microcosm that reflects all the change and discontinuity in our current economic, political, and cultural state worldwide. The workplace is being turned upside down and is certainly out of touch with our desired reality, our perceptions and expectations.

We gain insight when we realize that today's changes are not independent of each other. Our career problems are systemic, interconnected, and interdependent, too complex to be understood by one simple theory or discipline. If we view our careers, work-life issues, and changes as separate from our environment, we can't design a coherent, effective response to problems. Lacking some kind of systematic framework to understand these clashes, we navigate blindly. For this reason it is important to have an overview of major changes in our life and work as a reflection of our more cosmic chaos: the current happenings on a national and global scale—specifically economics, politics, business, education, and other cultural and social values.

We must recognize and accept that we are experiencing change more rapid than most of us can comprehend. The status quo has erupted into the unfamiliar and unpredictable. Understanding career problems and how to solve them is a real challenge.

In more stable times, when the pace of change was slow and predictable we could live in our own world, our particular geographic area, our profession or industry, and feel secure. However, this is no longer an option in an era when change is our only constant. There are no simple formulas from the past to direct our career success.

What is happening that is creating individual career shock and the failure of the traditional career formula? As we race into the twenty-first century, we are perched between two ages—the familiar that is dying and a new and unknown order that is only gradually shaping in outline form from the chaos. Our world is reshaping swiftly, even as we walk upon it, technologically, environmentally, and culturally. We have experienced deeper change in the past twenty years than in any previous span of five hundred.

Of course, Americans in past generations experienced many changes. We moved from the frontier and a rural farm life to the city for jobs to meet the needs of the Industrial Age. These earlier changes, however, were not as dramatic or painful as today's since they occurred at a much slower pace. More importantly, we shared the traditional American Dream. Even those who had not achieved it strongly believed in it and felt that they could gain it. This continuity of values provided a shared sense of purpose and community.

Today our differences—discontinuities and diversities in cultural and social values, lifestyles, career opportunities, and new economic realities—are clashing with each other and with our former expectations. We are no longer sure what the American Dream is, if we have one or want one, or if we could believe or trust in it if we did. Many no longer search or seem to care. Others say that the American Dream is simply more diverse, that we are no longer a melting pot but rather a tossed salad or a mosaic. In our search for a new paradigm to rediscover or redefine our American Dream, we could view it as a search for the Holy Grail. It is the will to continue the journey—the search, not the actual recovery and possession of the Grail—that really matters.

To maneuver successfully through this watershed age, we as individuals must see and understand that it is a transitional age, the connecting bridge between the old and the new. We must also understand that transitional times are complex, difficult to understand and label, and therefore painful and frightening. When an era serves as a bridge, it deserves a special label. I call it the *dark night of the soul* for our entire nation.

Being neither here nor there creates anxiety, frustration, uncertainty, and fear in most adults, steeped as we are in the need for stability and security, schooled in certain formulas for living and working. But it is our time and place and we cannot ignore the events that will directly affect our life and work. Important trends will change the way we communicate, work, and play and eventually with wise leadership will create new and stronger patterns and values.

For millions who feel mindlessly trapped like Sisyphus, these changes may be welcomed, for in spite of the chaos, opportunities have never been greater. What we do need, however, is thorough examination and evaluation of the main premises and values of our culture as they relate to our individual work life. In other words, we are forced to be self-reliant and to make for ourselves the many critical judgments previously made by our family, culture, and church. This may involve the rejection of outmoded rules, a recognition of earlier discarded ones, and the design of new rules for our careers. To understand this multifaceted crisis, we must cultivate the wisdom to see our situation in the context of our human cultural evolution.

We must first understand that our current crisis is part of a transformation and that there is a strong connection among crisis, chaos and change, danger, opportunity, and rebirth. After civilizations have reached a peak of vitality, they tend to lose their cultural steam and decline (Toynbee, 1972). This loss of flexibility is an essential element of the breakdown, for when society becomes so rigid, it cannot adjust to changing situations. Growing civilizations display the Proteus Principles, with great variety and versatility in change. The Sisyphus Syndrome, with its uniformity, conventionality, and lack of inventiveness, is characteristic of disintegrating cultures with their attendant discord and disruption.

All cultures go through cyclical processes of genesis, growth, breakdown, and disintegration. Fritjof Capra, a physicist, writer, and early advocate of adding the spiritual element to science, says that at this last point, a creative minority usually steps in, but the forces are complex and the changeover is not easy. He finds that what we are experiencing today is identical to these symptoms. From his following summary, we can conclude that we are due for a transformation, "a sense of alienation and an increase in mental illness, violent crime and social disruption and religious cultism. These usually surface about three decades before the central transformation, rising in intensity and frequency as the transformation occurs and then declining" (1982, p. 28).

Doesn't this description well fit our societal problems today? Cynicism and crime have reached unbelievable records. We are experiencing the dejobbing of America, with unprecedented job loss and unemployment for an estimated forty-six million, increased work time and overwork for others, and the fluctuation of practically everything. At the same time, traditional career paths have been destroyed along with the loss of upward mobility and the disappearance of entire career fields. We are witnessing the collapse of industries and major companies, the loss of millions of midmanagers, and the breakdown of organizational hierarchy. We are seeing the flattening of the organization, along with the rapid growth of entrepreneurship, outsourcing, contracting, franchising, "temping," and contingency workers. The steady job of the past, with automatic annual pay increases and retirement at age sixty-five, is over. We must give up our outdated formulas if we are to maintain real creative control over our career.

Rosabeth Moss Kanter, for the *Harvard Business Review,* surveyed twenty-five counterpart publications in twenty-five countries on six continents. The dominant message from this study is, "Change is everywhere, regardless of country, culture, or corporation. Leaders have gone through the most pervasive changes in the last two years and report a decline in loyalty to their own companies" (1991, pp. 151–164).

How do these overlapping changes, the death of the Industrial Age and the birth of the Information Age, affect us as individuals? Our former paradigm valued conventional wisdom, stability, predictability, certainty, and maintenance of the status quo at all costs. What happens when the game changes rules at half-time? We are no longer certain we even know its name, much less understand how to play it by a new set of rules. At worst, many of us realize that we are forced to create the rules as we go. Handling a career "as usual," using the same rules with the same expectations, throws us directly into the Sisyphus Syndrome career path, feeling trapped, betrayed, and burned out by being forced to manage increasingly limited resources, having less time to do more, without hope of change or reward.

Coping with career shock and career collision is a serious issue because we feel like victims of our economy and are squeezed by the pressures of daily living. Coping is no longer about simple stress management: It is about survival. We have been told repeatedly in recent years that rapid change is inevitable in our world, and many have found the idea of change exciting. But we have not been prepared for the chaos that has preceded or accompanied these changes. While many need the excitement change brings, the challenge is to bind some sense of order and meaning to it.

Will our careers, our work life, be better or worse off in this age of change? The tools of technology, in combination with appropriate human action, may help solve many problems, but we don't yet know what problems they will create! Surely we are wise enough to know that technology won't fix everything that seems to be falling apart in our current decade. Human behavior is not technologically determined and may not need to be appropriately modified. Or will it? Will technology make our lives more difficult and complex?

The choices we make now are important. Education, the workplace, the environment, and other serious challenges will test our Proteus Principles, our foresight ability, and our ability to change. Ignore these human problems now and they will only worsen and return to haunt us and our grandchildren. We need action with courage, hope, foresight, and wisdom, not apathy, cynicism, and despair, to improve our present and future.

The early steps of real change are for most adults challenging and frightening. There are barriers and difficulties, real and imagined, psychological and external. There are crippling cultural beliefs and outdated policies to confront when refocusing and changing career direction. Many Americans may change careers with little difficulty, but of course I do not see them in my client base.

New Skills for a New Age

3

"Crazy times call for crazy organizations."

—Tom Peters

In the quote, Tom Peters summarizes his 768-page book on management, *Liberation Management: Necessary for the Nanosecond Nineties.* He continues, "No corner of the world is exempt from the frenzy. . . . In summary, the definition of every product and service is changing" (1992, p. 6).

Since our future workplace will not be an afternoon rerun of our past but a whole new prime-time series, the human skills and personality traits necessary for our career success in the coming years will vary radically from those developed in our former secure, status-oriented society.

The necessity to acquire the technical skills to move us into our Age of Information and Technology is becoming obvious to most, and though constantly changing, those skills can be acquired either in the classroom or on the job or they can be self-taught. However, many who lack the opportunity, confidence, or motivation may fail to learn these technical skills.

Recognizing and acquiring the nontechnical, "soft" skills for thriving creatively in our changing era—the necessary personality traits, temperament, and self-management skills—will be the greatest challenge. Acquired at an early age from family, community, and school, these skills create our compatibility with others and with our environment.

Our adaptive skills do change, but very slowly, and frequently only after an intense internal transformation process spurred by painful triggering events, trauma, or therapy. However, for a flourishing career in the future, we must make a conscious shift to a new way of seeing, thinking, and doing. For most of us, dropping former personality traits and acquiring different ones will not happen quickly or easily; changing these self-management skills is a complex process. But we must nevertheless develop plans to learn, unlearn, and relearn these skills.

First, living and working successfully in a world characterized by complexity and constant change requires us as individuals to be "the eye in the center of the storm." We must know who we are and what we want, be in charge of ourselves, an approach quite different from what was needed in the past. Alertness and mental health are fundamental if we are to seize and maintain creative control of our career. Marie Jahoda generally defines mentally healthy people as in touch with their own identity and feelings (their consistent "I"); oriented toward the future and over time fruitfully invested in life; with integrated psyches that provide them resistance to stress; possessing autonomy and recognition of what suits their needs; perceiving reality without distortion and yet possessing empathy; and masters of their environment—able to work, to love, to play, and to be efficient in problem solving.

We should ask ourselves, on a scale of 1 to 10, where we see ourselves in this mental health description (Jahoda, 1958).

Unfortunately, countless Americans will continue to struggle in their futile Sisyphus Syndrome with mounting career problems, using outdated, nonworking career success rules and formulas. But such a life does not fit our basic cultural archetype, our perception of who we are and what our lives are expected to be. Instead, on this brink of a new era, we have the option to redesign our careers, following the Proteus Principles of using foresight, changing as needed, and striking a healthy balance between work and leisure.

If modeling your career growth after a mythical Greek prophet seems too far-fetched for you, here is a more contemporary metaphor, a new personality type for our workplace, the Type CC Chaos Chaser. Presently, on one extreme we have the highly driven Type A, charging about and changing frequently merely for the sake of change, and on the other, the more laid-back Type B, passively seeking stability at all costs. Since neither of these types will thrive in our new environment, we need to develop a new personality model, one who can comfortably and creatively walk the fine line between complexity and disorder and wisely select the skills to thrive. These Type CC characteristics are learned as one moves through a successful career change process.

Not surprisingly, perhaps, these Type CC personality traits are remarkably similar to the traits we associate with the earlier self-reliant American frontier spirit and also with our more contemporary successful entrepreneur. They already form a strong part of our American cultural archetype and are therefore not foreign to us. However, perhaps we have neglected or simply forgotten them since they have been little valued, encouraged, or even tolerated in education or the workplace in the last seventy-five years. But because they are a natural part of our spirit, adopting the Proteus Principles or becoming a Type CC Chaos Chaser will not be so difficult once we begin the process. First, however, we should recognize the initial but temporary panic we experience when forced to realize that we are now on a new global frontier and the 1950s womb-to-tomb career ladder has collapsed for good!

THE TYPE CC CHAOS CHASER PERSONALITY PROFILE

What are the critical Type CC personality traits for success in our new frontier? The critical "C" characteristics for our future are control, creativity, change, challenge and competency, common sense, confidence, courage, curiosity, commitment, and cooperation.

Control

> *"As long as we're directed by the internalized voices and dictates of others, we're not in touch with our own will: We're not in control . . . reaction rather than an action."*

—Gloria D. Karpenski

Frequently expressed as independence, control is the first major Type CC personality characteristic affecting our careers. We are beginning to insist more on controlling our own destinies and having options. The need for the freedom and autonomy of the 1960s has not disappeared, but perhaps it has been dormant, especially during the "greed is good" decade of the 1980s. However, this need for control over our destinies is peaking today because of the chaos and disorder in the workplace and in society. Working ourselves to death is being recognized as absurd and self-abusive.

Many, materially successful but emotionally cheated, searching for something beyond this kind of success, ask, Must success cost so much? However, the general attitude in our culture is that materially successful people don't have serious emotional needs; consequently no one takes their problems seriously. A typical response to attorneys expressing career dissatisfaction because of adversarial relationships, long hours, and dull paperwork is that they must be crazy to want out of a status profession. The need for control is spawning the growth of other options: entrepreneurism, temporary, full- or part-time; and contract, full- or part-time. Contingency work is expanding rapidly. The major characteristic of entrepreneurs is the need for control, not over others, but over their own life and work.

Today, since most of our former systems have collapsed and the old formulas for solving problems are outdated, to remain in creative control of our lives we are forced to create new ways to solve our complex career and work problems. In the past, the established upper levels of control made the rules and the majority of us learned to follow them well with little question. In school, always raise your hand and ask permission was the rule. In the workplace, the message has been, Sit down, shut up, and do as you are told. The boss was the authority. We were also taught that the majority is always right, which may be exactly wrong in many cases. However, this passiveness and deference will not work for individual or organizational success in the future. To become a Type CC Chaos Chaser, we must rethink our definition and take action to develop our own creative control.

How do Type CC Chaos Chasers manage to create order out of chaos? They fit Johoda's and Masterson's definition of the mental healthy adults; their goals originate from within and are not based or dependent on outside needs or social conventions, which shape most people in the culture of today's work world. They have their own clarity of purpose and the courage and commitment to do whatever it takes to reach their goals. Psychologists call this an internal "locus of control" and estimate that 20 percent of adults have it.

Creativity

> *"The idea that will reshape our times and our careers, the most powerful catalyst of our age, is that each individual can be the predominant creative force in his or her own life. . . . Once you have discovered that, your life will be changed forever."*

—Robert Fritz

Creativity or some form of self-expression is a second Type CC characteristic required in our current age. Creativity is both a major motivation and a personal and organizational skill fundamental in the search for workable solutions to our challenging life and career problems. Currently

95 percent of my clients who work through a career change have a high need for creativity, as documented by the validated personality inventory they complete in the Self-Assessment process. A majority are surprised and initially bewildered at that report, and some even protest having any creative potential. The creativity requisite for a Type CC Chaos Chaser is not limited to painting, drawing, acting, and writing but is a much broader ability to perceive patterns and scout out and invent new ways of solving problems and living lives. Jonas Salk summed up the creative approach in Philip Goldberg's, *The Intuitive Edge*: "It is always with excitement that I wake up in the morning wondering what my intuition will toss up for me, like gifts from the sea. I work with it, rely on it. It's my partner" (1983, p. 23).

Seeing creativity as arts related only indicates that society's definitions and vocabulary are too limited and our self-concepts too frozen. Contrary to what many of my clients believe, creativity is not usually something totally new or original but a different configuration, or a new synthesis, or seeing something in an unusual way. Many of us think that creativity is reserved for those gifted in the arts or inventions, not a resource that ordinary people can cultivate and tap into. In reality, creativity in the arts is only a small part of the range of creativity.

Bernie Siegel, a physician and surgeon, describes the direct connection between control and creativity: "Becoming your own person releases your creativity. Freed from bonds of convention and the fear of what others may think, the mind responds with new solutions, new goals. . . . You become able to take risks, to experiment with your own life" (1986, p. 168). He stresses that all have the opportunity to live inventively in their work. "People who develop their full individuality often change jobs, moving from a career that bores them but gives them security into one that brings meaning to their lives and provides them with a way of giving something to the world rather than just getting something from it" (p. 168).

Creativity, acquired through a process, not a structured program, is based on intuition, foresight, and inventiveness, traits long neglected in our Western rational machine and muscle era. Albert Einstein emphasized, "The really valuable thing is intuition. Through meditation I found answers before I asked the question. Imagination is more important than knowledge" (Goldberg, 1983, p. 15). While most people have the potential, the instinct, and the brain for foresight and intuition, it is usually discounted, underdeveloped, and underrated, and only about 20 percent of our population use these abilities consciously.

Intuition is the quality that introduces alternatives and possibilities. With practiced intuition, we gain critical insights into ourselves and our environments, and we evaluate choices for the future. An awareness that precedes wise choices, the part of us that "knows," intuition gives meanings to cues, depth to understanding, and quality to judgment. Insightful people detect motives, feelings, and attitudes, both in themselves and others, and also from the environment.

Insight

Insight, apprehending the true nature through intuitive understanding, is a penetrating mental vision or discernment, the seeing into inner character or underlying truth. It is the perception, understanding, or grasp of a situation or person below the surface. Through insight, we maintain our contact with reality and distinguish between symptoms and causes. We see behavior specifics and comprehend the core values of ourselves and others. Insight is a prerequisite for real growth and is the center of meaningful interpersonal relationships.

Creative intuition and imagination allow us to make peace with uncertainty and trust our ability to deal with it. Decisions made solely on cold reason are usually made to satisfy others. Those of us who would thrive in chaos cannot let critical clues go unnoticed. Unfortunately, uncontrolled feelings, overspecialization, and overconcentration frequently distort cues necessary for insight. However, our intuitive decisions, sometimes even if others think they are off base, make us feel good and bring the real rewards in our life.

Foresight

Foresight, the gift of prophecy based on this intuition, is the heightened ability to see and synthesize trends from the past and present and project them into the future. It is an integration of the creative and imaginative but also the practical and logical, putting together what we see happening in our current environment and projecting these trends forward two, three, five, or ten years. The person with keen foresight will have the ability to understand, value, and integrate human nature and its forces in interaction with the environment. Intuitive foresight is conceptual, requiring that we see the whole, not just the isolated scattered parts. For example, moving from the immediacy of the bottom line to foresight is an increasing necessity in a successful business today (Naisbitt, 1994). Though difficult to predict the future, it is important to "best guess" outcomes into long-term plans. However, making precise predictions may not be possible or wise at this time.

Both foresight and insight are abilities requiring intelligence but are not highly correlated with IQ scores. Bright people may have neither ability, and those with mediocre minds may have high intuition and fore-sight. Frederic Flach, a psychiatrist, says creative people tend to be inde-pendent in thought and action; have a strong self-esteem; are open to new ideas; exhibit many interests; tolerate uncertainty; and commit themselves to life, work, and people (1988, p. 113).

To tap our creativity, it is imperative that we rearrange our in-terior patterns and reform self-defeating behaviors that block our self-expression. We must come up with different views of both old and developing issues, problems, and ways of being and thinking. Our age needs pattern-makers, not pattern-followers. Creative people who see relatedness and connect ideas, information, or situations in different ways to see, understand, and solve problems: These are our new pattern-makers.

Developing creativity within our own lives means that we have dis-covered a powerful point of view, a more direct perception of the world, a superior way to tune in and use our human instinct, according to Marilyn Ferguson, publisher of the *Brain/Mind Newsletter*. Creative peo-ple know how to deal effectively with change, how to take action and risk and how to recover, detect, and track trends and patterns, and they are fearless in their forward movement. Creative individuals are usually real strategists, perhaps not planners, but visionaries who synthesize rather than analyze. They develop ideas for the future and they program action. They are catalysts who urge and teach others to act.

Becoming a creative strategist with our career and future is impera-tive. In our former age of stability, when rules were established and remained unchanged, creativity and new solutions were not as vital. Previously we could walk rather passively through the system with few, if any, major career problems.

Never before have adults so needed to initiate the creative process in solving personal and career problems. By learning how (and creativity can be taught and learned) to access and use our insight and foresight, and by having the courage to act, we can thrive in the future using the creative process. In a private conversation, Marilyn Ferguson said, "From the psychology and biology of change, we are learning that the brain designs its own software to handle new challenges" (1996). We must learn to trust our own software!

Henry David Thoreau, in *Faith in a Seed* (1993), visualizes a future change, a forest from a few seeds that were scattered by the wind. In our fast-moving, stressed-out, overloaded lives, can we recognize the seedlings of new ideas and new ways to shape our future? Can we cre-atively visualize new ways of doing and thinking? The new and valuable rarely come with a flourish of trumpets.

Flexibility

Flexibility is essential for creativity: the ability to play with an idea, try it on for size, see different angles, argue with ourselves about it, bypassing the habit of using only one approach to the problem. To be creative and handle our careers in the future, we must push beyond the limitation of our past answers, not only those received from outside but also those imposed by our own fixed ideas and compulsions. As we creatively search and visualize our future, we change the way we see ourselves now. We can detach ourselves from our conventional paradigms and systems, from the abstractions and traditional solutions that others use, and from the routines and fixed customs of those around us. Becoming an authentic pathfinder is the real challenge.

Psychologist Frank Barron's studies of creativity found that healthy creative personalities have the following traits: a sense of humor, personal courage, a certain innocence of vision and a spontaneity of action, honesty of thought, social responsibility, acceptance of the past, no fear of the future, and a capacity to be able to contribute something of human love to the world. He concluded that soundness is not an absence of problems, but a way of reacting to them" (1963, p. 5). George Vaillant (1977), Director of the Forty Year Grant Study of Adult Development that researched prosperous men, drew the same conclusion on adaptability as Barron: Although the men in the Grant Study were successful, none had problem-free lives.

Ferguson writes that the ancients believed that fire, since it first occurred by accident from lightning, was a gift from the gods (1980). Then they learned how to make and use fire. So it is with creativity. In the past, creativity has been viewed as a gift from the gods, given randomly to some individuals. However, we know now that creativity can be learned and used as a valuable tool in our everyday life.

Change

> *"The heavens and all below them,*
> *Earth and her creatures,*
> *All change,*
> *And we, part of creation,*
> *Also must suffer change."*

—Ovid

Change is the third characteristic for the emerging Type CC Chaos Chaser of the future. This means the ability to embrace change and to use it creatively and confidently, rather than to fear or to try to escape from it. Pathfinders, Type CC Chaos Chasers who are comfortable with rapidly changing times, ask, What can I learn from this new frontier, this different age? What and where are the patterns, the underlying order and meaning for self-renewal, for moving myself and others to a higher level? This is especially true for adults nearing midlife because a mind-set of rigidity and opposition to change may be a very strong tendency at this time. Taught that stability is desirable and change at midlife a "crisis" sets us up to become dinosaurs holding on for the Ice Age. Yet real change, the emotional and psychological transformation that allows us to become significantly different, to move from our pain to our personal power, is achievable, although difficult at any age.

Csikszentmihalyi (1990, p. 192) describes an "autotelic self," possessed by those people who can change, who have within themselves the purpose of their existence. Such people have a knack for turning negative experiences into positive ones, translating potential threats into enjoyable challenges, and, in doing so, maintaining inner harmony in times of chaos. As creative survivors, they have the courage and ability to change and to overcome hardships. This ability seems a very rare gift, but it is a talent we desperately need to develop fully to thrive. Achieving and maintaining a sense of personal power, an "autotelic self," despite seemingly overwhelming odds, is a quality that Americans greatly admire.

Pain of change has great power to motivate—or to paralyze. A Type CC Chaos Chaser can see change as the opportunity for a fresh start. It is the opportunity to redefine and recover a part of our lost self, perhaps to create a life unfettered by former expectations, burdens, and defeats. Transcendence, the internal shift following a deep change that will move us successfully into our future, goes beyond the common experience, pushing us to surpass and exceed our preconceived limits. When we connect and establish a relationship to our natural, most instinctive self, we are given a new life regardless of age or circumstance—not a superficial change in behavior but a true shift in our life orientation. More than a transient peak experience, transcendence is much deeper and life-altering. When transcendence occurs, it creates possibilities never seen before in one's work life. This is the goal of every career change, although not every one contains such power.

Type CC Chaos Chasers can accept that the past is over and so may be its matching job, career, relationship, or self-identity. More critically, however, the Type CC personality is based on such discoveries and on integrating them. Knowing our own core being, our bedrock, our "I," discovered under fire, which will remain consistent, will provide the sound base for the direction and stability we need in a changing world.

We are unaware of possessing such power to change our lives and our history, partly because for too long we trust what we are born with. We think that if we do what we have been programmed to do, all will be okay. It is only when we free ourselves from this basic conditioning that we can start living.

Type CC Chaos Chasers accept the reality that no world is ever easy, and maybe all times seem troubled to those living them. Going underground or becoming the embittered cynic are not options if we are to capitalize on opportunities in the current complexity and move to a higher level for inner security and personal self-renewal.

The Type CC Chaos Chaser is first and forever the change-maker. The ability to experiment, risk, and change, in spite of fear and an uncertain future, and to see the underlying order and opportunity emerging from complexity and chaos, is personal power in its highest form. The Type CC personality can adapt and move swiftly back and forth from the status quo to the visionary, with creativity and speed. As author Robert Bly says, "You must change your life . . . to resist all change is worse than a waste of time: it is dangerous" (1988, p. 1).

Challenge and Competency

> "Sixty-five percent of the corporate jobs that will be created
> in the next ten years will be to perform functions we don't
> yet even know."

—Eric Miller

Challenge and competency are Type CC personality traits for the future. Challenge, the opportunity to bring out the best in ourselves, and competence in using our strongest skills and staying on a lifelong learning curve, are the next two major related career needs. Challenge and competence, directly tied to growth and achievement and to a high learning curve, are vital. Type CC Chaos Changers are not those who can settle in, plateau, and maintain well and, in fact, could be labeled trouble makers if in a learning environment. Building our competencies and staying on a learning curve is essential, even though direct job advancement and growth up the ladder may be limited today.

Growth in skills and competencies increases knowledge and stimulates ability and personal development, increasing our sense of being skillful in our work. This development creates new attitudes toward our career. Since our career is usually our major means of self-actualization or self-fulfillment, if we aren't growing and learning in our work, we are setting ourselves up to be underdeveloped. As our career grows, more identity is invested in the career role. Creation of new aspects of self, choice, growth, and involvement form a spiral, with each feeding back on the other. As we become more competent and challenged in what matters in our world, we become more involved, and this in turn increases our self-esteem and satisfaction. It is critical that our work and our career help us value ourselves. If self-esteem is high, we will seek success and develop and grow. If self-esteem is low, we focus on avoiding failure and protecting self and tend "to quit while ahead."

Lifelong learning, our ability to learn and unlearn and relearn throughout our entire life span, is our major security for the future. Keeping on a continual learning curve about self and our external environment is a future skill that cannot be overemphasized. True, our learning may not be a labor of love, but it is imperative that we learn what we love. Two weeks should not pass without a significant personal or professional learning experience, thought, or insight, internal or external. New information or new insight into the familiar as well as the novel, on a continuing basis, is absolutely essential for a Type CC Chaos Chaser.

Peters calls this *brainware,* the application of what is above the shoulders. "Your ability to improve your skill base and make yourself more marketable, whether you are a teamster or a neurosurgeon, is the only thing you've got" (1993, p. 102). In the past, we have acquired degrees, the more the better. Today we need to focus on learning skills on a continuing basis. Learning to solve problems, to think, rethink, redefine, make up our mind and then to change it based on new learning, are essential skills for our complex future.

Where we learn this information, whether in a structured classroom, on the job, or on our own, is not important, as long as we are building our skill and knowledge base. Based on our less than glorious success record as youngsters, we often fear the more structured classroom learning. But it is a completely different experience when older adults with a focused goal return for more formal education or training. Adults who barely slid through school return and make excellent grades. The first steps—gaining the career focus, making the decision to return to the classroom, and then actually getting enrolled—are the most difficult. The traditional enrollment procedure, with its bureaucratic system and long waiting lines, can be anathema to entrepreneurial adults or to independent personalities who don't relate to time-consuming or "nit-picking" policies.

Common Sense

"To sustain hope, one need not blind oneself to reality.
People need to know the worst—about the evils to be remedied,
the injustices to be dealt with, the catastrophes to be averted."

—John Gardner

Common sense—realistic, tough-minded optimism in facing our present age—is another major trait of the Type CC Chaos Chaser. Whether the winds of change spark us or overwhelm us depends more on our attitude and our expectations than on the nature or the severity of the actual events. Type CC personalities realize that our earlier, highly valued natural American optimism needs to be mixed with some tough-minded realism and that in the future, we don't need the kind of high hopes that are dashed by initial failures. Dealing realistically but optimistically with our failures as learning steps is an important future skill. More critical and complex than our attitudes toward the future are the attitudes we have about our capacity to affect that future.

Wisdom promoting well-being for the future means learning to choose our battles—knowing when to challenge and fight and when to serenely accept "what is," remaining *realistically* positive. Fatuous optimism and foolishness are not the goals of the Type CC. Nor is obsessive control, for when there is no flexibility or realism, we are set up to fail.

Our pioneer ancestors had a strong and optimistic sense of the future, a trait that seems dramatically missing from our present world. They felt they were part of an exciting drama; a good future beckoned and reflected their confidence. Today, confused and under pressure, many feel victimized. Certainly many American workers today, a reported 43 percent feel cynical and defeated, with limited personal power to affect their future and "see selfishness and faking as core of human nature" (Kanter and Mirvis, 1989, p. 1). Furthermore, "confidence in business and business leadership . . . is 15 percent today" (Kanter and Mirvis, 1989, p. 5).

Type CC Chaos Chasers have a realistic, tough-minded optimism about the future and their ability to direct their affairs. They act with purpose as individuals or in groups and feel they are riding a wave toward a positive future. Responsible and pulled by dreams and hopes, they take action to do something they believe strongly in and let realistic optimism guide them.

True, it isn't easy being a realistic optimist. It's a challenge to feel that our actions can make a difference when daily we are confronted with violence, homelessness, illiteracy, and inhumanity. However, Mother Teresa's philosophy is meaningful here: "I never look at the masses as my responsibility. I look at the individual. I can love only one person at a time. I can feed only one person at a time. Just one, one, one. . . . So you begin . . . I begin. I picked up one person . . ." (1983, p. 79).

Confidence and Hardiness of Spirit

> *"If you haven't the strength to impose your own terms*
> *upon life, you must accept the terms it offers you."*

—Sir Claude, in *The Confidential Clerk* by T.S. Eliot

Related closely to Type CC personality—realistic optimism is the need to develop strong *confidence and a hardiness of spirit,* capable of enduring fatigue, hardship, and exposure, while still feeling vigorous. This reflects a "can do" spirit and a trusting approach to life, the opposite of the weak, timid, and victim traits.

A confident, hardy, spirited approach is one that believes in the basic goodness of humankind, that most people will be kind and fair in their relationships with others. This type is probably slow to anger, neither seeking evil in others nor expecting the worst of them, nor spending much time feeling resentful, irritable, and angry. Those with trusting hearts treat others with consideration and kindness.

Just as our research has shown that the pessimistic, hostile heart is at risk of disease and premature death, it also can reassure us that the confident, trusting heart appears to be hardier and to protect itself against these outcomes. According to Redford Williams, a pioneering researcher in linking hostility and coronary heart disease, those who have this trusting heart are more likely to remain healthy throughout most of their lives and to live long (1989).

Do most people feel a hardiness of spirit and believe they can influence and exert some measure of control over their lives and their world? Daily I meet outwardly successful adults who internally feel weak and powerless. They see that they are barely hanging on, both personally and professionally, and they fear that if they slow down to really examine their lives, their world will crash in on them. Others have varying degrees of belief in their capacity to control their lives and influence the world around them. This confidence greatly increases their spirit of hardiness and health and the likelihood of a sustained effort in taking charge of their careers in chaotic times.

Type CC Chaos Chasers know they can solve their problems because that is the nature of being human, and they see failures and frustrations not as reasons to doubt themselves but as cues to strengthen their resolve. However, they accept that life sometimes involves unrelenting effort and a continuing willingness to try.

Type CC personalities, confident and hardy, are designed to climb, but they do not set themselves up with expectations so high that in order to be a complete person they must acquire countless objects: an employer, organization, status career, complete health benefits, trophy wife or husband, model kids, etc. Outside dependencies negatively affect our confidence and spirit.

Courage, Hope, and Resilience

"The future is shaped by people who believe in the future and in themselves. Leaders must help people believe they can be effective, that their goals can be accomplished, that there is a better future that they can move toward through their own efforts."

—John Gardner

The Type CC Chaos Chasers, to thrive in this current and future age, will need the *courage, hope, and resilience* to learn how to manage their lives in spite of unrelenting change and chaos. A review of hundreds of experiments in social psychology, which linked hopeful illusions and well-being, found that people who function well tend to hold onto hope (Brown and Taylor, 1994).

Courage

Courage is neither the opposite nor the absence of despair but rather the capacity to move ahead in spite of despair and indifference, to face difficulty and pain with firmness and fortitude. Do we have the courage to create our own future? Our recent past has hardly encouraged us to be courageous in dealing with our careers. In our diverse world, we must each have the courage and will to determine our own definition of success rather than wait for someone else to define it or to rely on another's model. Unfortunately, our educational system has stressed rote behavior, and the structure of the workplace has continued this.

A Type CC Chaos Chaser has the courage to ask hard questions, not reduce matters to pat "quick-fix" answers, and to strive for balance between head and heart. Courage is daring to feel the vulnerability of being human and authentic, being willing to discard former beliefs, if necessary, rather than be a slave to them forever.

In a private conversation after the APA convention (July 19, 1996), John Holland, when asked about the successful characteristics of a researcher after receiving the award for "Distinguished Professional Contribution to Knowledge," used the words entrepreneur and *courage*—to put out information, then reappraise and reevaluate, and not fear the critics. This is the kind of courage needed to take the first steps and learn along the way.

In considering the quality of courage, how is it that some achieve harmony of mind and grow in complexity, even when some of the worst things imaginable happen to them? Why do some people during a crisis remain faithful to their ideals while others drift with the current?

Courage is to ask ourselves, What can I change and what do I maintain in spite of this crisis? Making the decision when and where to give, adapt, relax, flex, maintain, and change requires courage. It requires courage to say no to the rules of conventional wisdom and former beliefs and behaviors and yes to what we intuitively know and honor from our success criteria list.

Hope

Hope, the feeling that what we desire is possible, is implanted in our earliest years and later is nurtured by our experiences in life. If not learned voluntarily in younger years, to become a Type CC Chaos Chaser we must learn what it takes now. Hope is the faith that life serves an ultimate purpose in the universe, the confidence that there is a connection to a higher power that we can call on as we go through chaotic change.

Resilience

Pushing on and beyond in spite of difficulty is the Type CC trait of *resilience.* This psychological and biological strength, a major adaptive characteristic, is strongly needed for successful change now and in the future. It is the quality that allows us to recognize, face, and endure pain and adversity: to acknowledge its purpose and to recover or rebound and return to our original or even a higher or renewed form. Resilience lets us rise above, while forging lasting strength from the struggle. Adults, in going through the successful career change process, are responding to their need for a change and are developing and refining a deep and powerful resilience to achieve this.

Traveling through the process of a successful career change, we learn we have greater capacity for surviving and thriving than we ever suspected. We learn we are not victims, with no options. We can weather great odds, feel fear, anger, despair, and pain while we sometimes stumble in the dark in search of meaning and structure, and through all of this, ultimately grow stronger and more in charge of our lives. This is what it means to thrive creatively—and this is what we feel after surviving a successful career change.

Flach, whose work focuses on resilience, says, "Managing emotional pain is more difficult than we might assume, calling for survival strengths of faith, hope and the will to live" (1988, p. 29). If we deny, ignore, or mask with drugs all the reality of our emotional pain, we lose part of our spirit and perhaps even create physical illness. We certainly can't grow beyond a certain stationary point.

Resilience is self-trust and self-respect and the ability to restore self-esteem when it is diminished or temporarily lost. It is the creativity to see new ways, to tolerate pain and grow from it, to develop insight into ourselves and what we are going through, and it is the resourcefulness, spirit, and ability to solve our own problems.

Curiosity

"The future is uncertain . . . but this uncertainty is at
the very heart of human creativity."

—Ilya Prigogine

Curiosity and ability to deal positively with contradictions and uncertainties are major Type CC personality characteristics. Dealing successfully with ambiguity and paradoxes, seeing not one but multiple right ways, requires the ability to be curious and nonjudgmental and indeed to value the paradoxes that continually surface in our age. Black and white answers do not exist in complex times, but we need judgment to weigh and balance the paradoxes we confront today.

For example, in our society, we define success as money and status yet at the same time feel guilty about it. Other conflicting messages with which we live:

- In rejecting your weaknesses, you cancel your strengths.
- You don't have to change by yourself but you must do it yourself.
- Positive transformation and rebirth are preceded by pain.
- Information overload creates information starvation.
- Be autonomous and self-reliant but conform.
- Be independent but connect with others.
- Gain external recognition with status based on internal meaning with value.
- Keep your head in the clouds but your feet on the ground.
- Be loyal to the organization but mind your own career.
- Death of custom brings birth of the self.
- Creativity and common sense are strongly related.
- A strength carried to the extreme is a weakness.
- We crave freedom and autonomy but dread the responsibility of it.
- We need to know but fear knowing.

With all these contradictions and paradoxes, we must develop wisdom and trust in ourselves. Gardner (1990) writes of two seemingly contradictory ingredients that are at the heart of sustained morale and motivation: positive attitudes toward the future and toward what can be accomplished through one's own intentional acts; and recognition that life is not easy and that nothing is ever finally safe.

Practicing the art of inquiry is a future skill related to dealing with contradiction and uncertainty. It involves asking the right questions without rigid emphasis on one right answer. It is the ability to suspend judgment, to juggle and become comfortable with unanswered questions and unresolved differences. Be wary of seeking quick simple answers to complex issues, of moving into small, comforting, familiar boxes that close out the rest of the world and therefore critical insights and messages for our future.

"The certainty of misery is better than the misery of uncertainty," says the cartoon character Pogo, a favorite philosopher. Frequently,

adults remain stuck because they prefer to accept the pain that is familiar rather than pain of the unknown. Remaining positive in times of insecurity, when outcomes are uncertain, is closely related to realistic optimism and hardiness of spirit as necessary skills for the Type CC personality. Chaos Chasers must be at peace with uncertainty and some risk.
This means expecting the best but having a contingency plan. However,
the worst seldom happens. This again is a common sense approach.

In a hierarchical bureaucratic system, the main emphasis was on fitting in, intuiting what the boss wants, and cranking it out. The master
plan was left to the company and Big Daddy, with additional duties
handled by Santa Claus and the Tooth Fairy, while we frantically dashed
about to achieve goals we hadn't thought through for ourselves. For all too
many, little or no conscious or unique thinking has been put into our
careers, either in selecting or managing them. Moore (1992) emphasizes
that fulfilling work, rewarding relationships, personal power, and relief
from symptoms are all gifts from the soul. But we have not given the soul
a place in our values; consider it only when it is disturbed by neglect and
abuse.

Commitment and the Search for Meaning

> "I don't know who will lead us through the '90's, but they
> must be made to speak to this spiritual vacuum at
> the heart of American society, this tumor of the soul!"

—Lee Atwater

Commitment and the search for meaning, connection, and community is
a real hunger for Type CC personalities. Though each of us defines *meaning* differently, the search is almost universal with people in career
change. The best use of instinctive and preferred abilities for a committed
purpose and connection with a community is our common goal and is the
most overwhelming need expressed by adults in career unrest today.

Finding our calling is a search for spiritual connection, for soul, and
for tangible goal. Such a search goes beyond religion or a set of beliefs
and rules to a deeper sense of belonging, connectedness, or participation
in a community. Bernie Siegel (1986) sees spirituality as finding peace
and happiness in an imperfect world, feeling that one's own personality
is imperfect but acceptable. From this peaceful state of mind comes both
creativity and the ability to love unselfishly.

To thrive in our coming work world, many will consciously seek more meaning from their work. Moore, a professor of religion and psychology, stresses that our emotional complaints of emptiness, vague depression, disillusionment about marriage, family, and relationships, a loss of values, a yearning for personal fulfillment, and a hunger for spirituality all reflect a loss of soul. He says, "We yearn excessively for entertainment, power, intimacy, sexual fulfillment, and material things, and we think we can find these things if we discover the right relationship, job, the right church or therapy. Without a connection with soul we will not find all these satisfying" (1992, p. xiv).

When we say, Now there's a person with soul, we mean someone who has highly developed sensitivities and is creatively compassionate and deserving of our respect and admiration. We sense a spiritual and the emotional side to them, high-mindedness, warmth, spirit, and courage. That person meets challenges, maintains grace under pressure, has courage, dignity, and wisdom.

Our focus on the soul lifts us beyond the machine paradigm of the last 100 years, when much of the human spirit was obscured by the smoke of the Industrial Age when the machine paradigm was also the accepted human model. Moore assures us that with acceptance of soul we can "deal with everyday problems without striving for perfection." Soul is "an approach that is more accepting of human foibles and sees dignity and peace as emerging more from that acceptance than any method of transcending the human condition" (Moore, p. x).

The possibilities of technology will likely increase our need for human interaction and connection. It is critical that people who use technology see it is a tool that meets a human need. There are technology specialists who are so intrigued with the possibilities of technology that they are happy just being in the environment. A career problem may surface when they must focus only on the routine part of their work, which may have little interest for them.

However, a high percentage of those in serious career unrest are employed, highly trained, and experienced computer technology specialists who have discovered that what they do every day is in itself not enough to provide meaning for them. Some deal in sophisticated but routine business or financial issues for large corporations, or perhaps are creating technological applications for expanding organizations. Many, however, have social service, creative, or investigative needs that are not in any way related to their daily use of technology. Healthy, balanced personalities will increasingly view technology as an effective tool for problem solving in their particular field of interest but not as an end in itself.

Many searching for meaning have faced or are facing some major trauma or life-changing experience. Passing through a "dark night of the soul," they realize their need to connect with and help others. Such devastating events can initiate a fruitful search for deeper meaning in our work lives. Joan Borysenko (1993) says that our wounds can be gateways to a transformation of the spirit and that they nourish our soul and bless us with the potential to help our world.

To become a healer we must move beyond being the trapped victim or even the mere survivor to being the creative thriver in our world. Only then can we use our true transformation of the spirit as the potential to help others. We can convert our experience into a healing process for others feeling the despair that we so well understand. Our own transformation vividly confirms for others that recovery and renewal is possible. Our own transformation of the spirit also gives us the potential to help others since we have received help ourselves.

Maintaining our soul demands attention, but our world sets us up to ignore it. For some, nourishing the soul involves walking, for others, listening to music, traveling, reading, public speaking, painting, volunteering, teaching, looking at art, washing the car, painting a room, helping a neighbor, planting a garden. Whatever centers us is a necessity, not a luxury.

Meaningless work can disturb the soul. On the other hand, fulfilling work and the health of our soul cannot be separated; our work can be the greatest expression of our soul, involving deep issues. But in our fast-moving, stressed-out lifestyle, who has the time, energy, or imagination to search for meaning, soul, and spirituality? Admittedly difficult, discovering and honoring the unique need of our soul increasingly rates as a top priority for many contemporary Americans. But as clients search for and discover their future image (discussed in detail in Part III), they are naming their mission and meaning, their commitment and soul food.

Unfortunately, for many adults thinking of changing careers, there seems to be a pervading perception that if we meet the needs that nourish our soul and spirit, then we won't be able to make a decent living. The old either/or dualism of money or meaning so extremely active in our decade may pose some problems in gaining both. Type CC Chaos Chasers look to combine meaning and money and know it requires creative and positive thinking. This is the problem that a career change must resolve to be successful.

What are some modern practices that are damaging to our soul and spirit? Moore lists "psychological modernism," an uncritical acceptance of the values of the modern world. He also includes blind faith in technology, attachment to gadgets and conveniences, total acceptance of scientific progress, "devotion to the electronic media, and a life-style dictated by advertising" (1992, p. 206). This tends toward a mechanistic and rationalistic understanding of human affairs, which takes us back again to our Industrial Age machine view of humans.

Also, there is a strong inverse relationship between information and wisdom. We want to know about other people, but we frequently fear real connection with them. Some clients who say they are searching for meaning in their work want to solve this issue with a quick fix, without investing time or emotion. They deal with the surface issues only, and their deeper instinctive needs are neglected.

Mother Teresa, when awarded the Nobel Prize for Peace in 1979, said, "The most terrible disease that can ever strike a human being is to have no one near him to be loved. Without a heart full of love, without generous hands, it is impossible to cure a man suffering of loneliness." Of the Western world, she said, "I have walked at night in your streets, I have entered your homes. I have found in them more poverty than in India. I have found the poverty of the soul, the lack of love."

Type CC personalities seek to unite with some higher part of themselves. Meaning and money can indeed be united for the Type CC Chaos Chaser, the new personality of the future.

Cooperation and Collaborative Teamwork

Cooperation and collaborative teamwork are understood by the Type CC Chaos Chaser as being as important as independent action. It is critical to be flexible and skilled enough to go both ways as demanded by the situation. Collaborate effort, coaching others, sharing information, teams, quality circles, and employee stock ownership are trends critical to the developing work world.

All these are examples of the life-long trend from competition to cooperation, and are designed to help people work more efficiently together. Mergers and joint ventures, nationally and internationally, are rapidly growing. Actually, the competition is creating the necessity for companies and employees to cooperate. These cooperative ventures are not takeover-type mergers with one company reaping all the profit at the expense of the others. These are more alliances designed to improve each partner's long-term growth prospects. A Conference Board Survey of 350 multinational CEOs found that geographic expansions and market share are the leading motivators as well as speed and cost *(John Naisbitt's Trend Letter,* 1994*)*.

Kanter (1994, p. 96) describes a three-year study she made worldwide, which uncovered three fundamental principles of business alliances:

1. Must yield benefits for the partners

2. Involve collaboration (create new values together rather than just exchange)

3. Require a complex system of interpersonal connections that keep people learning.

Their research found that North American countries are too occupied with the finances and economics of the deal, and they "frequently neglect the political, cultural, organizational, and human aspects of the partnership" (1994, p. 97).

While the increasingly complex and expansive global area signals the growing need for a fundamental strategic shift to collaboration and cooperation from competition (*Trend Letter,* 1994), this teamwork implies mutual respect, open communication, and well-chosen, well-treated people—no easy feat in today's business world.

Fortune, in their issue "Managing Amid Chaos" (Huey, 1993, p. 44), describes the culture shock of an ex-IBMer, now chief executive at Taligent, the joint venture of IBM and Apple. Creating the technology to compete with Microsoft and Next is the challenge, but creating a new corporate culture out of the collision of two diametrically opposed operating philosophies is tough, a kind of "Big Blue comes to Steve's garage" culture (p. 44). The conclusion is that the changes needed in individual cultures to make this a success are next to impossible.

However, let me caution, the consensus of my clients in the corporate world is although there is much talk of "teamwork," the reality is still the old cynical formula: You move up by stepping over dead bodies!

Type CC adults facing the current realities of their careers in collision can begin to accept the necessity to change and develop new skills; however, the emotional pain of change, irrational and frequently mindless, is an unexpected and very real factor.

THE PAIN OF CHANGE

Dark Night of
the Soul

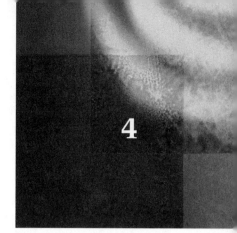

The Challenge
of Change

4

"Resistance to change is a universal phenomenon and when pitted against change, it gives rise to fear that ultimately intensifies the conflict."

—Frederic Flach

Fear of change, especially a career change, blocks us from taking creative control of our work lives. We must understand the human side of change, our resistance to it, and how this negatively affects our career decisions. So far, this issue has not been adequately addressed.

Change, for most people, is essentially a four-letter word. Our leaders, even our presidents and would-be presidents, have had problems with change. President Woodrow Wilson said, "If you want to make enemies, try to change something." Adlai Stevenson remarked that "change is inevitable, change for the better is a full-time job." President Kennedy said, "Progress is a nice word, but change is its motivator. And change has its enemies." In a recent speech to forty thousand Americans, President Clinton stated that Americans are resisting change and turning inward, away from dealing with community problems, because of job insecurity. "I hear a longing for yesterday," he added.

RESISTANCE TO CHANGE

Reared in a world that for the past seventy-five years has defined career success in terms of one job in one organization with forty years of security in a clearly defined career path, many adults today find our current environment almost impossible to understand. This risk-averse definition of success is thwarting our ability to accept and to deal creatively with the rapid changes in our new economy, which require us, sometimes very quickly, to make major realignments in our career/life values, views, and expectations. Although some people adapt to change more readily than others, resistance to change is currently the common barrier to effective career management, as well as organizational restructuring.

We hear daily that change is the only constant in our age, and certainly the greatest cause of career failure will be our inability or unwillingness to change. We must not focus only on the chaos and disorder that change initially creates. To succeed now and in the future, we must learn to embrace change as a positive force and to scout for the emerging needs and opportunities it creates.

WHY WE FEAR CHANGE

Why do we fear change? The reasons are as varied and complex as human behavior itself. With change comes the unknown—risk, readjustment, success, failure, and pain. We are forced to leave something familiar behind, but we may not know what. Many of our messages on our values, needs, and expectations have come from external sources so that we have no internal core instincts and being—no consistent "I" to guide our behavior. Our current revolutionary speed of change also greatly adds to the complexity and chaos.

James O'Toole lists thirty reasons relating to the root causes of resistance to change (1995, p.161). They range to homeostasis—meaning that continual change is not natural, therefore resistance to change is healthy—to inertia, self-interest, fear, lack of confidence, unpredictable cynicism, ego, myopia, and habit. The despotism of custom and the collective denial experienced by our most rigorous researchers and scientists, as pointed out by Thomas Kuhn (1970), demonstrates that real change is a challenge.

Mixed Messages

Mixed messages and lack of leadership fuel our fear, as we Americans face a number of confusing paradoxes relating to change. We hear that we will be required to reinvent our civilization to deal effectively with all these changes. However, millions lack the confidence, information, and strategies to release the patterns of the former age, and we have no reliable guidebook on how to move on to the new frontier of the Age of Technology and Information. While we hear in speeches and slogans the value and the necessity for change, few, if indeed any, leaders have spelled out any real specifics. Unfortunately, those recommending all these changes are not coaching us on the "how."

Alvin Toffler (1980), in *The Third Wave,* provides five hundred pages of excellent details of the rapid changes in our era but only eleven pages on the psychological issues of the future. Apparently we are expected to jump into major change with only a vague, generalized command to do so, as if change is simply a rearrangement of our internal and external world, an automatic act like blinking our eyes. Or else it seems to be assumed that we already know how to maneuver cheerfully and successfully through an increasingly complex world.

Lack of Control

When employees perceive change as out of their control, unfair, or arbitrary, they become resistant and cynical. These changes that we do not design or are thrust upon us unexpectedly, which we can't control or understand—that is, most changes in our work lives—can be overwhelming. Since many individuals feel so little control over the rest of their lives, the need for control over their work life becomes more important.

The leaders of organizations trying to bring about massive change seem to have little insight into the resistance and apprehension, both overt and covert, with which these changes will be met. Many employees perceive such changes and reorganization as making it difficult for them to do well the job they value. They are trying to adapt to changed procedures and policies with little communication or feedback from management. Sometimes resistance to changes goes underground but is still active. Initially, 75 percent of the working population will resist change, actively or passively. Twenty percent of employees may make the changes gradually, but only five percent may really welcome them.

These days, many executives are saying the right words but those words are proving meaningless. In working with people on all levels, I have gained much respect for their innate intelligence and insight into the reality of their workplace; they resent being misled and manipulated, and leaders would be smarter to "tell it like it is." In fact, the problem with massive changes in organizations is often the human factor, not the restructuring plan itself. Many large corporations were predominantly nonchanging, so they frequently fail to adequately consider this human factor now when reorganization is occurring. Feeling betrayed and abandoned, employees vent anger by ingeniously stalling the changes being attempted by the organization. Assuming that people will follow them because they are right is an error that trips up most potential leaders before they get to the starting block. When employees see change as out of their control there will be great resistance to it.

Going Counterculture

Being different, deviating from our past is another major reason why changing careers is so difficult. Change directly challenges the dominant stable personality culture of our workplace, our family teachings, and the larger environments these institutions inhabit. To change careers involves going counter to our expectations. To introduce a countercultural practice such as a radical career change, we need to combine thoughtful insight, power of conviction, and a forceful personality.

Negative Internal Conversations

We often have negative internal monologues relating to changing, which is another reason we resist change. Generally in the past, change has not been seen as a growth opportunity. We may say we can successfully change careers and make a decent living while doing something with real meaning, but then a little voice from our earlier generation silently says, Are you kidding? What do you expect from life? Work isn't supposed to be enjoyable, just do it. Perhaps this goes straight back to Plato, who viewed change as evil and cleanliness as a lack of change. Many, especially if they are in a status career or caught in the "golden handcuffs," express feelings of shame and guilt for merely considering a career change.

Quick Fix

Some expect a one-step solution and have difficulty handling the tension and timing involved in moving toward their future image: They want to do it in one giant, easy leap. Frequently they have struggled for years with a major career problem, and now they want to solve it in two weeks. Constant rapid changes and the diversity of our options today create complexity and therefore a decision-making crisis for many who want simple, immediate answers and results. The act itself of jumping into a new career field may not be so difficult, but changing or redirecting your career successfully for lasting satisfaction is not easy. We do have multiple options, once we really begin to pick up on them, so using time wisely and choosing can become an issue.

Information, both the lack of it and the rapidly increasing overload of isolated data and information, is a major problem in dealing with a deliberate career change. We need creativity, determination, synthesis, and a strategy to sort through possible matching career patterns, and to understand rapidly developing current and future opportunities. To understand what information is useful or crucial, and what is merely peripheral, outdated, and misleading, creates tension and frustration and requires creative but pragmatic problem solving and decision making. An ongoing internal monologue is needed to sort out the real from the garbage.

Lack of Visualization

Change is difficult if we can't see it in our mind's eye. To change successfully, we must have an intuitive but well-informed vision both within us and externally. A balance between inner conviction and a realistic view of conditions, trends, and opportunities in our outer environment is critical.

An awareness and understanding of what we want to change and of the barriers to change, and a redefinition of the attitudes and behavior that we want in the future, helps us visualize change. When the direction is clear, we can feel a measure of control and move forward more confidently. During this process of change, as we are struggling with our problem solving, it is most critical that we learn to use our intuition and not just our learned behavior. Many seeking career change are simply unaware of their options, while others believe themselves to be victims like Sisyphus, with no way out of their current work situation. Still others have a sense of unworthiness, believing that they are undeserving of better. Surprisingly, many high-placed professionals cannot visualize a successful career change. Their career identity programming is so strong that they seem unable to focus their creative problem-solving ability on their own career problem.

Complexity

To understand our resistance to change and the difficulty in making major readjustments in our careers, we need to examine what happens when we change. Real change is a two-part process: first, the internal—our conscious and our subconscious, our spirit, mind, soul, psyche, hopes, dreams, motives, will, values, purpose, instincts, and competencies; and second, the external—our environment, workplace, history, geography, politics, economy, skills, colleagues, and culture. When we begin to shift both the internal and the external at the same time, especially when we have no clear picture of our next step, we can understand why a major career change is quite complex and sometimes seemingly impossible.

AMERICAN ARCHETYPES OF CHANGE

To explore and understand our response to change, we need to connect with a deeper understanding of how we respond to a cultural change as massive as today's. Our unconscious images, our particular archetypes of change may help us understand our reaction to making a successful change.

The research into American archetypes by G. Clotaire Ropaille (1976), a cultural anthropologist and psychoanalyst turned archetypolist, could give us clues here. Briefly, his work focuses on the transitional years of early childhood, from ages one through six. Children, according to Ropaille, are shaped by forces and people around them, and they begin to take on the qualities of the men and women they gradually become. Language is a very important part of this assimilation. As children learn a language, they grasp the meaning and the emotion through the external events that accompany the words, and these imprint on them. We lose that specific memory imprint as we get older, but the language and emotion created by the imprint are important in programming the subconscious.

Carl G. Jung, in discussing universal archetypes, found that all humans possess certain instinctive reactions that are biologically structured at birth. People sharing the same culture generally share similar or identical imprinted structure for many words. These are an original pattern, a model prototype, and so are the same for a given culture.

Working from a foundation of Jung's universal archetypes and Freud's ideas of the individual unconscious, Dr. Ropaille developed the concepts of the cultural unconscious and cultural archetypes. Consciously people aren't aware of their imprint structures, yet these archetypes influence and affect our decisions both conscious and unconscious. Ropaille also found that we are not aware of our response to these imprints, since they exist at a much deeper level than we realize. He contends that there are patterns for all aspects of human life, and they will vary from culture to culture.

Changes on the *conscious* level—what people believe based on their current knowledge and opinions—happen with great frequency, but as we move into the unconscious, which is the seat of these cultural imprints, the rate of change decreases dramatically. The cultural *unconscious* can change but at a very slow pace—perhaps over centuries. These cultural archetypes have great stability. They reveal information deep inside the mind, behind the emotional reaction.

Ropaille's original study (Zuckerman and Hatala, 1992) specifically set out to find America's notion of "quality." They discovered "quality" was a highly emotionally concept for Americans and that Americans are vulnerable to what others expect and want. Specifically, Ropaille found that such catch phrases as "Do it right the first time" and "zero deficits" are more debilitating than motivating; they make people feel restricted and controlled. This is because innately and culturally, Americans live according to an unconscious pattern, and as much as they want to do things right the first time, an internal voice tells them that things simply cannot be done right the first time. They resolve this internal conflict by taking few risks.

In other words, in America, perfection has unpleasant connotations and is not the same as quality. In fact, the classic American success story is that of the underdog who becomes a champion, who overcomes great odds—but who fails the first time.

According to Ropaille's research, the words *new, change, possibility, opportunity,* and *breakthrough* excite us and stimulate positive feelings associated with creativity and innovation. If Ropaille's research is correct, that these words are deeply embedded in our archetypes as Americans, then why do so many adults today resist change, especially in their work life? This enigma is certainly worthy of research.

Also, according to Ropaille's research, Americans see painful beginnings as good news; the initial pain fuels the ultimate drive to succeed. Success results from overcoming obstacles, from transforming negative emotion into positive energy. However, to authors Zuckerman and Hatala, this transformation of negative emotion into positive energy is automatic, may not happen in some cases, and certainly is not happening to millions of Americans today. Many talented people are not seeing crisis and change as opportunity but as the breakdown and failure of our entire American Dream and cause for cynicism and despair.

There are three phases to this process of transformation of negative emotion to positive energy, according to Zuckerman and Hatala. The first phase is crisis, failure, and disorder. In this emotional phase, people are closed to learning. The second phase is gaining support from others, and so we turn to teachers, coaches, and mentors, who guide and direct. The third stage is the champion winning out over difficulty, and the celebration of success.

Zuckerman and Hatala say that supposedly Americans, deep down, thrive on and value change and don't fear early failure. Why then is change initially so frightening to so many adults today? Could it be because in the last fifty years, fed with Depression-era stories and our corporate career model, we have been programmed with messages about stability and security, and thus our first reaction is intense resistance to change? However, when we begin to work through this conscious level and get deeper, down to our archetypal imprints, perhaps the fear will decrease and defuse. In other words, perhaps our fear comes from our conscious-level training, not from our cultural archetypes. Perhaps when we Americans let go of our surface teachings, designed for an age far different from the twenty-first century, we can deal with change and new beginnings creatively and powerfully.

For these complex reasons, changing careers successfully takes time. We need to peel away several layers of our conscious beliefs so we can realize and name what is uniquely us—our DNA fingerprint. But we don't go to this deeper level unless we are under intense pressure, forced out of our current comfort zone.

Here is another paradox: We perceive resistance to change as a mature response to facts of life, since we often view people who make frequent changes as somehow unstable or immature. Whether change is sought or resisted, whether it happens by chance or design, whether we look at it from the standpoint of individuals or institutions, a majority of us are ambivalent about it. Perhaps this is the clash of our conscious learned responses to change with our archetypes, our unconscious responses. It seems that our will to adapt to change has to overcome an impulse to restore our past.

CHANGING CAREERS AND THE THEORY OF CHAOS

Liberating knowledge, information that provides understanding of change in order to overcome what seems like an innate, natural resistance, can come from unusual sources. Twenty years ago, I encountered new developing theories from science and physics that provided major professional and personal insight for understanding and accepting change: the scientific theories and writings of Kuhn, Toffler, Capri, Ferguson, Assagioli, and Prigogine, concerning the theory of chaos, the changing face of science and scientific and cultural revolutions. Reading these authors provided powerful insight that freed me to explore alternative views of reality.

Specifically, the research of Ilya Prigogine, who became the 1978 Nobel Laureate in chemistry for his theory of dissipative structures—the basis of the chaos theory—was important to my insight into change. He found that most self-renewing organisms will eventually break down, fall apart, or die off. The new can then grow in their place and take the organism to a higher level. This self-renewal is the essential characteristic of all self-organizing and self-renewing systems. Human beings, unlike machines, are highly self-organizing, self-renewing organisms. The renewal does not occur, however, unless the former breaks apart.

Prigogine was a practicing physical chemist and a trained musician who had originally considered studying psychology. Consequently he saw this self-renewing theory applying not merely to science but also to philosophy and to the human condition. Since his early work in the 1970s, the chaos theory is now applied to literature, the environment, education, the stock market, systems analysis, brain research, and psychology. The process that follows the chaotic breaking apart is the process of rebuilding, renewing, and revitalizing ourselves. Change is a vital part of our growth as we build a new identity or system and move toward a higher level.

Prigogine's theory of dissipative structures is key to understanding the nature of change, recognizing and accepting its value, and conquering the fear of it. To understand change in ourselves and our careers today, it is helpful to relate this theory of chaos to the disorder that seems to come suddenly from nowhere. Where once all was predictable, now there are confusion and complexity. Perturbations and shifts that have appeared so small, incidental, and random, hardly worthy of notice, suddenly loom as major disorder, creating changes quite different from those anticipated at the starting point. Small shifts can eventually create great change just as, theoretically, the flutter of a butterfly's wings in California can eventually create a thunderstorm in Europe.

There are two prime features of the study of chaos that are helpful in understanding and accepting the value of change: 1) unpredictability, and 2) the variation of initial values, or the starting points. In chaotic behavior, when the initial conditions begin to change, the difference can increase rapidly, leading to dramatically different pictures of the same process. In other words, when we are seemingly in a stable state, changes that start out as barely noticeable or identifiable can very quickly multiply. What may be small changes in our existing systems or our individual worlds can create many different political, social, and biological systems. Today, with so many possible rapid and increasing changes from all directions and all fields, it seems impossible to predict where major shifts, with their disorder and chaos, will hit us next. It will certainly require all our foresight, intuition, and creativity to maintain a measure of control.

Thus, predicting results in a chaotic system such as our current work world is relatively difficult, and perhaps seemingly impossible, because measuring the initial conditions with infinite precision is not possible. Reality and prediction may have little in common. However, to my initial amazement, chaos, in all its seeming complexity and random patterns, actually has an identifiable pattern and order, and is not totally random. It can actually be tracked and graphed.

In dealing with the chaos and complex issues of our careers, we must learn how to act creatively in the face of uncertainty and this early disorder, while we consciously search for the basic fundamental order. While the reality of the future is unpredictable, it can be more manageable than we might initially believe. From science we know that microbes that learned how to cooperate with changing forces of a chaotic world, instead of going underground, brought a new level of complexity into existence. If we can learn how to identify, cooperate with, and integrate the changes in our workplace, we can certainly flourish.

Of course, another option we can take during this chaotic period is to try to go underground to hang onto our status quo, to try at any price to escape the complexity of change, forfeiting our creativity and career dreams and certainly not advancing. Choosing to change and find the order in the disorder is the wise choice ultimately, but it doesn't assure immediate success.

But if change for the better happens quickly and easily, maybe it is only temporary. We soon may find ourselves unconsciously reverting to our former status and remaining there. This we can avoid by not making a premature career decision in order to escape the immediate pain of a work situation. Change that is real and workable can take time—"Only that which is deeply felt can change us. Penetrating to the roads of fears and doubts, we can change radically" (Ferguson, 1980, p. 36). It is on this level that we must travel to change careers.

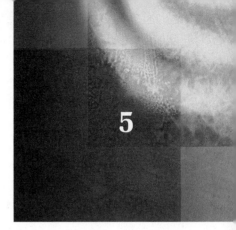

Career Unrest and Dissatisfaction

5

"One of the blessings of living in an age of anxiety is that we are forced to become aware of ourselves."

—Rollo May

The fallout of our current career shock, the collision between our current job and career reality and our past expectations, create extreme work dissatisfaction and career unrest. Much more than an occasional "blue funk down day" or the "Monday morning blahs," career unrest can range from occasional pangs, dull aches, feelings of loss, incompleteness, and questions such as, Is this all there is? to a prolonged emotional disability that will adversely and severely affect our physical, intellectual, and psychological health. It can directly curtail all factors related to work: creativity in solving problems, competence in using skills, motivation to learn and grow, career focus, direction and control, and foresight and awareness of emerging career opportunities and options.

If we continue to be trapped in this Sisyphus Syndrome, to see our world only in terms of entropy, fragmentation, and mindlessness, to believe that we have little or no control over our work life, we are victims. A victim mentally gives up, loses hope, feels and acts powerless, which kills the soul, intuition, creativity, and will. Emptiness, cynicism, and estrangement, forms of alienation caused by the feeling of being trapped and powerless, affect 32 percent of the work world and are the typical complaints of clients in severe career unrest (May, 1953, p. 185). Unaided by the rules, ethics, and formulas that guided other generations, we have become like early explorers, adrift without a map or compass in a frightening new world, with no "right" answers. We are being forced to face critical questions without society's former guidelines.

IS THIS ALL THERE IS?
AND OTHER PUZZLING QUESTIONS

In this time of chaos in career and in personal life, when there exist few standards for who we are and what we ought to be, we must undertake this search ourselves, first internally and then externally. Insecurity will force us to reexamine and redefine all our needs and resources. This provides new incentive to ask ourselves basic philosophical, cultural, and career questions, such as the following:

- What is the nature of being human in today's changing world? Are we hardy, resourceful, optimistic, and resilient or are we powerless, paralyzed, anxious, and apathetic? Have we lost our spirit and initiative? Need we be psychologically impoverished because we must change? Or have we the innate ability to judge, to choose, to act, and to change despite current chaos? Who or what is responsible for all this chaos?

- What do I owe myself, my community, my fellow human? Am I my brother's and sister's keeper? Should I expect the corporation or the government to be my keeper?

- What has real meaning for me in my work? How can I discover this? Am I expecting too much from my work life? Do I have the right to expect work that is meaningful and financially rewarding? On the other hand, do I owe it to the world and to myself to find work that provides enjoyment and worth?

- Am I overlooking sources of strength and the guidance I need in these very stressful times? What additional instinctive resources can help me thrive, not merely survive?

- What opportunities, challenges, and needs are evolving but overlooked in our environment? As the familiar drops away, what is replacing it?

- What are my unique career and life success criteria? What do I really want? What is the power source of my motivation, my energy, my payoff? What am I actually doing when I am unaware of the passage of time?

The questions keep coming, the answers are complex, and there are few educational and cultural resources to provide for this process of discovery. It can be lonely, but it is an absolutely essential search.

WHO CAN HELP?
THE BLIND LEADING THE BLIND

What happens when we feel extreme career unrest? We know that our work life is out of control, without direction, and perhaps actually provoking physical and emotional illness, but we have no clue as to what to do about it. We can try to ignore it, and join the ranks of millions of fellow Sisyphesians, trapped and dehumanized in our work. We do have the option of taking action to regain a sense of purpose and meaning in our work, but how and who can help us?

Our traditional profit and nonprofit organizations, in their own throes of falling apart, restructuring, and cutting back with an eye to the bottom line, cannot be counted on to provide employees with assistance in successfully managing their individual careers. If "downsized" employees are lucky, the company provides outplacement, aimed at helping them find a job in that same field. Outplacement services as they have been practiced in the past, though quite expensive, most frequently are provided to relieve the employers' guilt and are not equipped with the resources, nor geared for the creativity or commitment of guiding a searching adult through a successful radical career change.

Nor will the government, with its outdated work policies, be of much help. Frequently, our own families and communities still employ the old rules, beliefs, and standards, and unknowingly, in their questioning and advising, may discourage rather than reenforce. Society's major institutions that have always been relied on are at least two decades behind today's reality. We are on our own.

A major question we should pose is, Can we find or develop the strength within ourselves to face, understand, and conquer the insecurities in this changing, complex age, especially as it relates to changing careers? Indeed we are pathfinders on a new and rapidly changing frontier.

CAREER UNREST:
FEW CAREERS ARE IMMUNE

Before leaping ahead, let us take time to examine the universality of career shock and career unrest. As we live through the 1990s, we can count on a rapidly increasing epidemic of career unrest with no career immune. *The Cynical American: Living and Working in an Age of Discontent and Disillusion* (Kanter and Mirvis, 1989, p. 182) reports that

30 percent of the workforce in America has such a dissatisfied attitude about their place of employment that it directly depresses productivity and proves a serious drain on morale. A Louis Harris poll reported in "An American Renaissance in the Year 2000," (Cetron, 1994, p. 7) found that only 39 percent of workers say they intend to hold the same job five years from now. No respecter of economic level, age, or profession, work dissatisfaction—long well-documented among blue-collar workers—is stalking millions of "high-status" professionals also. The same source also predicted a career change every ten years.

Another study of one thousand successful American men reported that an estimated 70 percent suffered bouts of career unrest, of which 18 percent never recovered (Oliver, 1981, p. 3). Halper (1988, p. 16) found that 58 percent of successful businesspeople felt they had sacrificed their identities and wasted years of their lives. Many talked of making changes but didn't. They seemed trapped, unable to change, or even to visualize it. The National Center for Education Statistics (1993) reported in 1988 that only 40 percent of public school teachers said they would become teachers again, while 50 percent of private teachers felt the same.

A high percentage of my clients seeking career options are attorneys. A 1991 survey by the American Bar Association, released as a conference report at the A.B.A. annual meeting in Atlanta, found that only 33 percent of the nation's lawyers said they were satisfied with their careers, a decrease of 20 percent from a similar study compiled in 1984. Some 225,000 lawyers (41 percent), like those in Halper's study, said they would change careers immediately "if suitable alternatives surfaced." This phrase strikes an ironic chord, for it indicates a passive tone. Currently only forty thousand lawyers out of one million per year actually leave the profession. Lawyers with career unrest report that factors that contribute to their dissatisfaction include the stress of unrelenting long hours, an adversarial environment even among their own colleagues, increased competition, dull and repetitive paperwork, and most important, the general loss of professional status in the wider community.

For lawyers, another major factor has to do with finding meaning in the practice of law. Many went into law originally to serve an idealistic social need. However, something happens in law school, since after graduation most do not attempt to practice law in this manner. Instead, they go to work for large law firms at substantial salaries and long hours. For many, serious dissatisfaction arises regardless of high salary. In many law environments, the collegiate atmosphere has been replaced by adversarial, highly competitive co-workers. Paradoxically, many of my clients who are lawyers nevertheless express guilt at even considering the abandonment of law since it formerly enjoyed so much status.

In the past, it has been unthinkable for medical doctors to express dissatisfaction with their profession, but this is shifting very rapidly. *Dallas Morning News* (1993) reported that the Texas Medical Association, in a 1992 survey of six hundred M.D.s, found that 40 percent said that, based on their experience, they would not attend medical school again and would not recommend a medical career to someone else. This professional association publicly expressed surprise at the high number of disgruntled doctors, saying they felt it would be nearer 1 percent, and certainly not 40 percent! The doctors reported disillusionment caused by what they called the "hassle factors"—regulatory overload, insurance irritations, increased work overhead, an increasingly litigious society, and negative publicity in the media. The fact that the AMA finds this level of dissatisfaction a surprise indicates that frequently, perhaps, the very groups designed to monitor and further professional careers are out of touch or not choosing to acknowledge the career shock and unrest of their membership. Career unrest has hit the medical profession hard, and the radical changes are only beginning. Thousands of physicians are coming out of training owing six-figure medical school debts and have little chance of making the income expected in the past.

According to studies in the past, a high percentage of students entering medical school initially expressed an interest in family practice, but after medical training, few actually go into general practice. This is a repeat of the law school experience. What happens to this initial social orientation for law and medicine during the professional training years? In the 1950s, I observed my husband's medical school classmates from the freshman year through the period of internship. Seemingly in the name of scientific, clinical medical training, much of the human and social orientation was squeezed out of many of them. Only a few of them chose general practice in the face of their instructors' apparent disapproval. This could be the missing element that leaves so many in these professions open and vulnerable to criticism by the general population today. It could also account for the grave unrest expressed by many of these professionals.

My research, over a three-year period, in developing and delivering a diversity training project for the sergeants and lieutenants of a large urban police department revealed overwhelming job dissatisfaction and severe stress. Lack of strong leadership and professional management, little control and support in daily job activities, chaos and inefficiency in the court system, and again, low respect from the public, along with ambiguity in changing role expectations for law enforcement, have resulted in sharply escalating mental and physical health problems among their ranks. A recent popular T.V. news program reported that in New York in one year, more police officers died from suicide than in the line of duty. Sixty police officers took their own lives, compared with twenty that were lost on the job. High stress provoking extreme job dissatisfaction is a very real occupational hazard within law enforcement.

Research has also surfaced that the suicide rate for police officers is only matched by that of the dental profession, which is also currently experiencing severe career problems. "Many dentists and dental students suffer from depression, live anhedonic lives and relate to others with remoteness and discomfort" (Freedman and Kaplan, 1975, pp. 1069–1071). According to the Texas Bar Association, lawyers are now exceeding dentists in the suicide rate. To further understand career unrest, a physician friend has suggested a comparison of the career unrest of these three professions—law, dentistry, and police officers—with professions close to nature, such as farmers, foresters, landscapers, and veterinary medicine practitioners.

FALLOUT OF CAREER UNREST

Before examining specifically the sources of career unrest, we should examine its effects. Visible or invisible, career unrest negatively influences both the individual and the organization. Repressed creativity or self-expression is a major problem, as the employee ceases to actively learn and grow on the job. This precipitates a dramatic downward competency spiral leading to decreased motivation, increased boredom, detachment, and lowered self-esteem. This stalled growth creates countless negative reactions: "What if?" self-questioning, doubts about competency, dissatisfaction with responsibilities, possibly even conflict with co-workers, as well as feelings of career obsolescence, of being "over the hill."

How important is the relationship of creativity to career unrest? As mentioned earlier, my private clients in career change have shown a high need for creativity in their work, though not creativity limited to the arts but based in a broader need for self-expression. Many clients, having previously ranked themselves low on creativity, are initially surprised at their high creativity need defined by personality inventories and my observation. However, after examining the concept of creativity, and reflecting on their career needs, they recognize it as a major piece of their changing career pattern and at least a partial source of their career unrest.

Absenteeism, Lower Productivity, Increased Medical Costs

What begins as an individual's private sense of an intangible loss becomes tangible and concrete through reduced productivity for the organization as individuals enter into a maintenance-only mode. On the surface, they perform according to the job description but expend little, if any, discriminatory effort to confront and resolve problems that naturally arise, before they become full-blown. "Going the extra mile" is absent. Those in career unrest with repressed creativity tend to play it safe and do the job routinely with little extra thought or effort.

The real problem for the organization is that which is left undone, not doing the wrong thing or simply failing. Unused creativity resulting from job dissatisfaction results in a plateaued career and subsequently in "shelf-sitting," and perhaps even becoming cleverly camouflaged organizational deadwood. Such nonproductive employees become reliably mediocre and prove it possible to retire without resigning from the job. This can in turn create company cynics who focus only on petty political game playing. At best, they can become the passive-aggressive employees who always feel put upon or put down, who can justify performing only well enough not to be fired. While organizations believe that all the cutbacks and layoffs will eliminate marginally productive employees, they fail to recognize the clever game playing that some use to fake motivational and productive roles. The future of the world economy depends on tapping employee creativity, imagination, and curiosity, according to Peters, a management consultant (1993, p. 100): "Anything that enhances the creative side of the institution, from the factory floor to the accounts receivable department is a plus now."

While stifled creativity and loss of productivity is an important direct effect of severe career unrest and work dissatisfaction, there are additional effects. A direct cost to employers is that of increased use of medical benefits and absenteeism. Jerold Lancour reported to the American Academy of Orthopedic Surgeons in San Francisco at the 1993 annual meeting that workers who have poor job ratings and conflicts with their colleagues tend to stay home longer following a work-related injury.

Decreased Physical and Mental Health

Decreased physical and mental health, an alarming result of severe career unrest, are the strongest predictors of early mortality from heart disease. This is especially important since heart problems remain the nation's number one killer and the biggest health concern in the United States, killing more than 925,000 people each year. Nearly fifty-nine million Americans have some form of the disease, with high blood pressure and coronary heart disease as the most common (*Dallas Morning News,* 1995). The number of people suffering from congestive heart failure has increased, though the death rate is in decline. Research over the past thirty years points directly to work dissatisfaction as a major factor. The relationship of job dissatisfaction and physical health is well documented, according to Bernie Siegel: "People who suffer unsatisfying jobs are assuming the victim role" (1986, p. 169).

This feeling of victimization is the major cause of hypertension, according to Peter Schnall (Beil, 1995) of the University of California, Irvine. He began his search for causes of hypertension fifteen years ago after realizing that this disease, affecting 50 million Americans, has escalated only during this century and cannot be totally explained by medical factors such as diet, age, and genetics. He reasoned that an outside cause would have to be something widespread among the population that people are exposed to for a long time. He has labeled this outside factor job strain, which is more complex than simple stress. Schnall found that work that causes job strain has many demands and pressures, with no feeling of control over the situation or the outcome. People suffering from job strain typically work at jobs they dislike and have little peer support.

Men who were classified as having job strain were three to five times more likely to have high blood pressure than men without job strain. His data on women are not yet complete. Schnall told the American Heart Association during an annual 1995 science briefing that "although studies are still ongoing, our research group believes that job strain is a risk factor for heart disease."

A later study by Stanford and Duke Universities' schools of medicine may seem to somewhat contradict this. They found that coronary artery disease, a heart attack risk factor, was as common in patients with low levels of job stress as in patients with high levels of stress. Patients with high or low job stress were equally likely to suffer a heart attack or die because of heart disease. The scientists found that job stress was more common in patients with normal heart arteries than in those whose arteries were blocked. Job stress was more common among women than men in the study population, which consisted mostly of white-collar workers.

The researchers, who noted that their findings contradict previous studies, said that the lack of evidence linking heart disease and job stress should not be interpreted as proof that psychological factors have no effect on the development of heart disease. They suggest that other job-related stressors and dissatisfactions such as low job security or inadequate pay may need to be included in later studies. Also, a more exact definition of work stress should be formed for future studies. We do need to realize that all stress on the job does not necessarily translate into job dissatisfaction and career unrest, since some individuals thrive on stress.

Leonard Hayflick, in *How and Why We Age* (1994), which stresses the importance of curing heart disease, emphasizes that curing cancer would add only two years to the average sixty-five-year-old American's life. However, curing heart disease would add fourteen years! Heart failure costs Americans almost $40 billion in health care bills. Since career unrest dissatisfactions have such a potential to cause heart problems, and the resolution of these has the potential to increase longevity, it makes sense to look at work-related issues in a much more serious way now and in the future.

Increased Risk of Heart Disease

More than two decades ago, a special task force study, *Work in America,* commissioned in 1973 by Elliot Richardson and chaired by James O'Toole, summarized the dramatic results of major studies linking early mortality from heart problems to job dissatisfaction. The overall conclusion of these studies was that the best predictor of longevity is work satisfaction (House, 1972). In an impressive fifteen-year study of aging and how it is affected by occupational stress, Palmore (1969) found that the best predictor of longevity was work satisfaction, with the second being happiness. According to his study, job satisfaction predicted longevity better than physical examination, tobacco use, diet, or genetic inheritance. Controlling these variables did not statistically alter the dominant role of work satisfaction for creating longevity.

Why is job satisfaction one of the best ways to extend life? The factors just mentioned—diet, exercise, medical care, and genetic inheritance—may account for only 25 percent of the risk factors in heart disease, the major cause of death in the United States. It appears that our work roles, working conditions, and other social factors relating to work contribute heavily to this unexpected 75 percent of risk factors. Levinson states that "physicians as a profession have not caught up altogether with other powerful non-visible toxic agents—namely, feelings. It seems extremely difficult to grasp the idea that feelings are the primary participants of behavior and a major influence on health and sickness" (1969, p. 79). This observation has been increasingly validated in the more than twenty years since this was written.

Currently, given that heart disease accounts for about one half of all deaths in the United States and that sociopsychological factors may account for much of the risk, the critical question becomes, What factors in our work are associated most directly with high risk of heart disease? According to *Work in America* (O'Toole, 1973, pp. 79–80), they are, in order of importance:

- Job dissatisfaction, tedious work, lack of recognition, poor relationships with co-workers, and poor working conditions.

- Low self-esteem and excessively rapid and continuous change in employment, particularly where jobs are lost by downsizing and plant closing.

- Occupational stress, an overwhelming work load with much responsibility, and conflict or ambiguity in one's role or duties. Work overload could be caused by lack of resources, time, or ability; hence there is a risk of failure. This is overload stress, the norm for the 1990s. Responsibility for other people, not things, is also a big stressor in many jobs. Handling power without guilt is an emotional ability that many talented employees who find themselves in management roles have not developed.

- Incongruity between job status and other aspects of life. If we have a high educational attainment but a low job status, it can result in anger, anxiety, fatigue, and depression. This will be increasingly true as educational attainments grow but appropriate job levels shrink.

- Lack of stability, security, and support in the job environment. This creates a health risk for both blue-collar workers and professionals. Organizations do not meet these three needs for most employees today. The individual must learn to provide these for him or herself.

- Certain characteristics, often associated with a Type A personality, such as aggressiveness, ambition, competitiveness, and a sense of urgency about time. Notice that these are traits most frequently tied to successful men in our society. And we wonder why men die younger than women! Personality alone may not make all the difference, but jobs affect personality and jobs affect different personalities differently.

All of these risk factors as identified in the early 1970s have only dramatically intensified and are so rampant in the current workplace that in fact they read like a job description for millions. The effect of improved methods of treating heart disease could be canceled out by our current chaotic work environment; if we cannot relieve this continual stress of work dissatisfaction, we could experience a major epidemic of heart disease in the next decade.

Since these studies, summarized in the 1970s, produced such dramatic conclusions, I became increasingly curious why more attention had not been given to the relationship of early death and job dissatisfaction. I contacted the research department of the American Heart Association in Pittsburgh and inquired about their most recent research into the relationship of work dissatisfaction and early mortality from heart problems. A summary of research studies (Marmot and Elliott, 1992) published almost twenty years after the first compiled study, *Work in America,* documented the following working conditions that have the highest correlation for creating heart disease:

- Lack of support, little opportunity for development, boring, repetitive tasks, and little or no impact on decision making on the job. The lower on the employment scale, the higher the risks.

- Vital exhaustion—burnout, in lay language—a feeling of being emptied and unable to recharge energy. A young person prone to myocardial infarction would start a working career with extreme vigor, enhanced by cardiovascular reactivity to challenges. As the person grows older, vigor is replaced by inertia. The energy expended does not result in social reward despite "immersed" efforts. There is nothing to recharge the battery and it is operating on residual energy only. Shift work and long working hours also contribute to myocardial infarction.

- Chronic work stress, defined according to combined subjective and objective criteria. This was associated with an elevated ratio of low density lipoprotein cholesterol to high density cholesterol.

- Alexithymia, the inability to differentiate emotions. This may be related to hypertension.

- Poor decision latitude and poor social network. This correlates with high urinary catecholamine excretion.

- Poor social network and working on a job classified as boring. This contributes to elevated venous plasma adrenaline: heart attacks.

The poorer the support on the job, the higher the heart rate. Spontaneous variations in social support at work are associated with variations in mean systolic blood pressure during a working day. During periods of poor support, the systolic blood pressure is higher and vice versa. This research is based on men and women in six occupations, on four different working days, three spaced four months apart. Blood pressure was measured every hour during these days. They discovered that:

- The inability to relax is associated with a high heart rate during sleep, in addition to the progression of coronary atherosclerosis.

- Feelings of loneliness at night may activate the sympathoadrenal system.

How one handles adversity, disappointments, losses, and life changes has an impact on heart disease. Hostility has been a successful predictor in several studies. Episodes of cardiovascular illness could be predicted by means of a high life change score and high "chronic discord" score. Type A behavior, including hostility, the Sisyphus Syndrome, vital exhaustion, immersion, and alexithymia are all psychological concepts. A "hot reactor" is a person who has strong psychological reactions to challenges. This may or may not be Type A behavior; however, identifying this can be a preventive measure against heart disease.

Threat to Mental Health

Extreme career unrest and job dissatisfaction are not only related to our physical but also to our mental health. Mentally healthy people esteem themselves and feel that they are leading a rewarding life. However, 50 percent of Americans experience mental illness at some time in their lives. This includes depression, anxiety, social phobia, and alcohol and substance abuse. Antisocial behavior and psychosis are only a small percent of these mental illnesses (*Dallas Morning News,* 1994).

Arthur Kornhauser, in his study of blue-collar workers (O'Toole, 1965, p. 83), concluded after a twenty-year study that 40 percent of the adults in our society have had symptoms of mental health problems, and the key correlation is between job satisfaction and mental health. Kornhauser's numbers are generally considered an underestimate by his colleagues, and his study's findings have been corroborated by subsequent studies. He concludes that poor mental health happens if work and life conditions create continuing frustration by not offering the means for progress toward desired goals that have become an essential element of one's self-identity as a worthy person. According to this study, the unsatisfactory mental health of many working people consists in no small measure of their dwarfed desires and deadened initiative, reduction of their goals, and restriction of their efforts to a point where life is relatively empty and only half meaningful at best. In the end, for these workers and millions today, there seems only two options: to maintain high expectations from work, and thereby suffer constant frustration, or to limit their expectations, which produces a drab existence with little hope. Negative means of coping with these work problems, such as alcoholism, drug abuse, and suicide, are directly connected to work dissatisfaction.

There is definitely a strong positive association between job satisfaction and mental health, according to the work of the University of Michigan's Institute for Social Research. They found that a variety of mental health problems have been related to the absence of job satisfaction. These include psychosomatic illnesses, low self-esteem, anxiety, worry, tension, and impaired interpersonal relations. The factors correlating with these problems seem to be low status, little autonomy, rapid technological change, isolation on the job, role conflict, role ambiguity, responsibility for managing people, shift work, and threats to self-esteem inherent in the appraisal system (O'Toole, 1973).

There's no question that job satisfaction is important to physical and emotional health. The links between alcoholism, drug abuse, suicide, and working conditions may not be firmly established, but there is strong evidence that meaningful work is therapeutic.

The greatest consequence of career unrest, the most serious and the deadliest, is this decreased physical and mental health. To my surprise, it has scarcely been stressed in the popular literature, and the public is hardly conscious of it. I first encountered this research in the 1970s and was alarmed. None of my twenty plus years of career research has suggested that these findings are not valid.

In summary, this research concluded that the most common work factors that negatively affect health, especially heart disease, are lack of support, no possibilities to learn, and inability to influence decision making. These are the same issues I hear over and over from adults struggling with continuing work problems. Final conclusions of these many current empirical studies point to direct connection between meaningful work, a healthy heart, and longevity. Career unrest and dislike for a job, coupled with today's chaotic work environment, is an explosive combination for our human health and spirit. In an extreme form, it can be a major factor directly connected with early death. Career unrest and job dissatisfaction cannot be ignored from a physical and mental health standpoint!

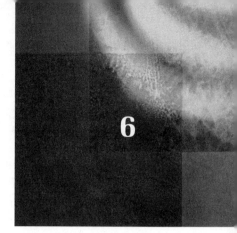

Discovering the Sources of Career Unrest

6

"The world will never be happy until all men have the souls of artists— I mean when they take pleasure in their jobs."

—Auguste Rodin

Perhaps you realize that career unrest is directly affecting your physical and mental health, and you must take action. Before seriously considering a career change, it is essential to identify the source of your career unrest and dissatisfaction, to know what you are trying to fix. Action without real insight is unwise. As you think about your dissatisfaction with your work life, it may be quite clear to you what the problem is. However, analyzing and identifying career unrest and its sources can be complex, requiring time and thought and perhaps professional help.

First, diagnose and understand as clearly as you can the career problem and the real source of your pain, and determine whether it is major or minor. If it is minor, treating it as major could create an even more serious problem. In the case of changing careers, "a little learning is a dangerous thing," both emotionally and financially.

DIAGNOSING THE SOURCE

Occasionally, some individuals will admit to a career problem but may want to avoid serious personal issues. They may view coming to a career change specialist as more acceptable than working with a therapist to solve personal problems. To identify the source of your problem requires some intuitive judgments. Ask yourself these questions:

1. Are you stuck, frustrated, or depressed because of work problems, or are the work problems created by personal and psychological issues? What do you see as the major problem in your career? Have you been under so much pressure for so long that you have little sense of the real issues? Have you thought things through and do you have a handle on the problem but simply don't understand how to fix it?

2. Are you considering a career change for a "push" or "pull" motivation? Is it a cry from pain or a call for purpose or meaning? Are you being pulled toward something that is more challenging and exciting, or are you trying to escape a difficult personal or work situation? Is the career unrest and dissatisfaction created by a healthy desire for growth and development at midlife? Is your restlessness a reflection of a healthy need to be on a learning curve, to develop a more meaningful life, to discover purpose, and to move to a higher level? Or are you avoiding a continuing problem in the environment of work, self, or both?

3. Is your career unrest related to poor personal coping skills on the job, lack of self-esteem or assertiveness, a wall of defenses, a false self, or other self-defeating behavior?

4. Is this unrest created by a lack of information on self and the work world? Do you need a process to surface, focus, and integrate this information into a usable form for you to make an effective career decision?

5. How did you select your original career? Did you base it on abilities, interests, and knowledge of the field, or did you slide into your career, perhaps by default or at someone else's urging?

6. Are you a victim of our now outdated career myths? Have the rules you assumed would bring career success simply stopped working, if indeed they ever really worked at all?

7. Is your career unrest related to unreal expectations of yourself and of the work world? Do you expect too much too soon, or are you such a perfectionist that you can never be fulfilled?

8. Are you considering a career change through necessity or desire? Has your career or job plateaued or disappeared, or did it simply never fit or provide enough for you?

9. Are you limited by an outmoded career system or only by your own thinking?

10. Are you currently on a learning curve in your work? Is that learning compatible with your self-concept? Are you learning what you love and value?

11. Are you searching for a career or for a job? While a job search and career search are related, they are two quite different processes. The job search in the new field is the last step of a comprehensive four-step career change process.

12. Do you have reasonable control of critical issues in your personal, financial, and physical lives?

13. Is your spouse or family supportive of your anticipated career shift? This support is a major factor in the successful undertaking of a career change.

14. Do you need personal therapy before attempting a career change? Are you at this time dealing with long-standing and possibly over-whelming personal problems rather than career issues directly? Are personal problems spilling over into your career, or have you worked through personal issues and now realize that your career was select-ed to fit an earlier "false self" that is no longer appropriate? Is restruc-turing your career part of the process of defining who you are becom-ing and not remaining a prisoner of the past deceased self? You may need to examine these personal issues before becoming involved in a career change process.

15. Do you have a drug or alcohol problem? Such problems must be dealt with successfully before beginning a career change process. Active drug and alcohol addictions are not compatible with a successful change process.

16. Do you expect a quick fix? Will you devote the time and consistent effort that it takes to make a career change?

These are questions to ask yourself as you begin to consider a career change. However, first it is critical to understand what is broken before we start to fix it. As a first step in considering a career change, determine the possible source of your career unrest by completing the rest of this chapter.

IDENTIFYING YOUR CAREER UNREST AND SATISFACTION

As shown in Figure 1, career unrest falls into four different levels: job unrest, organization/industry chaos, career content unrest, and career self unrest. A fifth level, personal life unrest, can spill over into career

FIGURE 1   COMPONENTS OF CAREER UNREST

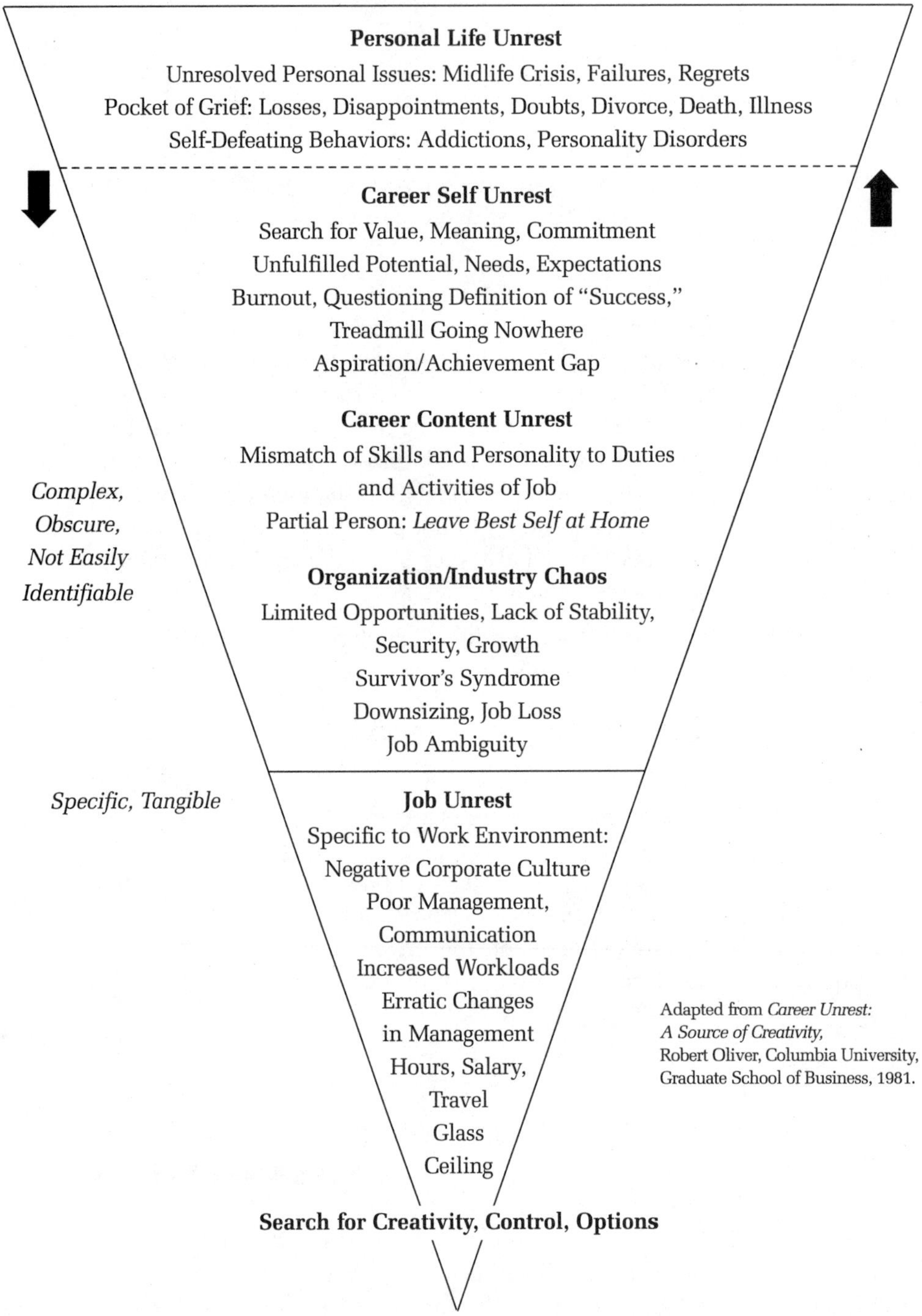

Personal Life Unrest
Unresolved Personal Issues: Midlife Crisis, Failures, Regrets
Pocket of Grief: Losses, Disappointments, Doubts, Divorce, Death, Illness
Self-Defeating Behaviors: Addictions, Personality Disorders

Career Self Unrest
Search for Value, Meaning, Commitment
Unfulfilled Potential, Needs, Expectations
Burnout, Questioning Definition of "Success,"
Treadmill Going Nowhere
Aspiration/Achievement Gap

Career Content Unrest
Mismatch of Skills and Personality to Duties
and Activities of Job
Partial Person: *Leave Best Self at Home*

Complex,
Obscure,
Not Easily
Identifiable

Organization/Industry Chaos
Limited Opportunities, Lack of Stability,
Security, Growth
Survivor's Syndrome
Downsizing, Job Loss
Job Ambiguity

Specific, Tangible   **Job Unrest**
Specific to Work Environment:
Negative Corporate Culture
Poor Management,
Communication
Increased Workloads
Erratic Changes
in Management
Hours, Salary,
Travel
Glass
Ceiling

Adapted from *Career Unrest:*
A Source of Creativity,
Robert Oliver, Columbia University,
Graduate School of Business, 1981.

Search for Creativity, Control, Options

issues, but it is not directly a career issue. What follows is a series of exercises that will help you identify which of these four sources of career unrest are most salient for you.

Job Unrest

This is an informal broad-brush exercise, but it will, along with the explanation of each level of unrest, provide basic insight into the source of your career unrest. If your total "no's" equal or exceed your "yeses," your overall career unrest may have several sources that definitely need attention on all levels. Or maybe the number of "no's" appears high in only one or two particular levels.

JOB UNREST—LEVEL I

	Yes	No	
1.	___	___	I have impact and control on most decisions affecting my work.
2.	___	___	Management provides adequate support for my work.
3.	___	___	I like the physical setting of my job.
4.	___	___	I like the hours I work.
5.	___	___	I like the people with whom I work.
6.	___	___	I am paid on a level equal to my responsibilities.
7.	___	___	My co-workers appreciate and respect my work.
8.	___	___	My company treats people fairly and ethically.
9.	___	___	I communicate well with co-workers and management.
10.	___	___	Management has reasonable expectations and goals.

Yes___ No___ **Total for Job Unrest**

Negative Environments

The questions on page 70 and 71 relate to *Job Unrest,* which is dissatisfaction with your specific working environment. Job unrest means that you are not getting what you perceive as needed and deserved from your particular organization or company and does not necessarily signal unrest with the particular career itself. It can be caused by a mismatch or conflict with the particular work situation, a negative or oppressive corporate culture, a glass ceiling and glass walls, no opportunities to grow and develop, lack of support, poor management, or the communication style of co-workers and supervisors. It can also be caused by the particular job requirements—too much travel, too many hours, or low pay for your industry. In the case of job unrest, a radical career change is overkill. Rather, the solution is to research other organizations, to find a company where the environment matches your particular requirements and needs, providing of course that you know what they are.

Frequently, clients from cold, critical, oppressive family environments gravitate to and remain in work situations that provide a similar environment. People who come from emotionally abusive families may find that their work environment repeats the same patterns. According to Anne Wilson Schaef and Diane Fassel (1990), this feels familiar but it is not healthy. There is no doubt that negative, difficult work environments are on the increase in this age of corporate survival at all costs. Market leadership, strong profits, ruthless management, and high stock prices certainly seem to count above all else to organizations, which may well be short sighted of them.

Ironically, most corporate executives in their public statements talk of the high value placed on their human resources—their "people"—yet it's just words. Perhaps these executives lack insight into the needs and motivations of people, especially their employees. Unenlightened managers may see employees as hardware or a machine to be trashed and easily replaced. For most companies, despite the verbiage, valuing its people has only rarely translated into reality. Employees, regardless of their educational level or job title, innately sense the truth. They fully comprehend the gap between what is said and what is actually felt and done by their employer. The realization of this gap is the source of much cynicism rampant among workers today.

What We Want in a Job

Just as Freud lamented, "What do women want?," in understanding our job unrest, we must ask ourselves what we really want in a job or from a company. What are our criteria for a good work environment? In 1983, a Public Agenda Foundation study (Naisbitt and Aburdene, 1985, p. 85) listed the following top ten qualities people want in a job (my experience validates these, except that today's employees use the terms *creativity, autonomy, control,* and *independence* perhaps more frequently):

- People who treat me with respect
- Interesting work
- Recognition
- Chance to develop my skills
- People who hear my ideas on doing things better
- Opportunity to think for myself rather than just carry out instructions
- Opportunity to see the end results of my [tangible] work
- Efficient managers
- A challenge
- Information about what is going on

Employees, in summary, want the satisfaction of knowing their work is competent, respected, and effective. Unfortunately, except in rare cases, a vast majority of our workplaces are not structured to offer this. Notice that job security, high pay, and good benefits, usually thought to be the highest priority as motivating factors, are not even on the top ten list, though they do make the top fifteen. Yet most companies today, as in the past, deal with people as if pay and benefits are the only ways to motivate employees. This paradox affects our work needs and reward system.

Organization Unrest

The second level of career unrest, *Organization/Industry Unrest,* is created by today's constant change and chaos within career fields and organizations. Though at one time the career field may have met our needs, the culture, expectations or challenges, and growth opportunities have now become severely limited, perhaps even nonexistent. Millions have lost their jobs through cutbacks and these jobs are not coming back. Notice your response to the following statements to understand if your unrest is being created by career shock and chaos.

ORGANIZATION/INDUSTRY UNREST—LEVEL II

	Yes	No	
1.	___	___	I can see myself in this career ten years from now.
2.	___	___	I feel I have creative control over my career.
3.	___	___	I can deal effectively with change and uncertainty.
4.	___	___	My career field has more opportunities than in the past.
5.	___	___	My industry is stable: I can count on keeping a good job.
6.	___	___	I have opportunities for growth and learning in my organization.
7.	___	___	I am aware of my options and have an alternate career plan.
8.	___	___	I can get what I need to achieve my career goals.
9.	___	___	I know changes and trends affecting my career.
10.	___	___	I know the steps to take to keep my career on track.

Yes___ No___ **Total for Organization/Industry Unrest**

For example, a client with a Ph.D. in English is exploring career change because, according to a new study of the American Association of University Professors (1995), nearly 40 percent of those teaching in U.S. colleges and universities are working part-time with little or no chance of advancement or job security. "I love my work and I'm an excellent teacher, but I want a full-time position in a challenging field, even if I must leave this career. My talents are not being used, I haven't grown intellectually in my part-time jobs, and of course I'm not satisfied with my income." For many who are changing careers, opportunities in their chosen field have disappeared, and as a result, they are forced in a different direction.

For many remaining in the workplace, all this change has created immense insecurity. Surviving the initial layoffs and mergers in an organization may provide some relief, but anxiety and fear of impending doom over additional cutbacks hover long after.

Executives in organizations, unless they have experienced it themselves, are not even remotely aware of the effects that cutbacks and downsizing have on the productivity and morale of the remaining employees. Those remaining employees suffer "survivor's syndrome" and feel guilt, anger, and sadness over the unjust way the cutbacks were handled by the organization and the very real loss of friends and colleagues. Alienated, they no longer trust the leadership of the organization and constantly wonder if they will be the next cut. One client of mine, a devoted, loyal, fifteen-year employee who took, as she called it, her "golden boot" or "early out," said she grieved over the loss of her family at IBM and missed the way the organization had been in the past. But her "family" had gone and she felt no sense of community in the new culture. It was not the same and she was happy to leave it behind.

Job ambiguity, uncertainty as to the nature and duties of the job after severe cutbacks, can be a very real problem for the remaining employees. A sense of competence for a job well done is a major need for productive employees, yet after layoffs and restructuring, they find themselves almost overnight laden with unfamiliar duties and lacking direction or control over them. Frequently they get little guidance from their immediate supervisor or manager since they too are probably confused, directionless, and alienated.

Another great source of difficulty is that these employees frequently find themselves burdened with the responsibilities that once belonged to multiple former employees. One client, in a corporate law department with eight other attorneys and with an already demanding work load, found herself the sole departmental survivor after a major cutback. There was no way she could even begin to know what was going on, much less do all the work. Since there had been no prior planning, she received no direction as to priorities on unfamiliar projects, and within a short time, overwhelmed and paralyzed (a natural response to such an overload), she was forced to take a medical leave.

As a longtime observer with connections to the business world, I seriously question the value of such employee-slashing by businesses. It may be necessary, but I wonder if it is only another passing fad, much like the mergers and buyouts of the 1980s. Like other quick fixes I've observed, they have ultimately created more problems than they solved. Some dramatic changes are necessary to meet new needs; however, these cutbacks could be only a Band-Aid, failing to provide a solution in the long run. Alternative methods, such as employee retraining or the use of part-time employees, while perhaps not quick or easy to plan and implement, could be a more productive approach in the long term. Careful, long-term planning is not characteristic of the style of most corporate executives. But this current "slash the troops" approach creates fear and severely limits productivity and creativity in workers that remain behind. Fear of job loss, or merely being grateful for having a job, does not spur creativity or translate into lasting motivation for human productivity: quite the contrary.

Not only are organizations changing but also entire industries and career fields are changing drastically, declining, and even rapidly disappearing altogether. Opportunities in manufacturing, law, real estate, banking, and finance have all recently changed dramatically, and many individuals involved with these may not have the skills or desire to accommodate these changes. Where they see their industry today, or where they see it headed, is not where they aspire to spend their future. Daily, I hear that the fields of law, teaching, banking, accounting, and medical practice are simply not what they were originally. As early as the mid 1970s, for example, of every nine Ph.D.s who wanted to teach at the college level, only one found a tenured track. This has not improved in the interim except that now there aren't as many Ph.D.s preparing to teach. A major change is coming for higher education, with loss of lifetime tenure almost a certainty.

This organization/industry chaos has left millions unemployed, confused, vulnerable, angry, and scared. Being without a job, and doing everything that the books, outplacement firms, and federal employment programs tell you to do to find a job only to discover that jobs in your career field simply are not there anymore, is like a minideath. Nothing prepares you for this pain and loss.

You know your industry is fast becoming obsolete. You have networked and shaken more hands than your local congressperson. Driven by stress and desperation, your disposition has soured. Your spouse and kids are worried about being on the streets and you've even had this nightmare yourself.

If you know your industry is fading and the jobs there are limited, a career change and refocus, though perhaps slow and painful, is your best option. In spite of the problems involved in changing careers, the goal is quite achievable. However, a note before launching into a radical career change: If you fit your career—if you love what you do and you see it as a very real need in the world—you should perhaps rethink your direction, acquire additional skills, and become more creative about making your current career work for you. Sometimes a different approach, not a career change, can solve the problem.

CAREER CONTEST UNREST—LEVEL III

	Yes	No	
1.	___	___	I like the type of work I do.
2.	___	___	I like the physical setting of my job.
3.	___	___	My talents are well utilized in my job.
4.	___	___	I enjoy my everyday work duties and activities.
5.	___	___	I feel that my personality matches my career.
6.	___	___	My work is building skills I enjoy using.
7.	___	___	My interests relate directly to my job.
8.	___	___	I am using creativity and self-expression at work.
9.	___	___	I feel successful and rewarded in my work.
10.	___	___	I feel I am in the right career field.

Yes___ No___   **Total for Career Contest Unrest**

Career Content Unrest

Career Content Unrest results when there is a mismatch of your skills and/or personality with the daily tasks and specific activities you perform on your job. Skills that you innately enjoy using and tasks you feel strongly competent in performing are either not used at all on the job or not used as much as you would like. Perhaps you perform the tasks and skills that are required by your job quite competently, but they may not come naturally to you. This is what I call an *overlaid function,* meaning the skills are learned but they are not your instinctive preferred skills. Consequently, they may seem rote, mechanical, unnatural. You feel no spontaneity, self-expression, or added flair when you use these skills. You follow the rules and do what must be done with little, if any, psychic payoff, and perhaps little, if any, extra effort. Notice your responses to the items above to determine the extent to which career content unrest may be a factor for you.

If we say that career content unrest is created by a skills mismatch, then we need to understand better the nature of human skills. Frankly, much work and research is needed in this area. However, we can say that there are three kinds of skills to match to the workplace for a good fit between person and occupation.

Technical Skills

Technical skills are acquired skills, the special knowledge skills and information we learn in order to accomplish specific tasks in a particular career or occupation that frequently requires formal training, certification, or licensing. These special skills can be self-taught, learned on the job, or acquired through formal training. Accounting, public speaking, medical technology, law, editing, writing, and speech pathology are some examples. Technical skills have a body of knowledge, theories, and a language or jargon of their own. They are consciously acquired and typically are the particular skills listed in a job description. While these specific knowledge skills are necessary for job success, for clients in career change they make up only about 10 percent of the skills that are important in changing careers, unless one moves into something like brain surgery or rocket science.

Functional Skills

Functional skills are those most needed for long-term success and satisfaction on the job, and certainly the most critical for a successful career change. Ironically, they are the most generally ignored in the job descriptions but by far the most important. They are innate instinctive skills—simply the way that we function probably as a result of both nature and nurture. These functional skills seem to flow naturally from us and are what we "have a knack" for doing well. These skills have not been consciously learned but are part of us, coming from what I call our DNA fingerprint because they are unique to each person. They are also called transferable skills because they are within us and accompany us to whatever environment we enter. These skills, which are used in working with data, ideas, people, and things in our work life, remain with us throughout our lifetime, though we may refine them and take them to a higher level.

Identifying our instinctive functional skills may not be easy for several reasons. Strangely, since these skills come so easily to us, we take them for granted, never stopping to identify and name them. Since they come to us so naturally, we assume that others have these same skills. Also, these skills can be latent, simply potential, if we haven't explored or developed the awareness to identify and use them consciously. It is essential to gain the vocabulary to name our functional skills so we can consciously use them. These transferrable functional skills claim at least 60 percent of the importance in making a career change. They will usually take us toward exhibiting great strength in working with data, ideas, people, or things. It is critical to our lasting success in our work to identify our major functional skills and the object or how we use these skills.

TABLE 1   FUNCTIONAL/TRANSFERABLE SKILLS

Data	Ideas	People	Things
Synthesizing	Innovating	Empathizing	Precision Working
Forecasting	Researching	Mentoring	Assembling
Budgeting	Developing	Appreciating	Manipulating
Auditing	Inventing	Consulting	Repairing
Categorizing	Problem Solving	Teaching	Inspecting
Compiling	Evaluating	Cooperating	Operating

Table 1 lists sample functional skills and the area of work activity they are most commonly used for.

Adaptive Skills

Adaptive or *self-management* skills, our personality or temperament traits, are a third group of skills critical to our career content satisfaction. These are the adjectives that describe us, our temperament and personality, a partial list of which is shown in Table 2. Our adaptive skills or traits are acquired early, genetically and/or learned from our family, our schools, and our culture in order to adapt and deal with our world. It is critical for us to understand these traits and match them to our working situation.

To understand these skills, these adjectives that describe you, ask yourself what major messages you received from your family and school about how you were supposed to be, to act, to become. For example, were you expected to be a leader: mature, independent, responsible, dependable, and a serious student? Think through these expectations, since they remain long with us and usually change only with therapy.

Self-management skills create the chemistry between people and the job. More people are hired and fired from their jobs because of these personality or adaptive skills than for any other factor in the workplace. People are frequently hired because those doing the hiring see their own traits reflected in the applicant and feel comfortable with them. People are fired most frequently not because they fail to perform on the job but because they do the job differently—too quickly, too slowly, too painstakingly, with a "wrong attitude" etc. They do not fit the expected norm of how the work should be performed, the attitude and style expected, or the image projected by an industry or an organization.

It is critical to match the expectations of how to be on the job. If we must perform in a manner contrary to our natural personality, if we must

TABLE 2   PERSONALITY TRAITS REFLECTING ADAPTIVE SKILLS

Reserved	Competitive	Trusting
Practical	Astute	Self-assured
Calm	Shy	Conscientious
Venturesome	Unpretentious	Controlled
Accommodating	Enthusiastic	Easygoing
Down-to-earth	Experimenting	Mature
Assertive	Tough-minded	Persistent
Imaginative	Genuine	Extroverted
Serious	Creative	Creative
Forthright	Resourceful	Innovative

wear a mask to work, problems will develop and eventually the mask will slip. In these circumstances, we are rewarded for not being ourselves, which can create very real self-esteem problems. Also, we may feel like outsiders and never really relate to or feel compatible with our co-workers.

Strong dissatisfaction from career content unrest, a mismatch of your skills to your career field, will not be solved by changing jobs or getting a new job in the same field. A career change or some serious restructuring should be considered. It is absolutely critical to clearly identify your strongest skills currently not used in your work and research carefully to see if you can match these to positions or opportunities in your present organization, especially if you like your organization and have tenure. Investigate carefully to determine if you can make a lateral move, a process that frequently takes research and connecting with co-workers throughout an organization. Some clients successfully change careers within their current organizations. Unfortunately, other organizations are not open to lateral transfers. Sometimes it's easier to make a career change by going to another organization. If the doors and minds are definitely closed and this repositioning cannot be accomplished in your current organization, then pursuing it in another environment is the next step.

If, after identifying the skills you wish to use but are currently not using, you determine that career content unrest is your career problem, you must then integrate them with your other functional skills, special knowledge, and experience. You may well have a unique package that will be highly marketable within your present organization, or with another one.

CAREER SELF UNREST—LEVEL IV

	Yes	No	
1.	___	___	My career provides meaning and value to my life.
2.	___	___	My career selection was based on my own aspirations and needs.
3.	___	___	I have a focused future image and a strategic plan for gaining it.
4.	___	___	I am learning new skills that I enjoy using.
5.	___	___	My work achievements are meeting my expectations.
6.	___	___	My work and personal life are well balanced.
7.	___	___	I enjoy gaining new insight in my career field.
8.	___	___	I keep abreast of activities in other career fields.
9.	___	___	My work makes an important contribution to others.
10.	___	___	I am growing personally and professionally.

Yes___ No___   **Total for Career Self Unrest**

Career Self Unrest

The fourth level of unrest, *career self unrest,* is a generalized sense of dissatisfaction related to one's work but directly connected to unmet inner needs. This unrest can be abstract, more difficult to define but very strong in its impact. It is a questioning of the meaning, value, and connection of one's work to a worthwhile purpose and as such is tied strongly with our deep value belief system of what is worthy and ethical. It is also related to vague feelings of unfulfilled potential, our aspiration-achievement gap. "I didn't start my life to end up doing this" is a frequent statement I hear from clients. There is a lack of connection between self-concept and current career. This issue of career self unrest will increase dramatically in the next decade. Respond to the statements above to gain a sense of whether career self unrest is a relevant issue for you.

A majority of "no's" to the above statements indicate you may be feeling career self unrest. Your work has little meaning or connection for you. It could be that you are on a fast-track career, but life in the fast lane isn't fun when you're running on fumes and you aren't eager to arrive at your destination anyway. In reality, you see yourself on a treadmill, racing hard to go nowhere, certainly not anyplace where you want to be.

Another source of career self unrest could relate to having had therapy, gained stronger mental health, and realized that the career that may have been adequate earlier does not fit the you that has emerged. You may be examining your priorities: Must success cost so much? Is there something beyond this? You are questioning and redefining your former idea of success.

However, you could feel strongly or perhaps only vaguely that something is missing. Your employer is okay and your job is okay, but you want more than okay in your life. You have no idea what is missing or what else you could do. You would like out—but to what? You don't know your options or even whether you have any, and you are fearful of searching them out. You would like to have creativity, control, and autonomy regarding your career, but what if your expectations are unrealistic? What if you search and can't find anything better? What if you discover what you really value but can't make a decent income from it? It may be wise to count your blessings and your money and slide along! You can retire in twenty years, but what will you do then?

In summary, your career self unrest may spring from three sources: 1) the search for commitment and meaning in your work; 2) the search for a sense of wholeness; or 3) self-defeating behavior or poor personal and professional coping skills. Career self unrest can relate to having felt successful earlier in a career but now discontented and unsatisfied. Or perhaps you are simply tired and burned out in a career selected at age seventeen, which is no longer appropriate for you at the age of forty. Perhaps you have grown and changed but the job and the career field has not. Or it may be the reverse—the career field has changed and is no longer satisfying.

Commitment and Meaning

As mentioned earlier, most of my clients in career self unrest have a need for meaning, but their career, as they see it, provides little or no opportunity to meet this need. They seek a move away from work as a means to an end and frequently ask, "Is it too much to expect my work to provide meaning and purpose for me?" Many were driven toward success but now face the disquieting realization that something is missing and are looking inward for the first time. I hear, "I don't know what is missing from my life and work, but there must be more than what I have now" and "I've been so focused and driven to arrive at the top that I've no idea who I am or what is important to me." Many say, "I want to make a difference in my world. I'm not contributing anything except to the bottom line of a faceless corporation. Who cares?" One attorney made this classic statement: "I tired of doing the worthless for the unworthy!"

Because the search for meaning in our careers is a basic need, we should ask what we mean by *meaning*. While the object of the search for meaning varies widely from client to client, it has in common a search for intentional significance, a reassurance of our uniqueness, that we are not just another grain of sand in a meaningless universe. Most of us want to know that we are here for a reason and that we contribute to something special—however we may define it—that we matter, that the world is better because we are here. We want to feel that day by day, step by step, we work to make a difference for ourselves and others.

Frequently the need for meaning is expressed as a need for creativity, challenges, growth, and learning. We want to exercise and to grow our talent and skills that we most delight in using, not in mere busywork but by doing something with a purposeful intention. It may not necessarily be an achievement for all the world to see and value as long as we know and feel its worth.

Daily, I deal with adults who are searching for this meaning in their careers. Are these people maladjusted misfits? Absolutely not! These are the best and brightest, frequently in highly responsible positions, some with annual incomes of more than $500 thousand a year. Most have all the outer trappings of success, but they know that something is missing. Even in the best of times, there was an abiding sense of discontent. Now, this sense has become more acute. These men and women are searching for more but have difficulty defining it because it has to do with the human spirit, the soul. They have a deep spiritual need to connect with work that matters to us personally. This very real need has not been factored into our definition of contemporary success, certainly not in the 1980s, the "Greed Decade." Many who long for work that fills a spiritual need may in fact feel some guilt because they cannot fit this into their current meaningless career—or they feel guilt for wanting to leave a stable profession.

As mentioned earlier, people in the workplace have been viewed primarily as operating under the machine model, as disposable separate parts that could be removed and replaced if they malfunctioned. I was actually told by a personnel director twenty years ago, "Dr. Harkness, you fix people. We don't do that—we throw them out and get new ones." The human spirit, the concept of human beings at their best, suggesting courage, dignity, commitment, and the will to live, lifts us beyond this machine paradigm. Currently, millions of Americans are searching for meaning beyond the primitive machine model, for a way to prevail creatively in spite of problems. They are not content to seek spirituality only in organized religion but insist on integrating it into their work life.

Pursuing Wholeness

Another need of the personal inner self connected to career self unrest is the need for wholeness. People make the decision to change their careers because an essential part of them has been thwarted, lost, or isolated. They feel they leave their best selves at home when they go off to work and more and more refuse to make these tradeoffs. Their work no longer fits their self-concept. Many of my clients feel this strong career self unrest because they are tired of bringing only a small part of themselves to a career that supposedly reflects their identity. Even if they are rewarded, it is for being only a small part of what they long to be and what they are capable of doing. They see their potential as much greater than their position.

This partial-person feeling is affected by work that is so fragmented that people cannot see a connection with the whole or the end result of what they do. "I never see myself at the finish line" was the way one client described it. Their world is too compartmentalized, and so are they. We are now beginning to value the whole, rather than the small specialized expert as in the past.

It can also be that when we do see the results of our labor, we ask, Is this worth all the effort? One young woman accountant said, "My first job at a Big Eight accounting firm was really a doomsday job! There were four of us on a big project and we worked ten to twelve hours a day, six or sometimes seven days a week for six months. When we finished, all we had was a bunch of numbers on pieces of paper! What real difference does that make in the world? Who cares?"

As we leave behind important parts of ourselves to build a career, issues of balance, growth, learning, and the longing for what was left behind begins to surface and demand recognition. "I lost myself twenty years ago," lamented a successful retail executive experiencing extreme burnout and assessing her next step. She had gone into retail simply because she had little information and career focus in college. She had studied Spanish and lived one year in Mexico and loved it. At twenty-three, she moved to Mexico to live and planned to enter retailing there;

however, a top retailing executive, an authority in the field, advised her she should come back to the United States to work because it would be better for her career growth. To her later regret, she took his advice and jumped on a high-achiever's work path. It became an endless treadmill, and she never returned to Mexico. Six years ago, she walked away from this career that demanded sixty to seventy hours per week. Now, twenty years from the beginning of that career, after a thoughtful assessment process, she fully realizes that her success in the retail business provided her with money but no meaning. Her original goal of studying language, cultural, and social issues was left behind when she left Mexico. She is now determined to move toward a career that has real meaning for her—which is *not* conventional retail in the United States.

For many today, partial isn't enough, especially as we near midlife. While there are some people who enjoy zeroing in, focusing on being the specialist and not needing to hook into the final results of their work, most, the specialized experts as well as the generalists, want to see the effect of that work. We have been taught to methodically break problems apart to solve them, to fragment the world logically and analytically. Such an approach is supposed to make problems more manageable, but we pay a high price for it, especially today, for we no longer see the entire consequences of our actions. When this happens, we lose our sense of connection to the whole. We try to put the pieces back but it is somewhat like trying to repair a broken mirror. The finished product is flawed and distorts the image.

The world, our lives, our careers are not made up of disparate elements of an unrelated focus but are directly interrelated. Many are rebelling against working on one small part of a product or problem and never actually seeing or realizing the final product; most of us, especially the creative innovators, need to see the whole in order to realize the impact of our work; this is essential in order to build on it. Intuitively seeing and connecting interrelationships into a coherent whole will be a major skill for our future success.

Compartmentalized work was not a problem growing up on a farm. The entire family prepared the soil, planted the seed, tended the crop, harvested it, canned it and later ate it together. This was a challenging and directly rewarding process, different from simply buying and consuming the product. This is not a suggestion that we return to the good old days. But people need work that allows them to see more of the final product as farmers did. This creates a sense of ownership, control, and purpose.

What are the results of this lack of wholeness on the job? Clients can feel powerless as a result of leaving part of themselves at home and using only part of themselves in their work. This is not a natural state, and it makes it difficult to create a working strategy for our lives and our self-development. Human beings have an innate need for balance and wholeness, but finding out how to gain it can be a great challenge. Attaining wholeness in our current chaotic, frenzied work world is a process that most of us have not learned. Wholeness includes inner needs, outer needs, and integrity—faithfulness to one's commitments and expression of creative potential at work. People who stagnate in poor physical and emotional shape and do not assert themselves, who fear connecting, do not feel whole.

We have been consistently told that to be successful we must specialize in school, be good in one small niche and forget the rest, focus on learning more and more about less and less. This approach isolates us, and as a result we fail to use many of our talents. The unused part of a person, however, doesn't drop off or go away—it festers and creates dissatisfaction and unrest, even illness. When the innate need for balance of the whole isn't honored or respected, we can expect problems.

Some people, sliding into a career early on, never really thought about options. Although considered successful by themselves and others, they now find enjoyment and satisfaction in their work is missing. They may realize that their jobs are well below their competence and potential. A learning curve may no longer exist for them in their job, and they may lack opportunities for growth, or the nature of the tasks may be a mismatch for their skills and consequently hold no interest or challenge for them. Many need a better use of their creativity and the development of their competencies and skills, for without these they feel stagnant. The need to grow is an almost universal desire among my clients; without growth they feel a deep sense of malaise, they are bored. They may suspect unfair treatment and see organizational success as climbing over the bodies of their co-workers. They feel they could be fired at any time and are pessimistic about the future, not knowing what they really want, seeing only the chaos and not the opportunity, unable to relate to co-workers, and thinking that everyone views them as failures.

Some are seeking options, focused career information and direction. They have thought and daydreamed about, perhaps even seriously studied options, but nothing appeals to them for long, or else everything has a vague general appeal. They can't seem to spark a strong commitment to any career direction. This is partially due to the rapid changes in our external environment and the value changes that have occurred in the past twenty to thirty years, or even in the past ten years, which have left us with no sense of direction. Traditional ways of behaving, handed down from our parents and grandparents, are not working yet we have no idea what *will* work. We need information and direction to assist us in leading lives with meaning. Many people have lacked a career identity from the very beginning of their careers, and this lack is being felt acutely now.

Developing a balanced lifestyle is directly related to a sense of wholeness. People are now seeking balance for family and self, for community and spiritual needs. They are beginning to question the time spent pushing a career at the expense of the family. Many whose life circumstances are in flux due to illness, divorce, death in the family, children becoming independent, a working spouse creating more free time, or early retirement, must make dramatic shifts in their work lives. An example is the homemaker/volunteer forced or self-directed to change focus to a paying position.

Gaining career and life control and security is also a seeking for future balance and direction. Some like their work but also have the foresight to detect that their career field is in decline and want to gain more control and power over their career direction. This is one of the strongest needs of my clients in career change. They see themselves as being potential victims, having little control over or impact on decisions involving their work or position. Someone else makes the rules, and the decisions can be short-term, bottom-line, quick-fix solutions, frequently seen by clients as not being in the best interest of the customer, the organization, and their own careers. Many find their career sidetracked because massive changes in a field have wrought limited opportunities, and they understand that they must plan now to move on. The question is, move on to what?

Self-Defeating Behaviors

A third major problem that can create career self unrest is poor career and life coping skills. This self-defeating behavior usually bubbles up strongly in the personal self, described in the next section. Here, however, we are concerned about how our behavior can negatively affect the career itself.

Some workaholics and extreme type A personalities have addictive needs related to their work lives. Type A people, impatient "control freaks," want a quick fix. Sometimes hostile and stalled, they will not take time to solve problems. They may have little real awareness of themselves and are driven by irrational values and their own addictions rather than developmental or maintenance needs. Some workaholics reach a point in their lives where their manic activity is no longer working for them, or the object of their workaholic tendencies is no longer available to them.

Of all the poor career coping skills, the perfectionist trap creates a multitude of career self unrest problems. Perfectionism in this context refers to those trapped by unreal and rigid standards and expectations of their performance. Frequently, critical, judgmental parents gave them a mixed message: Don't do it if you can't do it perfectly. Such perfectionists never risk starting if they can't see a perfect finish line, and this eliminates all learning along the way. These clients frequently remember only their failures and mistakes, give little credit to themselves for what they do right, and seldom, if ever, celebrate their successes. They can tell you readily about their failures, faults, and weaknesses but are speechless if you ask them to discuss their strengths and accomplishments. Their expectations of themselves, others, and the workplace may be quite unrealistic. Frequently, they exhibit crippled self-esteem, suffer from intellectual paralysis, nagging self-doubt, regret over lost opportunities and perceived failures, and procrastination in making important decisions and initiating or completing projects. In their personal lives, they may well suffer from inability to form and maintain intimate, genuine friendships and love relationships.

Steven J. Hendlin (1992) writes how deeply ingrained perfectionism is in our achievement-oriented culture and therefore in most of us. He says that the act required to keep us from falling into the perfection trap is like dancing on a razor's edge. It can be a positive that becomes a negative very quickly. Hendlin outlines the many perfection traps: the desire to shape the perfect child, work perfectionism, the driven perfectionistic boss and company, competitive perfectionism at play, marital and sexual perfectionism, the search for the perfect relationship, and the emotionally and financially ruinous yearning for the best material objects.

Perfectionists think that anything short of perfect in performance is unacceptable. They are not motivated by desire for improvement but by fear of failure. Achievement brings them no real joy. They are running from the negative, not toward the positive. They have an all or nothing mentality; they generalize on the basis of a single incident; and they constantly use the words *never, always, must,* and *should.*

Perfectionists dismiss their positives as "not counting" for one reason or another. David Burns (1980, pp. 40–41) says the perfectionist may jump to a conclusion from negative interpretations even though there are no facts to support such a conclusion. He says this goes in two directions: 1) mind reading, the arbitrary, almost paranoid assumption that someone is reacting negatively to you; and 2) fortune telling, anticipating that all will turn out badly and seeing your prediction as an already established fact.

Perfectionists seem to carry an innate fear of being exposed as phony. They judge themselves harshly and think that others will do the same. According to Hendlin, they lack the inner resources of self-confidence but create a surface of competence and control that hides their turmoil. However, as they move to higher levels of achievement and responsibility, fear eventually cracks the veneer.

Having escaped many (but not all) of the traps of perfectionism myself, I can safely say that the feeling of freedom that follows is worth all the therapy, trauma, and insight that it takes to dump it.

Arthur Freeman (1994, p. 7) provides the following list of the most commonly occurring distortions, self-defeating attitudes, and self-talk that create depression. Notice that many relate directly to perfectionism:

- I'm afraid of failing.

- I'm a perfectionist.

- I can't ever control my life.

- I value security and avoid risks.

- I'm shy.

- I'm too old to make changes.

- I avoid conflict.

- It's a dog-eat-dog world.

- I'm overqualified.

- I compare my achievements to others.

- There's no fit for me into today's world.

Other poor coping skills related to problems in career self unrest are seen in clients who

- Have hit the glass ceiling and walls: plateaued, stopped growing, retired without resigning

- Are searching for the next step and have no idea which way to move, lack ability to formulate steps and strategies for career control and motivation to follow through on their own, thus requiring a strong coach

- Feel like hopeless victims—typical trapped Sisyphus with no options

- Lack any internal mirror: their meaning is all external

- Were fired, laid off, are in a state of shock, and have avoided until now taking responsibility for their career

- Maintain a facade of career success, outwardly self-confident but inwardly feel worthless and phony

- Seem upwardly mobile, doing all the right things but privately carry a deep inner fear of being a loser

- Are passive-aggressive, feel victimized but expect others to rescue them

- Believe that any different new career will solve all of their problems, but end up repeating the same negative pattern due to lack of recognition, attention, and correction of poor skills and attitudes

- Have low self-esteem, lack assertiveness, are subjective and too vulnerable

Identifying and beginning to deal with these poor coping skills before making the career change is critical.

Personal Unrest

Personal self/life unrest deals with internal needs and issues directed primarily at our personal life rather than our career. These highly personal issues will spill over into the career since the two cannot be clearly divided. However, it is important not to confuse these and make a career change if that is not the real source of the dissatisfaction. If you have a majority of "no's" for the following statements, your personal self/life unrest is high.

PERSONAL SELF/LIFE UNREST—LEVEL V

	Yes	No	
1.	___	___	My personal life is positive and I am a happy person.
2.	___	___	I understand myself, my needs, strengths, and weaknesses.
3.	___	___	I am comfortable with who I am at this point.
4.	___	___	I have supportive family and/or friends.
5.	___	___	I have high self-esteem and relate to others in a genuine manner.
6.	___	___	I handle loss and change effectively.
7.	___	___	I learn from my mistakes and move on.
8.	___	___	I take informed risks based on my own judgment.
9.	___	___	I am responsible for my own life and decisions.
10.	___	___	I see myself as a "survivor" and "thriver" in life.
	Yes___	No___	**Total for Personal Self/Life Unrest**

Pocket of Grief

Personal life unrest may be a "pocket of grief," a pervasive sense of loss from an accumulation of major disappointments, doubts, regrets, failures, divorce, illness, and death. These are losses that come to us all and remain with us. We stash them away in a side pocket of our lives; only rarely do we take them out and examine them, then put them away again. These losses will always be a part of our lives, and this we cannot change. Our pocket of grief is a major problem only if we can't seem to wrap up its contents, put it aside much of the time, and move beyond the losses. This means not denying or hiding but merely moving these hurts from centerstage. Otherwise the contents in our pocket of grief can seriously detour us.

Personal life unrest may also be connected to poor coping skills related to childhood trauma, family problems, or personality disorders, loaded down with depression, guilt or shame, or an overdeveloped need for security and approval. Social structures and relationships may be built on self-denial, repression, and authority. Such people have learned to lie, especially to themselves. Many clients seeking career change have severe personal problems related to a personality disorder, drug and alcohol addiction, eating disorders, sexual and psychological abuse, vague feelings of abandonment, and alcoholic, critical, noncommunicative, or perfectionistic parents. Some need medication, intensive rehabilitation, or extensive psychotherapy, and pursuing changing careers is not their next best step.

False Self

To survive and to cope in their life and career, many have assumed a "false self," a persona that early on served as a defense mechanism to help protect them from severe pain, but the presence of this false self in adulthood eventually retards or freezes the growth of the real self. Many in personal life unrest are accomplished fugitives from themselves, so they wear this false self and frequently exhibit self-destructive behavior. Some can't risk or experiment; they settle into rigidity, which leads to lost hopes, sense of failure, unfulfilled dreams, and despair. Their false self serves to make them feel safe, to avoid the fear and depression that would result if the real self did emerge. Those wearing the false self are fatalistic, cynical, negative, and fear the future. With this iron-clad mask, they are strangers to themselves and have great difficult finding their "I," their consistent self-concept that is essential for a fully satisfying and successful career change.

Those with a false self can be successful in solving career problems if their defenses are not so thick that they cannot begin to get through to their real self. Many are overachievers with rigid standards and expectations of perfectionism and success, while others have a victim mentality and chronic low self-esteem. This spills over into their career and makes a successful career change more difficult. With time, we can work through these self-esteem, self-assertion issues, but clients must be highly motivated.

Many adults have sound mental health and a strong self-image, though it may be temporarily eroded by their current career problems. They may have succeeded exceptionally well in their career to date but now intuitively realize they may need to take a different path. At the other extreme are clients with serious personal life unrest, exhibiting negative and self-defeating behavior and personality disorders that have always plagued their personal and work life but which have now reached the breaking point.

In analyzing your responses to the exercises presented in this chapter, determine whether the issues most relevant to you are primarily career related, personal life issues, or both. It is critical to understand the specific problems being faced. While career and personal issues are not separated by thick black lines, our primary focus here relates to career redirection and change, even though it is not always possible or desirable to completely separate a career problem from a personal problem. A career in crisis is usually a reflection of a person in crisis. Career unrest and personal self unrest are all part of one related system of our work and our life, and when we move one part there is a movement throughout. For this reason, a career move must be a synthesis of the internal and the external, a well-thought-out and planned integration of work and personal issues.

Who Changes
Careers and Why?

7

"Work is the great equalizer, the philosopher's stone that transmits all the base metal of humanity into gold. The stupid, it will make bright; the bright, brilliant; and the brilliant, steady. To youth, it brings hope; to the middle age, confidence; to the aged, repose."

—William Oster

Tolstoy, in a letter to Valerya Aresenyev (1856) described the value of work this way, "One can live magnificently in this world if one knows how to work and how to love, to work for the person one loves, and love one's work." Sigmund Freud narrowed it down to *lieben* and *arbeiten* (love and work) in defining the two elements fundamental for maturity. Abbie Hoffman, long before he became a stockbroker in the 1980s, said, "Work is the only four-letter dirty word in the English language." Our national specialist on stress, Hans Selye (Siegel, 1986, p. 168), said, "If you do what you like, you never really work. Your work is your play."

To understand the process of changing careers, its pleasure and pain, we must have some real insight into the meaning and role of work in our lives. In essence, relationships and work make up our lives. While love may be the favorite subject for poets, work may be the prime candidate of importance for most adults. Studs Terkel, in his vivid interviews for *Working* (1972, p. xxiv), portrayed work for many of Americans as dull, frustrating, and "too small for our spirit." However, he was constantly astonished by the extraordinary dreams of ordinary people.

Work can bring meaning and usefulness, new clarity, self-respect, and satisfaction to our lives. Though we may take our work for granted, it is the instrument for us to provide great value for others and for ourselves. Like fine silver, we need to polish our work regularly to keep it bright. While the nature of work is changing rapidly in this country, it remains central to financial and psychological welfare for most of us.

As emphasized earlier, satisfaction with one's work is one of the best overall predictors of longevity, and extreme and continuing dissatisfaction with work is a major cause of occupational health problems. A good job can indeed be "therapy."

WORK AS OUR IDENTITY AND SELF-CONCEPT

Work plays a crucial and perhaps unparalleled psychological role in the development of self-esteem, identity, and sense of order and form to our lives. To be denied work is to be denied far more than the things that paid work buys: It is to be denied the ability to define and respect oneself. The opposite of work is not leisure or free time: It is being victimized by some kind of disorder, which, at its extreme, is negative chaos. Losing a job, so central to bringing meaning to our lives, can be a devastating experience.

However, if most of us managed our business or money the way we manage our careers, our productivity and our financial resources would really be in trouble. Most adult Americans, including high-powered executives who spend years organizing, directing, and controlling the fate of people, equipment, and capital, probably spend less than one full day per year applying similar systematic planning techniques to their own careers.

Annual physical checkups are routine, but many people are remarkably passive in allowing their current work environment to determine their career direction. Depending on automatic guidance from the conventional established system and on our own commitment to our job to provide our career direction is unwise in an era where an accelerating pace of change and chaos in our personal and business world is the norm. Cruise control is not designed for detours around construction sites. When the work world is upside down is not a time to leave our careers to the gods, fate, chance, or nocturnal elves.

When we think about it, our career is probably the greatest single financial and personal investment we will ever make. Frequently it determines our lifestyle, our friends, our environment, and certainly our financial rewards. Multiply the number of years you will likely work, say at minimum forty years, by an anticipated average annual income of $50 thousand, for example, and the lifetime earning capacity is at least $2 million.

Amazed at your multimillion-dollar investment? If the management of such a sizable investment were part of your job responsibility and if you could pocket only the interest from this investment, you would apply great ingenuity, time, and energy in making decisions. You would read, observe trends, consult financial specialists, and keep a running account of all activity. Yet how many of these resources are you investigating in planning your own career direction? What really reliable information have you acquired in the past month or the past year on the trends shaping your industry and therefore your future? What new skills have you learned; what actions have you taken as a result?

If money is not your major motivator for taking creative control of your career, then think of your career as a mirror reflecting your identity. Right or wrong, for better or for worse, in our culture we *are* what we do for a living. If you feel uncomfortable, or don't like what you do, it will negatively affect your self-esteem and your sense of who you are.

Self-concept, the mental picture we have of ourselves, is a very important part of our identity. Wise or unwise but nevertheless true, our social status has long been equated closely with our job. This may change in the future since there may not be enough status jobs to go around for those who want them. However, I have many clients in apparently successful, high-status careers who carefully avoid telling others what they do for a living because they want to hide their work identity. Not feeling comfortable with your work is like wearing ill-fitting clothes.

Our work has many functions besides paying the bills. It provides both physical and psychological sustenance, affiliations with society, recognition, status in a group setting, the lifestyle of the individual and family, and a way to relate to others. Any activity of such major importance will carry with it many concerns. Frequently, our career self-concept may have formed in elementary or secondary school, and we have spent years moving toward that image. When we're in our forties or fifties, however, we must change it, sometimes very abruptly, and that is very difficult though we may recognize the absolute necessity.

Nevertheless, as a result of all the changes in our work life, changing careers or radically restructuring them is becoming necessary and desirable for many working Americans on every social and economic level. We are being forced to face unexpected problems in our work life and to do so with little or no insight and preparation.

We change careers because we understand what it is possible to get from our work life, realize we are *not* getting it, and know we deserve and can take action to gain it. Work itself is the foundation of our lives; it grounds us to the world outside of ourselves and is a channel for our urge to fulfill our potential and to feel needed and productive. Work demands that we discipline our talent into a form that ties us to the real world and tells us whether or not our ideas and visions make sense. To develop our potential, we have to shape it in a way that relates to the community. So, actually, work and career are our ways of relating to the world around us. And of course when we see our work as not relating, not having any meaning to us or to the world around us, we feel dissatisfaction.

We hope our work will bring us the critical payoff that is important to us, either money, recognition, pleasure, appreciation, power, or fame, and when it fails to do this, we may well start thinking about alternatives. If we (especially men but increasingly women too) don't have work, we may feel marginal to society, uncertain of our identity, and doubtful that we can elicit the respect of others. Regardless of the reason for not working, the unemployed believe that others fault them for not being on the job. Perhaps unconsciously this is true.

Problems in the workplace in the past have been much more devastating to men than to women. For most men, functioning well at work is fundamental to functioning well everywhere. A man's identity and self-esteem in this society have traditionally been based on how well he can provide for his family and how far up he can move in his career. To have a place in society, a stable family, and people who count, it was and perhaps is still necessary for men to have work.

In addition to his work, a man's family is very important to him, and because of this, many will stay in jobs that are not satisfying because they see that as the way they take care of their family. In this country's culture, the male's self-esteem depends—perhaps too much—on this repeated success in the workplace. Though our values may teach otherwise, we admire overachievers and competitiveness in business, looking up to people who make it to the winner's circle. The greed of the 1980s is a recent example of this.

Women have not traditionally derived their self-esteem from a paid job, but this is rapidly changing. In the past, unfortunately, women derived their self-esteem through their ability to attract a man who could produce well in the workplace. So the self-image of both the male and the female have been tied to work, his directly and hers indirectly.

DEFINITION OF A CAREER

Research provides no finite definition of career change, nor are there reliable, definitive studies documenting who and how many Americans have made career changes, or who are currently trying to. Perhaps it isn't really significant to define a career change as long as we can make it successfully. But since changing careers is complex, maybe we should understand what we are changing. What is your definition of a career? Do you view your career as:

- Advancement via a clearly-defined ladder, where only up is good?

- A specific profession, with only certain occupations such as lawyers, doctors, or teachers classified as careers?

- Paid employment in a lifelong sequence of jobs, and only people who work for money have careers?

- A mixed bag lumping together the terms *occupation, profession, vocation, career, employment, job?*

- A sequence of roles, related experiences, and activities; student, wife, parent, citizen, employee?

I view a career more as the last definition, in a holistic system including lifestyle, aptitudes, competencies, and aspirations. It is a broad sweep of all the activities we perform, paid and unpaid, and the roles we play in all the stages and settings throughout our lives. Since career comes from the Latin word *carrus,* meaning a vehicle for transporting, a career can be viewed as the vehicle or means to take us toward our mission in our life and work. For example, in your career you may have played many roles: child, student, spouse, parent, grandparent, teacher, consultant, researcher, therapist, department manager, business owner, community service worker, and public speaker. Some of you have been paid in money and others in love, respect, and recognition. Classification of career as simply what we are paid to do is too restrictive because it excludes such important activities as rearing children and volunteering.

This discontinuity between our perceived self and what we actually do has been created by the varying concepts of career and success in the past few decades. Frequently a career has been interpreted as a nine-to-five job, a means for paying the bills, encompassing one life and one occupation that extended generally from age eighteen to retirement at sixty-five. Any life outside that nine-to-five job was usually unrelated to one's "career." The career in turn was isolated from family life, leisure time, or anything not related directly to the job. Basically, our perception of career was quite narrow.

It is now imperative that we define a career not as the sum of activities we do between certain hours for which we receive money but as a much broader, more comprehensive course of action and activities throughout a lifetime.

WHO IS EXPLORING CHANGING CAREERS?

A navigator set on reaching a certain port has a definite course to follow. Always alert, however, to possible changes in weather conditions, the navigator has in mind optional routes to take if needed and flexible time scheduled for reaching the destination. This metaphor describes your backup career contingency plan. If a major storm develops, to stay straight on course and ride it out is perhaps the best alternative. However, taking another course may be the best option, and the navigator may decide to shift to another port, depending on his or her objective. If a destination has never been clear and one cares little to arrive at a named port anyway, one may drift with no destination in mind.

So it is with a career. Americans are being forced to become their own career navigators and are increasingly having to rethink career direction and consider changing courses. Their decisions should be based on their destination and their purpose in traveling in the first place. If you don't have a career contingency plan in today's chaotic work world, you are playing Russian roulette with your career.

Those exploring career change come from a variety of career fields, ranging from highly trained, experienced, financially successful professionals to the entry-level job holder. They include lawyers, physicians, psychologists, business executives, sales people, accountants, bankers, systems analysts, actuaries, engineers, computer programmers, college professors, recent graduates, public school teachers, musicians, actors, dancers, social workers, entrepreneurs, mechanics, homemakers, secretaries, and volunteers. Individuals who work with me in career change have ranged in age from twenty to sixty-eight, with multiple degrees and credentials and annual incomes ranging from zero to several million dollars.

Many have invested years in school and dedicated work on the job to reach their career goals, only to discover that the reality is not what they had anticipated. Some are unemployed or underemployed, the victims of outside forces, such as chronic high unemployment, downsizing, and cutbacks, while others are simply burned out, fed up with careers for which they may not have been suited in the first place. Some have never had a career identity though they have had many jobs. Whatever the reason, all want to gain or regain meaning and a sense of competence and success that has been misplaced or never achieved during their working lives. Those exploring careers and needing information represent different age groups.

College Students

This is a growing group of clients exploring career options, picking a college major in order to select their first career wisely. They are facing the reality that it is much more difficult to simply slide into a good career field than it was for their parents. Without direction, information, and special attention, they may flounder and drop out for several years. Also, the rising cost of tuition is reducing the number of parents who can afford to pay the expenses for their children to take different courses, exploring to discover the "right" career by chance or trial and error.

While I don't necessarily recommend precise career selection too early, it is possible and desirable to determine the general areas that fit a young adult so that exact focus can evolve later without reeducation. Having some early assessment of aptitudes, skills, interests, and values, coupled with exposure to the realities of a variety of targeted career fields, can be helpful in directing young adults into the right areas, if not the specific career. Later they can take up intern opportunities and learn more specifics.

Newcomers/Initial Starters

Young college graduates entering their first full-time job need much information, direction, and focus, with assessment to identify their natural skills, motivation, needs, and interests. These must be matched with emerging opportunities if they are to have options above the lower level service-oriented jobs. Young graduates can flounder getting into the job market today and easily end up in low-paying, dead-end jobs. More information and resources should be directed toward helping them make this transition. Also, research indicates that it is very important that their first job be under a good manager, that it be challenging and demand a strong learning curve, for this sets the tone and style for later career accomplishments.

The Reappraisal Age

Many dealing with serious career issues today are between the ages of twenty-eight and thirty-five. They have been in the workplace perhaps for several years in a career they thought they wanted, or they may have simply backed into it by default, and now they are wondering if they are in the right career field. Some are merely curious and want to know their options, while others are dissatisfied and anxious to do something else.

All had a limited knowledge of the work world and of career fields when they started their careers and, boxed into one field, have since learned little about other careers. While they are beginning to reappraise their original career direction, they need information. Some of this group, with internal and external insight, and after thoughtful career and personal assessment, readjust to their current career and remain in the same occupation or perhaps move to a similar position in a different-sized organization. Sometimes they discover they are in the right place and they settle in to learn new skills to build their competencies in their current career, for the reappraisal has provided them with a sense of direction and focus. By the time I meet them, however, most of them are anxious to explore making a significant career shift. I hear, "If I don't do this for the rest of my life, what am I going to do? What's out there? What are my options?"

Midcareer Restructure Age

Around their fortieth to forty-fifth birthday, many experience either "a call and a pull" or else "a cry and a push" motive to shift their career direction. A "cry and a push" motive simply means that they are highly dissatisfied, can't tolerate their present work life any longer, and want out. The mask they have donned every day for years has slipped, for whatever reasons. They may have no future focus or direction but want to escape their present situation.

The "call and pull" motive means that they feel a deep need to do something they see as more worthwhile. They may have been in their career for eighteen to twenty years and they want to refocus, some very radically. Perhaps earlier their career was okay; it mostly met their needs; but maybe it has plateaued and stalled, or they feel that they have other talents they would like to use. On the other hand, maybe their career has never been a good match, and they now need more from their work life. Both groups are looking at some significant career shifts. Jung predicts these changes when he says, "We cannot live the afternoon of life according to the program of life's morning, for what was great in the morning will be little at evening, and what in the morning was true will at evening have become a lie" (Jung, 1976, p. 17).

Early-Out, Corporate Retirees

Around age fifty-five, some are searching and curious about their options. They represent an increasingly growing number making career changes. Some of them have children through with college and are ready to try something new but don't know what. They may want to build a career in a different direction and are considering the option of an "early-out" retirement package being offered by many organizations. They may have no intention of quitting work

One client, Stephen, spent twenty years as a highly paid engineer for a large high-tech company. During that time, he spent six years, going part-time, to get an MBA in a highly data-oriented specialty. After a self-assessment process, he realized the happiest he had ever been was managing people in a very nontechnical role. His volunteer church work with its general responsibilities had earned him much respect and given him great pleasure. He had the extroverted, generalist, natural traits and skills of a talented manager; he was not an analytical, technical specialist by nature. Nothing in our conversation or our formal assessment process indicated a fit to the introverted specialist engineering role in a large worldwide technology company. When the opportunity to take early retirement surfaced in his company, he began to consider getting out. Then his minister approached him and asked if he would like to take a position as a full-time administrator for his large church, to handle all the day-to-day responsibilities except the pastoral work. Stephen was ready for this; because of his assessment process, he knew it was right. His new salary is not high but in combination with his retirement is equivalent to his former company income. He is now elated about his job. He says he does a little of everything, from managing the office staff, handling the financial responsibilities, and setting up computer systems, to repairing the bathroom plumbing. A natural organizer and manager, this is the best time of his entire career. Stephen sees that he can continue this for the next twenty years an entire career lifetime.

Traditional Retirement Age

Many adults in their sixties are thinking of retiring but want to retire "to something" not merely "from something." For many, doing nothing is not an option, financially or emotionally. They have had busy lives and didn't plan for retirement, so they haven't developed outside interests. But shuffling around the house waiting for death is not on their program. Such retirees will be a rapidly growing group.

In 1960, the year John Kennedy was elected president, there were 16.7 million Americans who were sixty-five and older. In the past thirty years, that number has increased by 87 percent to 31.2 million (*Dallas Morning News*, 1994). By 2025, the forty-five-to-sixty-four-year-old group will jump to 80.1 million from 46.7 million in 1990, an increase of 71 percent. This means that millions of U.S. workers may well expect to change careers in their mid-fifties and sixties. These changes will lead to new jobs and services, for as the baby boom generation enters midlife, new businesses will be formed to help them plan new careers.

Just as important, unless millions of people rethink their finances, the golden years of their retirement may turn out to be tin. The saving habits of many Americans will provide only a fraction of the money they will need to retire in comfort. Nearly 40 percent of American households have no retirement savings. According to the *Naisbitt Trend Letter* (1994, p. 7), Americans have one of the lowest savings rates in the world—a mere 5 percent of their after-tax income. In addition, in fifteen years, one-fifth of the U.S. population (forty-five million people) will be in retirement. Savvy individuals know that the government or the company will not take care of them in their twilight years, and if they keep healthy, that span of lifetime in retirement could be eighteen to twenty-five years.

As for Social Security, it is generally known that today's retirees receive about four dollars in benefits for every dollar they paid into the fund. Tomorrow's retirees if they're lucky will get only one dollar for each dollar contributed. With pensions and Social Security benefits shrinking, retiring may not be an option because of these financial considerations. Working full-time or part-time in a position one values and enjoys may also be the best life extender one can find. In the past, we know that many men who retired to full-time leisure after a long working career did not live long.

Downsized, Rightsized Adults of All Ages with Lost Jobs

Downsizing is both good news and bad news, depending on whether we are losing a job or making an organization more efficient. On the bad news side, since 1987, U.S. companies have wiped out 4 million jobs, and more than 375,014 workers lost their jobs in 1995; this has especially hit the midmanagement-level professional who was on his or her way up the corporate ladder. Advancing technology makes it possible to eliminate their jobs, and competition makes it necessary. While this group makes up 5–8 percent of the workforce, 15–20 percent are losing their jobs (*John Naisbitt's Trend Letter,* 1996), and these job cuts will continue. While there is great distress, one wonders if downsizing may be a quick-fix fad so easily leaped on to make a favorable impression with the stockholders and Wall Street.

To see downsizing from another angle, if we look below the obvious drama of the headlines and the immediate pain of those who have lost their jobs, we discover that the job market, while highly chaotic and turbulent, has seen the creation of more new jobs than those lost. Since 1970, the U.S. economy has created about 50 million jobs, with more than 10 million created since 1989. (*John Naisbitt's Trend Letter,* 1996). The estimate is that even though 3 million jobs have been lost since 1989, there has been a gain of 7 million.

Many companies, after making drastic cuts, end up hiring new workers. The U.S. Bureau of Labor Statistics reports that the unemployment rate has averaged 5.5 percent in 1996—relatively low. They report also that 68 percent of the full-time jobs created from February 1994 through February 1996 paid median wages, and most of the new jobs were occupations in the top 30 percentage wage—more than half of these are professional jobs. Small to medium-sized companies are creating the most jobs.

In summary, job growth and downsizing will continue in our economy. However, a beginning positive trend is that many companies are creating in-house career centers to help employees with their careers choices within the organization.

Perkins (1987, p. 90) relates how 3,000 full- and part-time employees were given extra help in getting retraining and jobs after a company sale. This is somewhat similar to federal programs called Rapid Response, designed to retrain employees of plants that close.

Handy (1989) writes thoughtfully of the effect that corporate downsizing will have on the current structure of the workforce and the societal impact that downsizing will have on mature displaced workers, and also the growth of contract labor. He predicts a "shamrock organization," with the first leaf as a core of well-trained workers supported by outside and contract workers. The second leaf will be the specialty contractors and outsourcers, and the third leaf will be made up of part-time, temporary workers.

Handy's view doesn't focus on our current time when adults are feeling only the negative effects of the downsizing and the corporate changes. He sees that in the long run, once this adjustment is made, freedom of choice about our work lives may increase.

LEVELS OF CAREER CHANGE

All adults I work with are involved in change relating to their careers. About half make what I call a radical career change—moving from one profession and environment to another: the accountant who gets a Ph.D. in women's studies; the M.D. who works for a family-owned business manufacturing T-shirts; the attorney who returns to the university for a Ph.D. in psychology; the salesperson who gets an M.S.W. and goes into social work; the third-grade teacher who becomes an M.I.S. specialist in a Big 8 accounting firm; the nun who becomes a successful entrepreneur in a service business; and many more.

Others may restructure their careers without making such radical shifts. For example, the lawyer who leaves his large firm but continues to practice law independently two days per week and does freelance writing for the medical field in order to become the primary caretaker of his son; the attorney who leaves a highly lucrative and prestigious law partnership and opens her own small private practice in order to control her time and to work more closely with people she values; the tax appraiser in a large consulting firm who starts his own tax appraisal firm; the computer programer who moves into technical training in his corporation; or the the high school music teacher who retires after thirty years and writes and produces outdoor historical operas for cities. These clients remain in areas related to, but now different from, their former work. Do we call this a career change? I would say yes, for even though the general industry remains the same, the environment or the focus is quite different.

Another group stays in the same field, and perhaps the same job, but begin to shift their emphasis. What they change is their response to the work or the way they approach their work. They gain skills and insight and realize the problem was not so much the career field itself but perhaps the particular position they had in the organization, or the way they were handling it. Internal refocusing changes their response to the work and therefore changes their job satisfaction.

Clearly, a simple job change brought about by work environment unrest is not a career change. But if we talk about a career being a course of action or activities throughout one's life, there are many factors that can be shifted in making a career change, from making a very minor alignment to making a radical career reversal.

To use an automobile metaphor, the action required to solve career unrest can range from a minor tuneup to the purchase of a new and totally different model. First, before deciding specific career options, explore all possibilities. Career adjustments and specific action steps to solve career unrest can be in the same career path or can mean a shift in a career direction or a new career. Specifically, the levels of career change are as follows:

- Radical career reversal
- Changing specialties within a field
- Changing environments
- Becoming an entrepreneur
- Changing career path

Radical Career Reversal

This would be a total career change: changing one's technical content knowledge; acquiring new skills, becoming retrained and reeducated in a totally different occupation, such as from music to computers or from CPA to college professor. While this appears to be the most dramatic and radical career change, acquiring and learning new technical or special knowledge skills is only about 10 percent of the difficulty involved in changing careers, assuming that the new career is a good fit for our basic aptitudes, functional skills, and personality. Radical career reversal is going into a very different work environment in a different profession and dealing with activities that are quite different. Those radically changing their focus could be moving from education to law, music to psychology, accounting to counseling, teaching to managing information systems, music education to technical writing, or CPA to organizational behavioral psychologist.

Changing Specialties Within a Field

This means staying in the same general career field but changing specialties within the field—making a severe shift that involves changing a career path within an occupation. For instance, you stay within your same occupational group, such as teaching or accounting, but you pick up a different set of technical skills. An example would be a lawyer moving from real estate law to mediation practice, or one moving from a general law practice to being a patent specialist in a law firm or becoming a specialist in intellectual property.

Other examples of changing specialties or emphasis within one's general occupation might be a CPA comptroller who moves to the financial side of a business as a treasurer, or the teacher who becomes an administrator, or the electrical engineer in the defense industry who moves into the semiconductor industry. However, if this engineer goes to medical school, that would be considered a radical career reversal. A chief financial officer who moves into investor relations and corporate communications is staying in the business world, but he's changing careers in that he is picking up almost entirely new technical skills in public relations, writing, and media management. However, his past financial knowledge is a vital part of writing up the annual financial reports.

Changing Environments

This involves changing our environment dramatically while retaining the same technical skills. For instance, a teacher in a public school might take her teaching skills with her and move into training in a business environment. It is a real jump, certainly involving a change of vocabulary, but the skills are basically the same. An account executive might move from the advertising agency side to work within a corporation. The newspaper reporter who becomes a corporate communicator and writer is using the same skills, but in a different setting, and with some change in vocabulary. Another example of changing environments would be a manager in a for-profit organization who moved to management in a nonprofit organization, where the same functional skills of management apply.

One of my clients, a university professor in embryology with a twenty-eight-page curriculum vitae, after not gaining tenure eventually became director of an extremely successful fertility lab. His first move out of academe was to a private, nonprofit hospital, and then to a more traditional business setting. He took his same skills, his same knowledge, but pointed them in a different direction. Moving from a consulting firm specializing in compensation and benefits to a corporation setting up a compensation and benefits program, or from the private practice of law to a government agency doing a similar job, means keeping your same technical skills and area of expertise, but changing your surroundings.

Becoming an Entrepreneur

Moving from a bureaucratic environment to a small, fast-growing entrepreneurial organization is the career path of many in career change. This means taking your skills and your knowledge, perhaps gained as an employee, and starting your own business.

This could also involve launching oneself as a professional independent consultant or contractor. Sometimes this is a first step in becoming an entrepreneur.

There are varying shades of entrepreneurship and three obvious ways to go entrepreneurial: 1) You could actually start from scratch and create your own organization, 2) you could buy a start-up company that is already in existence, or 3) you might decide to buy a franchise. Naisbitt (1994) reports that one franchise opens every seventeen minutes in the United States and a 40 percent rise in foreign markets in the last decade (1993).

One client, a highly dissatisfied engineer with a Ph.D. in physics and twenty-eight years in a high-tech company, took early retirement, the "golden boot." After careful assessment and the identification of a life-long passion for writing (he had written but not published three adventure novels), he investigated and moved into technical writing. On the way, he learned all necessary computer skills in short courses and by self-teaching. Since then, he has made more money each year than he made in his regular engineering job, more importantly, he loves his work. At least 50 percent of my clients eventually go independent either as entrepreneurs, or as PICs—Professional Independent Consultants or Contractors.

Changing Career Path

A technical path could be changed to a management path. Or, if you are in management, you might want to become more technical. Perhaps you are working for a company as a manager or as a technical person and decide to change your career path and become entrepreneurial. You might change all of the elements involved in a career, or just a few. How you shift pieces of the puzzle will determine the degree—and perhaps the difficulty—of the career change.

Some options are as follows:

- Move vertically—up to a promotion. In today's work world, this is more limited than in the past since many career ladders have collapsed as organizations become flatter and less hierarchical. Actually, I work with many who do move up in their career after they really get into the process.

- Reshape job—add or drop tasks, enrich, grow in place. Frequently, after serious thinking, you will see that more options exist than you originally believed.

- Move laterally—across organizational lines in the same function.

- Realign—move down a notch to achieve a particular career goal.

- Reposition—change jobs and go to a new work setting within the company.

- Change careers—change industries and role, inside or outside the organization.

Refocusing or redirecting our careers is becoming a necessity, not an ideal option, as we make the many adjustments required in our workplace. Before making these adjustments, it is wise to examine and rethink many of our rules and expectations—the models that we have perhaps unconsciously built into our success paradigm. The following are key myths that, if left unquestioned, can sidetrack our career change at the starting gate.

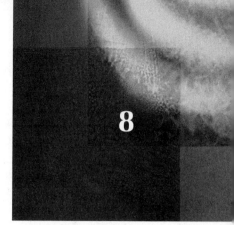

The Dozen Deadly Myths Defeating Contemporary Careers

8

"The thing to do is learn to live in your period of history as a human being. . . . By holding to your own ideas for yourself and, like Luke Skywalker, rejecting the system's impersonal claims upon you."

—Joseph Campbell

Myths are our narratives, our beliefs that unite us and keep our souls alive, bringing new meaning in difficult times. What happens when we find out that apparently our myths and stories, our rules and models, aren't working, that our former assumptions aren't even close to reality? In an age where change and disorder seem our only certainty, many Americans, midway through their lives, are becoming cynical and disillusioned as they realize the rules have changed and our former truths are half-truths or lies. The loss of our myths results in a loss of trust, belief, or direction.

Like the beams of a house, we can't see our myths from the outside, but they hold the house together so that we can live in it. When we discover they are invalid or superficial our first reaction is that all is lost: We have no structural framework to hold ourselves together.

When our collectively held stories are swept away, our individual identities collapse and we are left without direction or a sense of purpose. We experience anxiety, depression, powerlessness, and in some cases, aggression. The search for personal identity is widespread in our country today and can be seen in our personal and career problems. There are so many stresses that we flock to psychotherapists or rely on drugs, sex, food, shopping, or cults.

Past generations seemed to thrive on change. Our shared myth of the American Dream united us, and though from widely diverse backgrounds, we shared a sense of community, purpose, and history, a sense of direction that is dramatically missing today. Our current differences, discontinuity, and diversity in social and cultural values clash with our earlier teachings and, coupled with unbelievably rapid changes in technology, leave us with little sense of belonging or support.

Today, we are forced as individuals to deliberately do for ourselves what in previous decades was automatically determined by our unified culture. We must come up with our own system to seek meaning and make sense of our own lives—and this is no small order, especially if we are not aware of the necessity or confident of our ability to do so.

Myths, the stories that guide our lives, are problematic in today's rapidly changing age since they are so deeply ingrained that we never consciously think of them; they are archetypical, inherited from our ancestors. Unproved and unexamined, these collective "truths" are accepted uncritically and many times can be used to justify bad rules, ineffectual social institutions, ideas, or customs. Our current paradigm of career success is based on a system that no longer exists; therefore, using these outdated myths only adds to the chaos. Thus many feel abandoned.

These myths for managing our careers will be replaced eventually, but it is critical that we don't allow them to control our lives in the meantime. It is also critical that later we don't rush in and replace them with superficial or cynical myths that leave us unable to hope, create, and believe, since we need hope and faith for career motivation and sense of mission.

The following are a dozen deadly myths that have the potential to destroy our careers if we continue to follow them. They are listed somewhat loosely in the order of their importance in creating problems in the process of changing careers. Myth 12, though seemingly abstract, is the fundamentally flawed foundation of the others.

MYTH 1   Our current chaos and disorder is temporary—it will pass and the good old days will return.

MYTH 2   One life equals one career. The work we selected, or somehow backed into, perhaps in our late teens, is a lifetime commitment.

MYTH 3   Old dogs can't learn new tricks!

MYTH 4   Increasing middle-class affluence and expanding opportunities are our inherent right.

MYTH 5   Career success, happiness, and high self-esteem directly correlate with status, money, and upward mobility.

MYTH 6   Planning a career isn't necessary because someone or something will rescue and direct us.

MYTH 7   Superior performance will be automatically recognized and rewarded in the workplace.

MYTH 8   A college degree is the key to a good job and career success: The more advanced the degrees or the more technical and specialized, the greater the guarantee of career success.

MYTH 9   Select your career on labor market projections: Go where the best jobs and most money and security are predicted to be.

MYTH 10   Successful people make no mistakes. Less than perfect is not acceptable so failures are to be avoided at all costs.

MYTH 11   Sacrificing your private life is the price of success. Dropping out of the corporate world is career suicide.

MYTH 12   There is only one right way to be, think, act, and succeed!

Let us deconstruct these twelve myths.

MYTH 1

Our current chaos and disorder is temporary—it will pass and the good old days will return.

REALITY   The more things change, the more they become different.

We would like to believe that where we are now in our careers, in our economy, and in the state of our social values is an aberration that will pass and allow a return to "normal." After all, haven't we always been taught that "The more things change, the more they remain the same"? We assume that the future will be an extension of our past—history repeating itself.

American values, until the 1960s, had actually changed little since our beginnings, but change seems our only certainty today—and our main failure may be our failure to change. Historians can see that the mid-1970s marked the real beginning of a shift from the Industrial Age to a whole new era dominated by diversity, social differentiation, the continuing acceleration of change, and, as many see it, the decline of the American middle class.

But no economic quick fix will work and the past cannot and should not be recaptured. New ways of understanding the roots of change have to be developed. For decades, we will continue to live with instability.

Our most passionately held assumptions may vary dramatically from the emerging reality. We are at the end of an age with no predictable straight line to our future but with two certainties: continuing technological change and the emerging insistence of individuals to control their own destinies. Our existing social institutions, rules, and policies are all dangerously inappropriate to these needs. We must look for new forms of work and new approaches for self-help, and we must invent new services. We must train for the future, not the past. We must develop mind, not muscle, brainware, not hardware. The new kind of worker will be more independent and resourceful, no longer an appendage of the machine.

How will all this change affect the way we work and live? Jobs will not be so compartmentalized and work not as divided. Routine, repetitive, fragmented work will no longer be efficient. Most manufacturing industries—auto, steel, rubber, textiles—are dying out in the United States. There is a corresponding rise in electronics, computers, biotechnology, aerospace, environmental recycling, service industries, lasers, optics, ocean science, space manufacture, and qualitative knowledge.

MYTH 2

One life equals one career. The work we selected, or somehow backed into, perhaps in our late teens, is a lifetime commitment.

REALITY   Millions of Americans will be forced to change careers. One life = one career is not an option.

While this may have been true in the past, it no longer is, regardless of how desirable one career may be to us. Certainly it has become evident that we will make many career shifts, moving more into composite or serial careers: one career building on another related career with major change occurring every five to seven years. This "one life = one career" dictum is particularly destructive today and is a major barrier to those in career change.

How ironic that in this country it's easier and probably more acceptable currently to change spouses than careers. While the rhetoric of our American culture has always valued change and innovation both on an individual and institutional level, we face several very real barriers to career change.

First, the "womb to tomb" scenario is directly related to the belief that one of the major tasks of youth is to select a single career, become trained on the job or in school, and go with one organization or company and remain a lifetime, moving step by step up the ladder. The fact that career fields are changing and the opportunities available earlier have shifted dramatically, or that one may no longer enjoy the work, are not considered relevant.

Another major impediment to changing careers is the belief that there are no options, no way to implement a change. Many adults are virtually blind to the process of changing their career, lack awareness of options that could work for them.

Many, toiling in demanding jobs that they dislike, burned out and numb with accumulated low self-esteem, have no idea what is happening in the rest of the world. Their ill-fitting careers demand so much time and energy that they have lost touch, not only with themselves but with their surrounding environment. Since we have never been encouraged to be curious about different career fields, we can't see possibilities and opportunities.

Unfortunately, in our culture, many see changing careers as linked with personal instability. Consequently, those exploring a career change may be viewed by family and friends as immature and irresponsible. Many have never had a clear sense of what they really want to do in their work life, and when forced to rethink a career direction they are fearful.

Changing careers involves changing our self-concept, discovering who we are, which can indeed be quite difficult and frightening. Culturally and socially in this country, right or wrong, we are defined by what we do for a living. The first question on meeting someone is "What do you do?" and we are immediately judged by our answer. Usually, the more education we have and the greater our potential for making money, the higher we are in the hierarchy of social status.

Changing careers successfully can be complex because it involves the growth and development of both the internal and external resources of individuals. Our internal needs and the external environmental realities must work together for us to achieve success.

In summary, for most Americans, getting beyond the one life = one career myth will require a major push beyond outdated policies and systems, past cultural barriers and our own fears of failure and the unknown. Weathering the criticism and questioning of family and friends is a hurdle and requires a strong creative plan built on sound research, information on ourself and the changing environment, and the determination to be in charge of our own life and destiny. As Thoreau said, we must became a majority of one. We must stop expecting the White Knight or the paternalistic corporation to rescue and guide us. We must guide ourselves with help from others. This is the ultimate in real creativity—the redesigning of our career based on our needs and the actuality of a different, changing world. Multiple careers are a reality for all of us; one life = one career is passé.

MYTH 3

Old dogs can't learn new tricks!

REALITY   In midlife or advanced age, we can launch into the most creative and productive time of our lives!

The key to thriving in today's world at any age is learning, unlearning, and relearning. Learning "new tricks" is a continuous process for people who are open to new ideas and who welcome opportunities to grow and change, regardless of chronological age. Crises in our lives— death, illness, divorce, unemployment—force sudden change upon us and provide us with the opportunity and the necessity to gain new insights into ourselves and new ways to handle our problems. When faced with the need and the challenge to do so, people at any age can learn and change.

The myth that we are "over the hill" at an arbitrary chronological age has been built into American culture and is fueled by our own individual self-concept and expectations in life. The media often portray an aging person as feeble-minded, stashed into a nursing home. We are set up for gradual decline and stagnation unless we challenge societal mores and say no to such a mindless myth.

John Gardner (1984) tells the following story about age and achievement: Once there was a fifty-three-year-old man fighting a losing battle over debt and past misfortune. He paralyzed an arm during his youthful military service, failed badly in his two government jobs, and was serving a prison sentence. Motivated perhaps by boredom, hope of gain and emotional release, or purely creative impulse, he wrote a book that has enthralled the world for more than 350 years! His name: Miguel de Cervantes. His book: *Don Quixote.*

We have cultivated a habit of speaking apologetically of "being old" when we reach the age of forty or fifty, instead of expressing gratitude for having reached the age of wisdom and understanding. I tell others that practically everything I've learned that I value and that has made a real difference in my life, I learned after I was forty years old! Picasso said, "It takes a long time to become young." We grow old, not by living a certain number of chronological years, but by becoming idle. We decay when we abandon our flexibility, our ideals, our talents, our life's mission, our involvement. We retire by buying into society's myth that "the best is behind us." We grow old because others expect it! The two most deadly assumptions related to this aging myth are that retirement is directly connected to the chronological age of sixty-five, and that mental decline begins at age twenty-one.

In 1953, Harvey C. Lehman, in his study *Age and Achievement,* reported a narrow age-range for artistic creativity (in the thirties) and said that the highest levels of leadership are reached in the fifties and sixties, although leadership can be observed at any age. It is clear that superior human accomplishments span almost the entire lifetime—aging is not a disease.

Adults have great capacity for growth and self-renewal. We need not relinquish as early as we do our resilience and capacity to learn and grow. Self-renewal depends on motivation, commitment, the values we live by, and the things that give meaning to our lives. We know little about the creative person and the environment that fosters creativity, but this we must research and learn.

If we remain poorly adjusted, we often become on-the-job retirees without resigning. We reminisce about the good ol' days, refuse promotions, live for time outside of work, daydream, and do unimportant tasks first. Frequently when we feel loss of personal control, we become defensive and domineering at work. We drink, smoke, waste time, complain about being bored, or find fault. This disillusionment can also result in poor personal adjustment. If we see ourselves as failures, we may talk of success but unconsciously seek defeat. Some, however, fantasize or leave families. Some postpone facing life's illusions. Some go through self-analysis to modify their dreams. Others spend the second half of life wandering in search of an unattainable goal, resulting in chronic depression.

Those who do take control of their work lives redefine their goals and modify career-related aspects of their dreams. Thus they engage in genuine self-renewal and growth; develop flexibility and a diverse identity across their life span that is helpful in retiring; and avoid engaging in self-destructive behavior and manage tension well. They fully understand that self-pity and resentment, on or off the job, are toxic.

MYTH 4

Increasing middle-class affluence and expanding opportunities are our inherent right.

REALITY   Rising expectations and declining affluence are clashing head on! Surpassing the educational and financial achievements of our parents is a fundamental archetype, a major cornerstone of the American Dream.

Postwar opportunities in business and the professions that flourished until the early 1970s are increasingly limited. Our relatively assured path up the career ladder started to collapse and is by now, for the most part, gone. The 1990s eliminated much of middle management, and executive positions and millions of other jobs are disappearing forever as the hierarchical organizational system flattens to meet changing national and global economic pressures.

The middle class, aptly renamed the "anxious class" by Labor Secretary Robert Reich, is having money problems, and continuing but conflicting data suggest that the American middle class is dramatically shrinking, being replaced by a "have" and "have not" reality. Less than ten years ago, Americans had still had high hopes for themselves and their children to continue to prosper, but unlike the 1950s and 1960s, the prospects are much dimmer today. We are witnessing a fundamental societal change: the first generation of Americans that are less educated and less affluent than their parents.

Since World War II, annual raises have been as much an expectation in our working lives as regular paychecks. However, today the average American's pay is falling, not rising, while workers in other industrialized countries are making gains. This is not what we would have anticipated with our history of success for the middle class.

There is increasing evidence that jobs in the future should be plentiful—but only in the areas of the paraprofessional, clerical, computer operator, retail sales, programmers, and janitorial, jobs that in the past have not been considered suitable for college graduates. O'Toole (1977, pp.10–11) reports that there has been more than a 100 percent increase in female college graduates employed as secretaries in the last five years, and 80 percent of college graduates are currently employed in positions that do not tap their potential. The old paradigm of career success—that the value and prestige of an individual is directly related to a position on the occupational ladder—will no longer work in a society where upper-level jobs are shrinking as rapidly as they are in the United States.

The development of alternative career paths and a new definition of career success is especially critical for the sons and daughters of those people who have achieved highly successful careers begun in a more prosperous time. It was assumed that the abundance of good jobs and expanding educational opportunities was an eternal given, and so many parents are slow to understand why their adult children can't get on track faster, easier—especially since they were given an expensive education and every opportunity!

Many financially successful people are working harder and longer and enjoying it less. They may work from sixty to seventy hours per week with little positive feedback, no appreciation, and a paralyzed, unpredictable economy. Many deal with a product they see as having little value. In return for the 1970s' standard of living, companies are now demanding far more hours, especially for production and nonsupervisory employees. To reach their 1970 standard of living, these employees must work 245 more hours, or six-plus extra weeks per year (Schor, 1991, p. 81). Many are living a life without time or opportunity to balance other interests, activities, and family needs. This lack of time and balance is making many of my clients rethink their career direction although they currently make high salaries.

These days, we distrust our government, our businesses, and our large institutions. The old dream of affluence that held us together is gone, as is our united sense of direction. We no longer believe in a classless society or that education is the key to occupational status and upward mobility. In the past, an abundance of middle-class occupational opportunities preserved the American values of democracy, opportunity, and individuality. Now, however, while many jobs continue to emerge, they have low pay, low prestige, low benefits—no future. The rapid advancement that characterized the postwar era has halted.

The expectations and assumptions about affluence, leisure, and growth that we held in the 1950s, 1960s, and into the mid-1970s, no longer exist. Our economy fluctuates between elation and depression, upheavals that mystify politicians, economists, and the average American citizen.

MYTH 5

Career success, happiness, and high self-esteem directly correlate with status, money, and upward mobility.

REALITY   Many experience failure or career success and personal failure, but there is no conclusive evidence that people who make the most money are necessarily happier or feel better about themselves!

Yet we do know that in this country money is a main barometer of status and success: the more money, the more successful, and therefore, we assume, the happier the individual. But for many, this is a destructive myth: They are making six-figure incomes but feel that they have sold out.

However, most of my career clients are seeking more meaning, a sense of competence, creativity, control, and commitment in their work, not merely more money. They are making plenty of money but puzzled about what's still missing. For most, after a certain level of income, money seems not to be a major motivating factor. If our work has meaning, lets us feel competent, and provides a reasonable income, money ceases to be such a high measure of success. We frequently use money to measure our success when our career is barren of commitment and meaning and we don't know what else to value.

Paradoxically, I have also discovered from my clients that the more rewards they garner, the more money they make, and the better they are at doing what they do not value—the less they like themselves! They feel they are actively selling themselves short or they feel like a fake, certain to be discovered. This inverse relationship negatively affects their self-esteem. One client, a successful account executive in a major advertising agency, secretly felt that advertising was of low value, that his customers were being "ripped off." The more praise and rewards he received for being good at his work, the less he liked himself!

Increasingly, men and women are recognizing that the drive to get to the top, however they define it, may not be worth the cost and trade-offs often involved. The idea that personal satisfaction will result from being at the top has played a major role in the formation of our society, and we have been the most economically successful society in history, so we find it difficult to discard this myth despite growing evidence that it is not universally true.

Clients say, "I want to be happy," but they can't define it. I hear, "I want a meaningful career, but have no idea what it would be." Breaking out of the tiny world of ourselves is a real challenge. We simply haven't learned to think creatively about our work life. Napoleon Hill, one of our first motivational self-help writers, defines success as the progressive realization of a worthy goal (1987). Success is a moving target we can grow toward, not a one-time event or final destination but a journey to achieve a goal that we see as worthwhile and valuable. But if this goal is established by an external yardstick (parents, society, etc.) and the rules are defined by someone else, if they fail to connect internally with us, they will not hold up to the "worth" in our definition. Finding one's meaning and mission may be the first and most critical step to happiness, however we define it.

Evidence abounds that mission, not money, motivates: The purpose principle within all of us is the need for a commitment to meaning in our lives. Only this fights our fear of nothingness.

The National Opinion Research Center of the University of Chicago reported that no more Americans report they are "very happy" now than in 1957. This group has stayed at one-third of our population since the 1950s, despite near doubling in both gross national product and personal consumption expenditures per capita.

Michael Argyle's comprehensive work, *Psychology of Happiness,* is summarized by Durning (1993, p. 21) in *The Futurist* as the three following conditions of life that make a difference to happiness: social relations, work, and leisure. And the establishment of a satisfying state of affairs in these spheres does not depend much on wealth, either absolute or relative. Unfortunately, the very sources of satisfaction get squeezed out as individuals pursue a high-consumption lifestyle. Affluence in fact may have broken the bonds of mutual assistance that adversity once forged.

David Myers (1993) reviewed 800 studies for a book on happiness. He cited self-esteem, optimism, and a sense of personal control as providing contentment. Happy people have good relationships, compelling work or hobbies, and spiritual tendencies. He says wealth is like health—if we don't have it we can be miserable, but having it doesn't necessarily make us happy.

MYTH 6

Planning a career isn't necessary because someone or something will rescue and direct us.

REALITY   You are in charge of your career! Absolutely no one is coming to rescue your career but you! If you are not in charge of your career, no one is!

The passive "someone is coming" syndrome has been the pervasive career attitude in this country for decades but it is far from reality today. Though this patriarchal approach may have been somewhat true in the past, and in isolated cases might be true today, it is not reality for millions in the workplace! There is no external system that will direct or guarantee your career success and happiness. Our manager, organization, university, fate, the gods, Santa Claus, the Tooth Fairy, Big Brother, or a benevolent father, none has the X-ray vision to plan and guide our career and then invite us to participate. We as individuals must activate our career planning process and take charge of our career. If we don't know how to take creative career control, our first goal should be to learn how.

The ultimate source for wisdom to guide our careers is self. If you don't know what you want or need for your career success, believe me, no one does. If you don't have this wisdom, acquire it! That is what career planning is all about. Some of my clients are angry because their organization or their manager is not providing them with what they want in their career. When I ask them what they really want from their work, they can't tell me. Yet somehow they expect their manager to have a highly desirable master career path laid out and waiting for them like an English high tea, and they have only to respond passively to the invitation.

We spend almost no time planning, directing, creating, or managing our careers. We don't thoroughly know ourselves—our product, our interests, skills, and motivation—or our market, the workplace environments. If they found the right environment, many would not understand how to gain access to it. There is much we haven't had to learn in the past, and this learning can be a lonely process if we perceive only chaos and uncertainty surrounding us.

We must recognize that we are currently without traditional support systems to guide us effectively. Rapid change creates great stress, and our systems, institutions, and workplace policies are years behind us, so as individuals we are on our own. The sooner we realize and accept this, the faster we can take control of our careers. Perhaps this is not the way it's "supposed" to be, but this is reality! Using the rules and myths of our former system are certainly not the solution.

To be passive and accepting is no longer the best bet in the workplace. Even if an employer can be responsive and provide information and a supportive environment, we must guide our careers ourselves. You are the someone coming to the rescue!

MYTH 7

Superior performance will be automatically recognized and rewarded in the workplace.

REALITY   If getting your reward or recognition in heaven is good enough, or if quality work is your main reward, then this myth is irrelevant for you. Superior performance and quality work should be respected and rewarded and we hope it is, but don't count on it unless you are very patient and willing to be disappointed.

The best jobs or promotions frequently go to those who are best qualified in getting the job or promotion, not necessarily those best qualified to do the job. The mind-set that quality and worth will automatically be rewarded today creates continuing frustration, cynicism, and failure. However, most of us are motivated by and thrive on the recognition of our colleagues and our managers. Listing this as a myth should not be interpreted as an attack on quality work, which is essential for all career success. There is simply more to achieving success than quietly doing a quality job.

Performing a quality job and being able to communicate and market this ability are two separate sets of career skills, both equally critical for career growth and development. For career success we must acquire both, especially in the coming marketplace. The first set requires competency, the actual technical or job content skills—knowing how to perform the job and doing it consistency well whether it be as a specialist or as a manager, and increasingly, for competitive people, high competence is absolutely necessary.

The second set of skills is purely nontechnical and relates to skills beyond those stressed in job descriptions and perhaps even in some performance appraisals. These consist of personality traits, the chemistry between people, and how we have learned to handle our environment. People are fired or have job problems not because they do not perform the work but because they are unaware and fail to understand how their environment works.

In summary, the best qualified people do not necessarily get the best jobs or the most money unless they have a keen awareness of how these things happen in their own workplace.

We are individually responsible for gaining the necessary skills for planning our career. If we don't know how, then we should learn on our own or get professional help.

MYTH 8

A college degree is the key to a good job and career success: The more advanced the degrees and the more technical and specialized, the greater the guarantee of career success.

REALITY   College degrees cannot be counted for getting a great job.

True, in past decades, we could have a degree and almost be assured of a good job. However, we need to reexamine this assumption today. A degree may be a necessary factor that helps us qualify initially for a job. In competitive times, it can be a standard used for advancement once attached to an organization, whether or not it's actually needed for the job. But it is definitely not the risk-free investment that it once was. A few decades ago, degrees were much more marketable and we could almost automatically obtain a professional job simply because of having them, but this has been slipping as an absolute for the last twenty-five years.

Parallel with the myth that the accumulation of advanced degrees will automatically assure upward mobility and career success is the myth that the only degree of value to a career is a technical or scientific one, or an M.B.A. To be successful, especially during times of severe change, requires both the basic foundation of the liberal arts and the more technically specialized areas. The imbalance of one type of degree over the other is ultimately destructive to the individual's personality and career and to our society. We can do both. The specialty, however, is very likely to shift in the future, while having the broader educational base helps us to realize and capitalize on our options.

Ranking people by class is antithetical to our American beliefs. However, the American middle class has had clear ideas about the worth of occupations and people and, if not actually ranked by class, we are ranked by level of education and profession. There has traditionally been a correlation among income, education, and occupational status. More significance was attached to occupations that required more education and it was expected that they would reward us with more money. A 1973 study by the Opinion Research Company found that when ranked according to status, physicians, ministers, lawyers, and architects are at the top (O'Toole, 1981). College professors, federal employees, engineers, accountants, and salaried managers in manufacturing comprise the next stratum. Foremen, supervisors, those working in sales, repair, secretarial, and clerical work come after these. (Ironically, housewives and entrepreneurs aren't even listed.)

While competition is increasing for the professional jobs that require college degrees, lower-level, service-oriented jobs are being created at a rapidly accelerating rate and are often being filled by college graduates. This change has come rapidly, and parents who have spent $75 thousand on a degree, only to have a son or daughter working in fast food or a movie theater, are having some sobering thoughts regarding their invest-ments. O'Toole (1977, p. 11), following his extensive American college graduate research, reported that "about 80 percent of college graduates fill jobs that were previously held by workers with lower educational credentials." Yet a college education is still considered an entryway to a satisfying career.

There are three major reasons why some people should return to higher education for an advanced degree:

1. It is an essential credential for their carefully planned career goal, a necessary part of their established career plan.

2. It is a vital part of their self-concept, an internal goal, a highly valued need.

3. It satisfies their love of learning for its own sake without attaching a monetary value.

Unfortunately, many of my clients who have wrestled with career unrest and job dissatisfaction have returned to the "womb" of academe, where career decisions can be avoided. They can concentrate on moving passively from one semester to another without any real long-term plan-ning on how to use the knowledge they are acquiring. Thus they don't solve their career problem and may even exacerbate it. Adults returning to higher education should be clear why they are going and what they want to achieve. They can spend time and money and come out with the same career decision-making problems, now compounded by having an advanced degree and large debts, but still not really knowing what to do.

The assumption that the accumulation of advanced degrees will automatically assure upward mobility, financial and professional career success, and career meaning must also be examined very carefully. Countless adults with major career problems have multiple advanced degrees.

Continued learning is an absolute essential! However, don't confuse learning with the acquisition of degrees. Formal education is a great vital-izing force but should be pursued with an understanding of its real value to us. Currently, it may not bear the material rewards or upward mobility as it did in the past, but it can be a major force, reordering our priorities and providing a deeper knowledge of self, nature, and society. It will not do this, however, if we wedge ourselves into a highly specialized narrow field. I used to tell my college students that the final, ultimate value of their college education was to teach them to be a good "crap detector," to be able to sort through their own, as well as that of others.

MYTH 9

Select your career on labor market projections: Go where the best jobs and most money and security are predicted to be.

REALITY   Readily available, great money-making careers today may be unavailable by the time you get there! To assure career satisfaction, select your career based on what fits your individual skills, interests, motivations, and values, and, after thorough research, balance these with the projected opportunities in that industry.

All career fields, including the best of them, go through expansions, contractions, and downturns in today's chaotic times. This boom and bust cycle has hit public and higher education, real estate, law, engineering, banking, oil, and computing. Indeed, no industry is immune.

Selecting a career is one of the most important personal and financial decisions of your life. It will be a major factor in determining your lifestyle, friends, and social status. It may even determine the kind of person you marry. Indeed, much of your future identity is directly tied to this choice. Does any of the following sound familiar?

- Dad thinks I should be a doctor. Since I don't know what else to do, I'll take his advice.

- My family is in business: I'm not certain, but I guess I'll keep up the tradition.

- My favorite teacher is my history teacher; why not major in history?

- I'm a good math student, so I'll major in accounting. (Math and accounting require opposing aptitudes.)

- Engineers are making good money these days, so I'll major in engineering.

- I'm good with people; I'll be a nurse. (But you may not like science or medicine.)

- I liked my first part-time job in a restaurant; maybe I'll major in hotel management.

- Computers are the wave of the future. I won't have to worry about getting a job. (In reality, numerous computer specialists are looking for more in their work life.)

- I wanted to be a writer so I picked English—in reality, I want to write about science. I should have studied both science and writing.

The major problem of many of my clients dealing with career problems at midlife is that their original career situation was based on what they, their family, or society perceived would be a money-maker, have high status, or both! Relying only on the judgment of others, or superficially matching your skills and interests to a career field for financial reasons, involves needless risk.

It is important to research what fits you, what ignites excitement and response in *you*. Find a career that matches your skills and motivation, and research the opportunities for making a living in it. Ask yourself these important questions in the order given:

1. What does the world need more of? What needs to be done?

2. Could I meet this need? Do I have the skills or could I gain them?

3. Would I value doing that? Could I feel a commitment to it?

4. Can I make a living doing this?

A note of warning: Much of the established information on projected career opportunities may be misleading or out of date by the time it is published. For example, the paralegal field has been predicted to need more people than any occupation in the United States. However, this projection failed to take into account the great number of law school graduates and their difficulty finding suitable jobs—with the consequence that today they are doing much of the work that was reserved for the paralegal in the past!

Never base a career selection only on the anticipated job market. If it isn't a compatible match for you, success in it will be difficult for you to achieve and maintain, and you may never value your success or translate it into high self-esteem for yourself. Read and be aware of labor market projections, but don't consider going into any field without a reality search into yourself on how the field will fit with you. Also, carefully research the day-to-day reality of the career field and current and projected opportunities according to people actually working in that field at this time. It is foolhardy to expend financial and emotional resources on a career that doesn't capitalize on your instinctive natural strengths, your motivation, and your values. You will never be outstanding or feel valued in a career that is a mismatch with your interests, personality, and skills.

MYTH 10

Successful people make no mistakes. Less than perfect is not acceptable so failures are to be avoided at all costs.

REALITY   The road to success for most successful people is checkered with failures, false starts, and frequently, grave mistakes. Addiction to perfectionism and fear of failure are deadly dictums to career success and creativity.

When the best is never quite good enough, it breeds fear of failure, and the result can be procrastination and unreal expectations of the world and others. One who makes no mistakes makes nothing! Real wisdom is knowing when to forego perfection. Fear of failure can create a paralysis even in making a decision to start a project. If not assured of a win/win situation, perfectionists play for small stakes, never risking failure.

Another way to state this myth is, Winning is all that counts. Only winning adds to our self-esteem; failure is intolerable. The parents of the 1950s passed this admonishment on to their children, which has helped to create overachieving workaholics, driven to trying to do everything perfectly, or paralyzed adults standing at the starting gate, too fearful to even begin.

Perfectionists, if they don't see a clear path toward success, don't begin. They have no permission to learn on the way, to take a trial-and-error approach, or to shape and reshape as they learn. This creates the paralyzing fear of failure that breeds procrastination and indecision.

Closely related to the myth of doing all things right all the time is the myth that *overcoming your weaknesses assures success.* But would a company spend its entire budget marketing its poorest product? If we spend most of our psychic energy and attention concentrating on our weaknesses, we will neglect our strengths. It is critical to understand your strengths—what you do well naturally and instinctively—and focus on refining and taking these skills to their highest level. We should find an environment that needs our strengths and that will pay us to use them. Don't continue to focus on a career where you are expected to work from your weaknesses.

Paradoxically, I have observed that a majority of adults can identify and articulate weaknesses and self-defeating behavior much more easily than they can strengths and accomplishments. Our strengths are frequently so natural that we are unaware of them.

Our weaknesses, our ineffective traits, usually surface unexpectedly when we are under pressure and paying the least attention to our behavior. But building on our strengths, our strongest product, is essential in competitive times. If we are not working from our natural strengths, we will never feel really strong and creative in our work.

MYTH 11

Sacrificing your private life is the price of success. Dropping out of the corporate world is career suicide.

REALITY In the future, there will be few, if any, ladders up. There are multiple alternative ways to career success. We can have it all, but not at the same time.

Success in both personal and career life is a juggling act for many today. To do this successfully we must identify, choose, and prioritize our "glass balls" (our top priorities) from our less important "rubber balls." Our glass balls are those we must not drop since they cannot be repaired later if cracked now. The rubber balls we can pick up at another time or simply chose to never pick them up at all.

Stepping off the corporate career ladder may not be a relevant issue in the future for many workers. Since the ladder has collapsed, there are no steps for moving up in a career by age and positions as defined by corporations in the past. The traditional career—from management trainee who selected a mentor and started up a designed career path to CEO and retirement with full pension—is over.

Even more important, small, fast-growing organizations, not large corporations, are creating a large majority of jobs. Alternative career paths, such as outsourcing and contract work, are all affecting the traditional corporate career. Today's career path should be viewed as subject to change, reevaluation, and redesign at almost any point. The new model is the serial career pattern with major but perhaps related changes every five years or so. Flexibility and a contingency plan are critical.

Over and over, the duality between work and family roles is played out by working adults. We are beginning to insist on love *and* work, the hallmarks of a mature personality. I emphasize the *and* since our society seems to insist that it be love *or* work, thereby forcing many adults to choose between a "successful" career and a balanced family life. Success in one area will not replace success in the other. Unfortunately, most workplaces accept that what is good for one's career or job may well be toxic for the family.

Healthy adults want and need balance. Time and stress on the job has increased sharply because of the job losses on every level, the loss of trust in our organizations, concern over fired friends and co-workers, and uneasiness over our own job situation. Fear-based motivation may move people in the very short term but isn't effective on the long haul, especially in an age that requires creative and innovative solutions to increasingly complex work problems. Stressed-out people dry up: They cannot and do not think creatively.

Working longer hours with low or no job satisfaction is causing many successful professionals to reexamine their original career direction. If we are highly committed and suited to our career, we may creatively survive and even thrive on the current chaos, especially if we can maintain some balance between our personal and work self. Realizing the necessity to do so, we will find our niche with its unique opportunities and be fueled by the challenges.

However, if we are only marginally matched to our work, we will begin to realize that the energy it would take to make ourselves successful in the difficult times, along with our basic lack of interest and commitment, is not a battle we care to fight. "If it's going to be an uphill battle, at least, when I get to the top, I want it to be where I choose to be," as one client put it. He is rejecting the Sisyphus role, the treadmill role going nowhere.

Fueled by mindless habit and fear, we seem addicted to stress and pressure, and we accept that this is the only way. Moments of real pleasure are furtive and guilt-producing. The world seems stuck on fast-forward, going nowhere, and many do not have the nerve to say, "There has got to be a better way" and to begin the search for it.

The American success story may become the exit line; wanting less is perhaps a growth trend. Japan is the only rich, industrialized nation where working hours are longer than in the United States. According to Schor (p.29), the average American is on the job an additional 163 hours, or a full month more than three years ago; men are working 98 hours more, and women are working 305 hours more. The work ethic is not gone—the actual productivity is double the 1948 level—but the nature of the work, the overwork, the lack of respect, and the deteriorating relationships between worker and workplace are very real problems (Schaef and Fassel, 1990).

MYTH 12

There is only one right way to be, think, act, and succeed!

REALITY   There are multiple, diverse, and wide-ranging ways of being, thinking, doing, and acting.

Each of these can be valuable, effective, and right, depending on time, place, purpose, need, and other factors in our lives and world.

There can be great strength and genius in the creative synthesis and integration of opposites, a skill that many of us have not learned. In my work, I have learned that this one-sided, habitual view of reality, so pervasive in our society, is the most common fundamental issue underlying the career problems of most adults in career change. Jung (1957, p. 19) says that we have learned to mistrust our instincts and to divide them into opposites, a practice that divides us up into parts that are frequently in conflict or isolation.

This either/or thinking is a real handicap in understanding self and our contemporary changing environment. Many have defined themselves solely by one specific job and can see themselves only in their present career role, as a teacher, accountant, lawyer, or engineer, even though they may have never liked or felt suited to that career field. Their self-concept is calcified, and it is difficult for them to gain a broader, more serial view of themselves and their work life. They experience the fear that "If I'm not the engineer I won't be anybody, so I'd better stay an engineer." This decision is made regardless of career problems created.

At every turn, our society has touted specialization as ideal, until we frequently feel polarized behind thick walls that are difficult to escape but easy to classify and stash out of sight. From behind these walls, it can seem overwhelming to creatively research another career field. Many teachers, for instance, believe that they have the skills and knowledge only for teaching. "If I can't teach, I can't do anything," I clearly remember thinking years ago. I defined teaching at that time within the narrow confines of a public school or college classroom. Today I am still a teacher, but in a totally different environment.

Business people believe they know and can be successful in business only; insurance people know only insurance, bankers know banking, lawyers know law only and probably a specific area such as real estate or family law. Each name carries a stereotype we can choose and put in a neat category so that thinking in specifics is not required or encouraged. This is especially true as our world becomes more unpredictable and complex. We try to simplify our complex decision making by saying that we have two options at most, and they are "either this or that."

These neat bipolar labels are endless: good or evil, dreamer or doer, mind or heart, conservative or liberal, love or will, reason or feeling, active or passive, order or disorder, winner or loser, businessperson or academician, intuitive or rational, weak or strong, for or against, masculine or feminine, rational or emotional, wise or foolish, in or out, success or failure, self or others, love or work, idealistic or realistic, head in clouds or feet on the ground. Extreme opposing pairs dominate our thinking and certainly curtail our options.

If we are to maintain creative control in our rapidly changing world, this dualistic "either/or" inflexible mentality must give way to a "both/and" paradigm—insisting on some of each, or all, in a creative integration of contradictions. Psychosynthesis, developed by Roberto Assagioli, is a comprehensive psychology that sees humans as tending naturally toward harmony with themselves and the world. He discusses the wisdom and the power to "play with opposites, the balancing and synthesis of opposites," to establish a dynamic balance without resorting to compromise (1965, p. 104). In journeying from rigid black/white thinking, we can learn to value gray. Many of my clients have been taught to think they can have either socially meaningful work with a marginal income or make money with no meaning. My approach is to be creative and ask why not have *both* meaning and money!

These are the twelve deadly career myths, our former truths, that have the power to destroy our careers if followed. Understanding their potential negative impact is essential for taking creative career control. Any significant change or growth to a higher level involves facing uncertainty and the unknown creating a "dark night."

The Dark Night
of the Soul

9

"In the middle of the journey of life,

I went astray from the straight road

and awoke . . . alone in a dark wood.

Ah, how hard it is to tell of that wood,

savage and harsh and dense, the

thought . . . renews my fear. So bitter

is it that death is hardly more."

—Alighieri Dante

Banished from Florence at age thirty-seven, Alighieri Dante was condemned to be burned to death should he ever be caught again in his homeland. On one level, his description is an allegorical reference to the entrance to hell. On another, this serves as the opening scene of a vivid description of emotional crisis faced as one is forced into making major life changes and finding a new existence.

Dante's dark wood, or dark night, is a reflection of his state of mind after being forced into exile, homeless and hungry for justice and friends.

That human beings reach heaven by journeying through hell and experiencing a rebirth or initiation is a reoccurring theme in our spiritual and literary thought. St. John of the Cross, the sixteenth-century mystic, used this metaphor in his spiritual canticle *Dark Night of the Soul.* He vividly describes going forth alone, "on a dark night with yearnings of love" (1577, p. 23). After being kidnapped and imprisoned, he wrote: "Horrible and awful to the spirit that we must take to move from the ordinary to the supreme." We can only reach the divine, and the blessings of the perfect union, by passing through severe trials and straits on the narrow way.

We learn in this passage that a time of chaos and perhaps of humiliation, chastisement, depression, and fear is an essential prerequisite to the full discovery of our own real values and meaning, our renewal.

Such "dark nights" are initiators into new ways of being. There is value to the darkness, for if we respond to the message, an awakening can develop. We can come out wiser and stronger with more personal power. This is the time when we seem to lose connection with our former inner source of peace and instead must face all of our fears and pain head-on.

THE CHAOS OF CHANGE

We can understand severe transitions and chaos as initiations into new ways of being if we see them as a ritual between two very different states of being, a process similar to the three stages of the rites of passage in primitive cultures, which are:

1. Separation from the status quo

2. Liminal period—the middle time between the old and the new

3. Reincorporation into the new role in society

The second stage, the liminal period, is the "dark night" and is compared to being in the womb, or in the darkness wandering in the wilderness, a time when parts of the old self are cleared away. At this time, we have no familiar routine to define role and self. The liminal person is stripped and owns nothing. Former unconscious adherence to the familiar beliefs that guide our lives is broken. This is the major step toward the rebirth or reincorporation into the new role, the third stage.

Mircea, in *Dreams of Life Renewed* (1958, p. 135), describes this process this way: "Initiation, restoration, renovation, a new beginning, lies at the core of any genuine human life. This is true for two reasons. The first is that any genuine human life implies profound crisis, ordeals, suffering, loss and reconquest of self, death and resurrection." Mircea says the second reason is that, regardless of the fulfillment that a life may have brought forth, at some point each will see his or her life as a failure. This vision does not arise from reality but from "an obscure feeling that he has missed his vocation; that he has betrayed the best that was in him." At this time of total crisis, the only hope that seems valid is the hope of starting life again. "This means, in short, that the man undergoing such a crisis dreams of a new, regenerated life, fully realized and significant."

This renewal journey manifests itself in some form in all clients who are making a thoughtful and therefore a successful career change. Like Dante, however, when forced to seek a new way, we imagine immobilization, powerlessness, helplessness, fragmentation, pain, and sometimes persecution and torment. However, we can choose to use this pain as a powerful motivator and forego the role of Sisyphus, the paralyzed victim. This is fundamental to learning how to change.

The meaning we ascribe to our "dark night" between our past and our future is central to how we emerge from it. What does it mean to have our career identity and source of livelihood swept away? Initially we may feel total hopelessness. Pessimism and depression makes it difficult to learn from experience. We can practice courage, not self-hate. "I don't know why this is happening, but I can deal with it" can be our refrain. At a time of extreme crisis, we have a choice: We can believe in either love or fear. Tragedy has the potential to tap a remarkable resilience in human nature and a deep reservoir of strength; therefore, most of us have the innate capacity to recover from monumental problems.

Tragedy and adversity create the need for meaning—from what is happening, we need to tell and hear new stories. Our ability to tell these stories is positively linked with our recovery from the pain of change.

Turning loose of an old career identity, a former self-concept, without having a new identity with which to replace it, as we must do to successfully change careers, can be difficult and often terrifying. In fact, if we hold tightly to the former career identity, we cannot begin to create a new image of ourselves in our mind. Juggling two identities, as I stressed earlier, does not work well. We cannot see ourselves in a new role. The former self-concept of who we are in our work life, though we know it does not really fit us, remains too strong. The old career paradigm is fixed, and though perhaps painful, it is what we understand. Creating a new picture—seeing a new image transposed over the old—distorts both. We get no help from our subconscious, the source of our creativity, in creating a new image if the messages are mixed and confusing, since it can only respond when we get our picture clearly focused.

The new image must therefore be allowed to be seen and felt without the shadow cast by the old. It is essential that we turn loose psychologically of the former career identity and allow the journey of discovery, the "dark night" transition, to occur. Though frightening, it is a very predictable part of the change process. The emotional and psychological stages of a career change, which I have termed the Chaos of Change, are demonstrated in Figure 2 and explained in the sections that follow.

Stage 1: Familiar Identity/Eternal Status Quo

The *Familiar Identity/External Status Quo* is the first stage in the Chaos of Change. This is our prechange or prechaos period. Prior to a major change, we may not be happy with our situation—life, job, or relationship—but it is familiar. We may be aware that we are professionally or personally plateaued, merely marking time, or we may be passive,

FIGURE 2   CHAOS OF CHANGE

> **FAMILIAR IDENTITY/EXTERNAL STATUS QUO**
>
> Plateaued   Passive Acceptance   Fear of Change

↓

TRIGGERING EVENT

Death & Divorce   Major Illness   Career/Job Loss   Psychological Shift

Life Will Never Be the Same

↓

DARK NIGHT OF THE SOUL BEGINS

Denial   Guilt   Anger   Powerlessness

↓

PARALYSIS   LIMBO   NOTHINGNESS

RUNNING TO ESCAPE   FORCED DECISION

↓   ↓   ↓   ↘

FIGHT	FLIGHT	FREEZE/FRET	FORGET
Go Back	Run	Inaction	Ignore
Excuses	Escape	Indecision	Deny
Hang on	Outward Motions	Procrastination	Mask, Deaden

POSTPONING   ⟶

FIGURE 2   CHAOS OF CHANGE (continued)

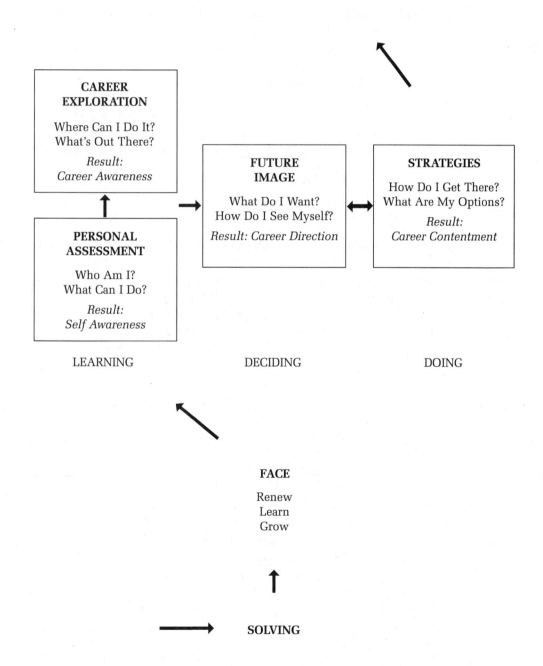

NEW IDENTITY
INTERNAL PERSONAL POWER

CAREER EXPLORATION

Where Can I Do It?
What's Out There?

Result:
Career Awareness

PERSONAL ASSESSMENT

Who Am I?
What Can I Do?

Result:
Self Awareness

FUTURE IMAGE

What Do I Want?
How Do I See Myself?

Result: Career Direction

STRATEGIES

How Do I Get There?
What Are My Options?

Result:
Career Contentment

LEARNING   DECIDING   DOING

FACE

Renew
Learn
Grow

SOLVING

unknowing and mindless, uninvolved with things outside our current narrow line of vision.

We may consider ourselves traditional and conservative and may have built walls to maintain a somewhat rigid control for protection from change. We fail to risk for we don't trust the outcome. Fear of change we cannot control, resistance to risktaking, and therefore little or no growth characterizes the response in this first stage. While unsatisfactory and maybe even uncomfortable, at least things seem predictable. If we think about it at all, we assume that everything will remain the same indefinitely. There are perturbations, small irritations, clear indicators that surface on the fringes of our consciousness, warning signs that changes need to be made, that disorder and chaos could be developing, but we ignore, deny, and postpone any real awareness. Many clients, after reflection, admit that they "sensed" developing problems intuitively but ignored and avoided them, perhaps even for years.

Stage 2: Triggering Event

Suddenly, from nowhere, a seemingly random *Triggering Event* shatters the apparently calm Status Quo state! This event initiates the chaos, our journey through the "dark night of the soul." This Triggering Event is a normal part of the change process, the pain that prepares us for the gain. As St. John of the Cross writes, this difficult and fearful dark journey makes it possible to fully accept and appreciate our eventual arrival. It begins to prepare us for lasting change in perception and behavior.

This Triggering Event can be compared to a bifurcation point, a physics term that indicates the moment of extreme change when elements become severely destabilized and when the eventual outcome is totally unpredictable. This powerful Triggering Event starts the Falling Apart process of major chaos identified by Prigogine (1978). It initiates a chain of chaotic events in our life and career that have the potential to move us to a higher level, a renewal, or it can send us to a more primitive state. We do have a choice here!

However, at the time when we are hit by a major Triggering Event, we are at great risk personally and professionally. We may quickly form a new system, a new identity structured around our current disability, our anguish and inadequate coping behavior, or we may set the stage for a more effective cycle of renewal, beginning our painful but possible move to Prigogine's higher level of being and working. Contrary to what we may believe, we do have that choice at this painful point of seemingly random chaotic disorder. Following Prigogine's model, this chaos begins the breaking down of the old that sets the pace for our renewal and growth. In our darkest moments, we are beyond pretense and actually closer to our essential nature, and this can lead to spiritual resurrection. However, the situation has the potential to get worse before getting better. Acts of chaos do not come in single packages, and real change is not a neat, predictable, linear process.

Career/Job Loss

For those with career issues, this Triggering Event can be losing a long-time job, being fired, being laid off, or being given the "golden boot," forced into early retirement. The Triggering Event can also be the realization of a severe career loss, a declining field that now provides little if any advancement, few job opportunities, or no challenge. In this case, the career field has changed forever—and it can no longer meet our expectations and needs. Oil, real estate, accounting, finance, teaching, counseling, health services, banking, law, manufacturing, and indeed almost all career fields have fallen into real chaos in this decade.

Psychological Shift

The Triggering Event can also be a psychological shift, the internal realization that the career does not meet enough of our needs for us to remain there. Maybe it's okay—but we realize that okay is not enough for us for a lifetime. There is a disconnection between meaning and our work. It may also be a sharp psychological shift if our personal life is spilling over into our career. An intense, internal reordering can result in the growing realization of personal or professional bankruptcy. It can be a realization of our earlier hoped for, but untapped or unused potential, causing an internal refusal to continue to live a life or career without meaning, creativity, and control. It can be a deep need for a new beginning. Perhaps this psychological shift is what a "midlife crisis" really is.

Death and Divorce/Major Illness

Triggering Events can also be a death in the family, a divorce, or a serious illness, all major events creating deep loss and leaving a lasting mark on our lives. Actually, sometimes all of these elements—the chaos from our career, illness, divorce, death in the family—all seem to meet at once, head on, and we may experience multiple Triggering Events, falling one after another like dominos. From the first major Triggering Event, though we may not realize it at that time, our life and/or career as we have defined it in the past is over.

Stage 3: Identity

The "dark night of the soul" in this time of career transition is the bridge of turbulent times when we must release our former identity, temporarily have *No Identity,* and begin to establish one based on the true self. But first we must discover the true self. This is the foundation to knowing what we want, which, in turn, is essential to gaining it.

A very real and deep sense of loss of trust and innocence is created when we perceive that the established system has failed us. We now realize that our world, the career, personal life, or both that we have so carefully built and guarded, is shattering, or perhaps has always been merely an illusion. We are essentially alone; no one is coming to rescue us from our plight. Our formulas, expectations, assumptions, and dreams about how things were to be are no longer reality, if indeed they ever were. The job, career, marriage, relationship, or our health, or maybe all of these, are gone. We think that if we cannot count on familiar rules, values, people, or organizations, then we can count on nothing. In the past, rules and values, though rigid and perhaps invalid, provided comfort and security, but when we face the reality that they are not working, and perhaps never did, how can we ever again trust anyone or anything, especially our own judgment? We long for a guarantee that all will return to "normal," although we know it may not be real or may be only temporary. While there were many negatives in our former status quo, we at least had a sense of someone being in charge.

In the past, most of us were conditioned to be passive in our work life, to find out what the boss wanted and to do that. With this straightforward formula for success, we would be invincible in our own small world. After the Triggering Event and the onset of our "dark night" with its immediate negative emotional downward spiral, we really are in great chaos and disorder. We are not yet far enough along in the process of the Chaos of Change to know that in the earlier Status Quo we were perhaps very vulnerable. Now we begin to wonder if that is the nature of all things in our world. We begin to glance cautiously over our shoulder and to wonder what else might we be overlooking that will knock us for a loop. All of life may take on an uncertain, temporary air.

"Dark nights of the soul" are periods of time when we feel we can no longer trust the ground we stand on, for it shifts with each step we take. However, if we can see this pain as a part of growth, as did St. John of the Cross, it can lead us to psychological and spiritual healing and revelation. A wound with meaning is much easier to heal than one that is meaningless or seen as divine punishment for our personal unworthiness. When we set our sights on a higher meaning for our pain, we are part of a "greater story," and are not Sisyphus, trapped, powerless, or unworthy. We are on a life's journey and when we arrive, we will have a story to tell to help others through their journey.

In this process of the Chaos of Change, we frequently begin to question not only immediate career issues but also deeper philosophical ones. For many, though adults, this is the first time we have ever stopped to engage in any real soul searching or questioning about ourselves and our place in our world. For most of us, devoted to finding and achieving the formula for success for the "good life," this is our greatest challenge. For the first time, we have no formula that defines us. We may know much about everything but little about ourselves. There are critical insights that are waiting to be uncovered, but we feel almost unbearable loss, pain, fear, and strangely enough, even shame. From the time of the Triggering Event, our lives will never be the same again. Frequently we do long for and attempt to restore the Status Quo. However, change cannot be avoided. There is a sharp sense of loss and of betrayal as we realize that the pieces of our life will never again fit together in the former way. This is especially difficult since most of us have worked so hard to maintain order, control, and security to keep the pieces all together whether they fit or not.

Stage 4: Falling Apart

Following the Triggering Event, we immediately experience a series of powerful negative emotions, and enter into a downward slide—this is the process of *Falling Apart* in real action. The intensity and pain that accompanies this downward spiral depend on our perception of the severity of the original Triggering Event, on our style of coping or adapting to life's events, and on our awareness of the importance of what is happening to us. The sequence of negative emotions will generally be in the following order but it is difficult to predict the length of each stage:

Shock, disbelief, and denial. You think, This can't be happening; I'm having a bad dream. Some people, when told they were fired and to clean out their desks by 5:00 P.M. and be out the door, actually continued with their work, fantasizing that the boss was only kidding or that the boss's boss would come and say that it was all a mistake.

Anger and revenge. Thoughts of revenge take over: I'll get even with that SOB if it takes forever. Fortunately, most of us only fantasize about getting even. However, violence in the workplace is rapidly becoming a frightening issue for many, and revenge killings are now a second major cause of injury in the workplace.

Frustration, anxiety, and fear of the unknown. We go from fretting—How could I have worked so hard at that company for ten years?, or I'm a stupid ass!—to a victim's cry of It's all so hopeless; I don't know what to do, and I don't know what will happen to me. There's nothing I can do. These feelings spring from abandonment fears.

Despair, powerlessness, and depression. We become gun-shy, with a deep loss of trust in ourselves, others, and the world. Can we ever really trust ourselves, or anyone else, again?

It must be stressed that these are normal negative emotions of loss and grief and should occur to some extent at this point.

We need to recognize, acknowledge, and move through and beyond these negative emotions with insight, not by merely slamming the door on them. As a rule, the depression and the downward spiral begin to shift gradually into yet another phase of the process.

Stage 5: Paralysis and Limbo

Paralysis, which plunges us into *Limbo,* a state of nothingness, characterizes the next stage in this Chaos of Change. You can't move—neither forward nor backward. Meanwhile, all around you everyone else rushes on, seemingly uncaring about your plight. Everyone seems to have a place and a purpose in the world but you; chaos seems to be happening only to you. You want to cry aloud, "Why me?" It is as if you are being personally punished, but for what transgression? What could you have done wrong, especially when you tried so hard to do it all perfectly?

At this stage, we feel caught in another dimension and suffer a state of existential loneliness that seems unbearable. We seem to have ceased to exist or to matter to anyone. We are at a critical crossroads. We have an irrational fear that we are at risk of disappearing into the void. Michael Novak, in *The Experience of Nothingness* (1970), describes this stage as frequently beyond the limits of reason, near the borderline of insanity. He says that at this time there is only darkness, with momentary beams of attention flashing like fireflies. What better description of our severe "dark night of the soul"?

Stage 6: Running

As the isolation of this state becomes intolerable, we begin our *Running Stage,* a time of frenzied activity. We frantically attempt to ease the pain of the loneliness and the fear of the unknown. This running, while normal during the change process, must be handled carefully and with awareness of what is happening to us. Major financial, personal, and career decisions need to be made very carefully, if at all, during this stage, for we are now in a highly vulnerable state.

Since we must run, it is a good idea to run to something that has the potential to be helpful in the long term, not self-destructive. I ran back to the classroom and completed eighty credit hours on a doctorate in English in a state of neurotic numbness, daily driving almost one hundred miles each way. If I had maintained this frantic Running Stage one more year, I could have completed my dissertation, while a zombie, in half the time it actually took. However, I became aware and actually changed from English to higher education in order to research and write about adults and career change.

We have the ability to self-destruct or to move to a new level at this time. Deliberately making a major change, especially a career change, is, strangely enough, a move toward freedom and discovering our uniqueness, even though initially we fear freedom because it could spell aloneness. This aloneness is another aspect of the "dark night of the soul," the time between letting go of the former career identity, the old way we worked, and discovering our identity in the new career.

It could be comforting to use the metaphor of the caterpillar: A lowly creature crawling on the ground goes into the dark chrysalis, its own "dark night," with no guarantee it will get out alive, and it emerges as a butterfly! The career change is a move from the former, unrewarding work life—the caterpillar role—to one that provides a sense of competence, creativity, control, and commitment, and the freedom to "fly." But it seems we really don't know how to deal with the freedom of having options. It has brought independence and rationality, it has made us isolated, anxious, and powerless. The isolation is unbearable, and we must either run from the burden of this freedom into new dependence and submission, or else accept the full realization of freedom, based upon our uniqueness and individuality.

Being free and having options can trigger a real crisis in decision making. Plato, in *The Republic* (1968), tells a story of people locked in a cave, but when one escaped, discovered freedom, and returned and told the others they could simply turn around and move toward the light, they refused, and chose to face a lifetime of darkness instead. Plato said, "We can easily forgive a child who is afraid of the dark; the real tragedy of life is when men are afraid of the light." What would we do if we no longer had our real and imaginary problems and burdens, our chains to hold us down? The thought of real freedom and options can be very fearful.

The "four F's" toward which we run are described in the next chapter.

TEARS AND A DARK NIGHT

"I am now beginning to see where I can do so much better than I have in the past—I see many options, but what I'm going through right now is that I am really angry at myself for my past lost opportunities. There's also a fear of what I can't become, or that if I try to become this and I don't make it or even worse, what if I do become this, and I do make it work and I become so absorbed that I isolate myself and become a loner from people I care about. What if I succeed and people begin to expect so much more of me? And what if I can't live up to it?"

In those few words, Steve, a talented young systems engineer bored with working on routine and traditional business problems, expressed frustration over past losses, fear of failure, fear of success, and more. He was amazingly insightful and verbal about his fears of change. He expressed the fear of loss of self and the grief over his past as he made his career transition, which was much more than the choice of a new industry. He said, "Before I knew better, I was not on the line. I was mindless—it didn't matter to me. My work was not me so it didn't have to be great, but if I make a deliberate choice for my work to be really me and I fail, it will be devastating—a real failure. What if I decide this is really me and I'm going to make it work and it doesn't work? What if I really try to take control and it doesn't wash? The lost opportunity will overwhelm me."

Steve's decision to search for his life's purpose and meaning was a commitment to find himself. Defenses must be dropped to get to one's real and honest self, but fear speaks, asking, What if I drop all the negative things I carry that both defeat and protect me, and what if I search but then find nothing that really counts? What if I don't like what I find out about myself? What if I can't even find it or name it? What if I can't make a living at it? Will I have to give up everything financially? What if I can't measure up?

Fears and questions abound. Dropping the false self, the state of mindlessness, and facing oneself means giving up the familiar and rejecting the perceptions of others. It is painful and frightening, but a key here is to see the former false self not as time wasted but as a building block. When we find the real self, we drop both the false self and the fear that there will be no one there when we look. This is a natural process of being in the chasm and tolerating the fear, panic, and uncertainty, the "dark night of the soul."

Facing and Solving the Career Problem

10

"In a dark time, the eye begins to see."

—Theodore Roethke

At this point in the process of the Chaos of Change, since we cannot long tolerate the paralysis, Limbo, and loneliness, and the Running to escape the pain, we are forced to make a decision.

The quality of that decision is critical. This conscious or unconscious decision determines if we are to really change and move creatively forward with our lives or remain caught in the response-cycle syndrome of grief, loss, and eternal postponement. This period is critical because when we are caught in the downward spiral of Falling Apart and the fear of being discounted, we also paradoxically are most open to new and challenging possibilities.

At this brief moment, seemingly suspended in time, we can choose to postpone action or to really change, and thereby alter forever our final outcome. This is our moment of truth—our greatest possible turning point. We must remember, though, that the capacity for turning hardship and adversity into an asset is a learned skill. It can be the beginning of our change and renewal. St. John of the Cross wrote that our being must be lost, and then found, to be truly appreciated.

TOWARD A POSITIVE OR NEGATIVE FATE

In describing this critical point, May (1975) says that human freedom involves our capacity to pause between stimuli—the point of pain and our reaction (in this case the breaking apart of the old and the start up of the new)—and in that pause to choose the response toward which we want to throw our weight. "The capacity to create ourselves based on that freedom is inseparable from consciousness or self-awareness" (p. 117).

I always compare this brief moment of decision to the climax in classical Greek or Shakespearean tragedy. According to classical tragedy, all of us carry within ourselves the unique seeds of our greatness but ironically also our tragic flaw, which can set us up for our own destruction. Our strengths and our character flaws are flip sides of the same coin; they cannot be separated. In other words, our major weakness or flaw can be seen as "too much" of our major strength.

Heroes in classical tragic dramas always face a "dark night of the soul" when they wrestle with their tragic flaw. However, in any great tragedy, there is always a moment as the conflict peaks when heroes or heroines have the choice to understand, to face their flaw, to change and overcome, or to continue mindlessly in the old behavior as they race toward their eventual tragic downfall. True heroes, not hopeless victims of external circumstances, have options. They can choose to know and change. Without choices, they are like Sisyphus, no more than pathetic victims whipped about by circumstance.

The eventual tragedy that results from mindlessness and lack of conscious awareness, could be averted if the heroic character could recognize the flaw, accept its reality, take charge of it, and change. At that climactic moment, the hero has an option, and the opportunity to change his destiny. We too have the freedom to choose. However, we can't choose our career direction wisely at this critical instant if we lack insight into our own strengths and motivations, and without sound, reality-based information on our environment. Remember that in our crisis point we can close down completely or become most open to the possibilities for change. This can be a time of death or rebirth.

So, at the very bottom of the stage of Falling Apart, at our darkest hour, we will make our critical decision! There are five decisions that we can make, either consciously or unconsciously, at this critical time. But before we decide to really change, we sometimes try the first four F's, which are negative decisions that delay any real change. However, these first four F's can be very much a part of the process of the Chaos of Change.

FOUR F'S FOR FAILURE TO CHANGE

FIGHT	FLIGHT	FREEZE/FRET	FORGET
Go Back	Run	Inaction	Ignore
Make Excuses	Escape	Indecision	Deny
Hang on	Outward Motions	Procrastination	Mask, Deaden

Fight

When we take this first approach, we remain locked into the old loss from our job or career, from family, divorce, or death. We hold tight to all the anger, despair, shame, and other negative emotions created by the Triggering Event. We do not release or discard the anger and rage but continually rehash, relight the fires, recycle the old battles and the wounds, and wallow in the ruins, creating a monument to our loss and thereby remaining an emotional prisoner of the past.

For example, in our personal life, we may know that our primary relationship is not working, but we stubbornly determine that we will make it work. However, we do nothing really different. We may get a legal divorce, but not an emotional one, since the actions of the former spouse continue to dictate our thoughts, feelings, and behavior for years. We are still involved in the identical fight. There have been no real changes in the internal script.

If fired from a job, we keep refighting the boss or the company, blaming, justifying, and retelling, but never gaining any real insight for resolving the event or moving beyond it. We develop a distrusting bitterness and cynicism that ultimately causes us more real personal and lasting harm that the original negative event.

It is impossible to move forward positively in a new job, in a different career, or in your personal life while still mired in negative emotions from the past. There simply isn't enough room in our psyche for so much negativity at a time when we are attempting to create a new identity. There's too much baggage, too much garbage and static to put together the clearly focused future image that is needed, and so we continue to recycle the old issues and hurts. We simply cannot be creative about our future while reliving the negatives of the past. We must move them from center stage.

Sometimes our fight strategy is going back to a career or a personal relationship in spite of the obvious and unaddressed problems. But this will not work for there has been no growth. With force, we keep trying to make the old way work, believing we can change a situation or a person by our control tactics. We work harder and become almost manic in our attempt to maintain tighter control, bargaining in groundless hope. We don't really change our behavior or response to the problem, to the Triggering Event, but fight harder to control the problem or situation in an effort to make it work out as we want it to. To do the same thing but to expect a different result is futile and foolish, for nothing really changes; we have only postponed the solution.

The fight strategy does not work, and ultimately we are back to deal-ing with the same old unchanging problem, only by this time perhaps it has deepened and become worse!

Flight

This is another postponing decision we can make following the Triggering Event and the Falling Apart process. If we choose the flight strategy, we quickly and mechanically run, even jump. We slam the door on the former situation as quickly and tightly as possible and leap into another job, another career, or another relationship. With no real insight, few second thoughts, or any self-renewal or self-understanding, this strategy is doomed to fail us. This is a distraction, part of our Running Stage technique. We think that if we can just escape the immediate pain, all will be great. Unfortunately, when we take flight, we take ourselves with us, so we repeat the process!

After a major loss, all can seem well on the surface, but we will still feel vulnerable and even unconsciously hostile, expecting and waiting for it all to happen again. There has been no real learning or internal self-rec-onciliation. We have changed our physical environment only and are still dragging all those negative emotions behind us. The emotional impact of the earlier loss has not been processed or healed. In fact, it begins to fes-ter and the poison spreads to our new situation, so that there is no recov-ery, only reoccurrence. Positive growth or change has been shut off. Taking flight without thought can be destructive, and, though it does relieve the pain on a temporary basis, it ultimately creates even more.

Within two weeks after being fired, and after a frantic but mindless search, one client found the exact type of job that he had lost in a simi-lar organization. He reflexively grabbed it, but only two months later was again discharged. His agony had only been dramatically postponed, since he had carried to his new position the problems that had created the ear-lier job loss. He also carried the deeper emotional loss, the fear and mis-trust of others, and the failure to work through these, which rapidly trig-gered the difficulties in the next job.

In a personal or work relationship, one can quickly fly from one bad situation to another, simply recycling the same scenario but in a different setting. Sometimes it can be startling to observe how we repeat the same mistakes, even in different environments and with different people, unconsciously typecasting ourselves. Both fight and flight are self-defeat-ing strategies that merely postpone the effect of earlier negative emotions that have arisen from a Triggering Event.

Freeze/Fret

In this mode, we alternate between frenzy and paralysis, making one plan, then another. We change our mind and jump between decisions, back and forth, taking no real planned action, making no real movement. Time after time, we go from hot to cold on what we will do, but the bottom line is that we do nothing but vacillate and worry. Our response of frenzied anxiety, daydreaming, indecisiveness, inaction, delay, and fretful procrastination absorbs all our thoughts and energy. In this vicious circle, we develop no focused plan and waste our energy and resources figuratively pounding on the walls of our self-made prison, then collapsing helplessly into the role of victim.

In this indecisive mode, our typical response is "Yes, but . . ." In this frozen state, we go up to the door repeatedly but don't open it and cross the threshold of change. However, before we can back away, something may happen that pushes us through. Again, we have made no decision; it was made for us. So again we can claim to be a victim in case the change doesn't work.

Forget

This is a way out for many facing change. As a response to the necessity to change, we may simply attempt to wipe out everything related to the problem, to ignore or deny the problem or our emotions. Frequently, in defense, we mask or deaden ourselves with drugs, food, alcohol, sex, shopping, workaholism, a new relationship, or even violence. We pretend that there is no problem. We hide the negative from others and even from our own consciousness. We build fences and attempt concealment—if there is no problem, there is no need to make changes. But the problems do exist and don't get resolved. Over time, it takes more and more to hide from ourselves. We wear a heavy mask, fear discovery, feel like a fake, and never find our authentic self.

Frequently, before we undertake a major change, we will try all of the first four F's, some in rapid succession, sometimes over a period of years, perhaps for a lifetime. These tactics of delay return to haunt us in an expanded form later. In using these, none of which are true solutions, there has been no rearranging of our interior self, no insight to help us in understanding our careers, human nature, our immediate environment, our world, or ourselves.

A major missing piece of our creative change is that there has been no understanding of what we ourselves have contributed to the problems we now face. Without this critical insight and awareness, we will continue to create the same problems for ourselves. On the surface, when we use these tactics of escape, it seems that all the problems lie outside of ourselves and therefore outside our range of control. We are victims caught in a crazy world. This is an important issue, for as victims, we are powerless, vulnerable, mistrusting of ourselves and others.

These four F's—fight, flight, freeze/fret, forget—are all failures and postponement of facing the real problem.

THE FIFTH F: FACE AND SOLVE FOR LASTING CHANGE AND GROWTH

However, we can make another decision—the fifth F! We can *face and solve* our problems instead of denying, running, masking, and procrastinating. In doing so, we begin to really change, first internally and then externally. When we gain insight into our own weaknesses, our contribution to the negative events that we're involved in, we can begin to feel some sense of power. Paradoxically, once we perceive our role in the drama we are living out, when we take some responsibility (not necessarily blame) for our scenario, we begin to gain a sense of our strength. When we know and genuinely understand the role we've played, we then can be in charge of this part of us in the future, and that frees us. We know that our life is not all random fate; we have choices and options. We are not mindless, powerless victims.

Once we gain real insight into how we unknowingly or unconsciously played a role in setting ourselves up, we know we don't have to recast ourselves in that role. Now we are achieving some consciousness of self, true creative insight that can help us gain control over our situation. We now realize that we don't need to control others. Knowing that we can alter our behavior and avoid repeating a situation releases our fear. Without that basic insight and behavior change, we are destined to repeat that same old behavior when under pressure. This robs us of our sense of power. Rather than suffer continual victimization, let us decide to use the fifth F as our model—to face, solve, and move forward from pain to personal power. In charge of ourselves, even in the most chaotic of situations we will prevail!

STEPS IN DESIGNING A NEW CAREER PARADIGM

Deciding to face, confront, and solve our career problems, to look for the underlying order in our career chaos, is the healthy decision for making a successful change. To identify and finally let go of our nonfunctioning career paradigm and begin the journey of change frees us to begin to turn loose many nonrealistic past expectations and losses and to start focusing on our future. The "dark night" isn't ended but we have realistic hope, and while we still feel some fear, we've resolved to shake off our Sisyphus Syndrome and to be a victim no more, either of a mindless system or our own self-defeating behavior. We can now begin to activate the first steps of career change, to think creatively and resourcefully about how to handle our future career. In spite of the current chaos, we feel excited and realistically confident that we can do whatever it takes to take charge of our career. While this confidence waxes and wanes during this change process, overall we know we are moving forward, even if ever so slowly. We don't know exactly what the focus and direction of the new career will be but we've finally made the decision to discover it. Having survived the initial pain of the "dark night" and released some of our old fears, we know we are in the process of moving beyond a helpless, trapped mind-set.

Of course, all our problems are not solved just by deciding to face the career change and to refocus. However, the beginning recovery from past loss and grief frees us enough to see that our crisis can be an opportunity to forge a stronger future career identity based on our own personal power and meaning, once we fully discover and name it. The situation has not changed, but we are changing our perception and self-concept so that the reality of options emerges.

By accepting the reality that there is no going back to the prechaotic, Status Quo stage, we must change our past behavior and those responses created by the earlier Triggering Event. This goal of creatively facing change and working through it can only be reached through a process of self-growth and internal discovery. We must discard many of our myths and false images about ourselves, the work world, and our former and current definitions and expectations of career success. We begin to acquire new insights into who we are, minus some layers of assumptions, and develop an understanding of the external working environment and the relationship and integration of the two. This process also requires careful and creative investigation into the realities of the environment now and into the future.

Facing and surviving a career crisis and regaining creative control over our work lives leaves us much more confident to take charge of our careers and our personal lives. Rather than living with a sense of loss, deprivation, and victimization, we can begin to feel the excitement of new possibilities for our career and our place in the universe. The "dark night" begins to lift when we decide to overcome and thrive creatively in spite of the current chaos.

Our intention becomes very strong at this point. Facing the problem and determining what can be gained from the pain of our change is the lasting solution. Recovery from loss requires that we see this crisis as an opportunity for discovery—a time to build our self-esteem and forge a stronger work identity based on our own internal personal power. Never again will we feel so powerless and fearful; never again will we passively count on someone else to be in charge of our career.

This decision to intentionally and actively face the change begins our steep learning and growing process for developing deeper insights into ourselves and the environment. This change process is not linear for there are few solid straight lines or fixed schedule times. Nor is the process all positive since it involves dealing with ambiguity and uncertainty. Change means moving from our stable comfort zone, facing our fear, building trust in our own interests, judgments, instincts, and perceptions, and not waiting for someone to do it for us. We must accept that we will make mistakes and at times fail. We must release our earlier frozen self-concept based on our former career and absorb new images and acquire a serial concept of self.

Real change, the search for meaning and method that goes to the very depth of our being, requires an emotional risk taken with courage and enough strength to feel the vulnerability of being human. It requires us to be open and ready to discard beliefs rather than remain enslaved in an old paradigm. Understanding that you always have options is an incredible source of strength. Mastering a career change involves learning how to avoid the excuses, the self-deception, the habits of self-defeat, and the crippling patterns of thought that have deadened us in the past. We discover and accept, as Jung named it, our "shadow self" that tends to surface from the unconscious only during extreme pressure. We identify our strengths as well as our self-defeating behavior, knowing that we have imperfections but being generous and kind to ourselves, and we allow space for growing and learning. Accepting ourselves and throwing off a mantle of shame, guilt, or failure for the necessity of making this career change is itself a creative art.

The career change process, even when undertaken intentionally, has emotional peaks and valleys, and so while our "dark night" is not yet over we begin to see light. During this time, we will vacillate between newly developing insights and interests and the fears that arise from beginning to accept new parts of and realizations about the self. Real change comes from a changing self-image and changing roles as well as real and imagined experiences. It must be internal, not peripheral, and it involves changes in perceptions, attitudes, and understandings of self and the work world. It is critical that in the process of real change we begin to listen to ourselves and beware the experts, family, and friends who question our actions and goals. We are learning to rely on ourselves, becoming more autonomous, yet continuing to hear and connect with others.

Facing the career change and the complex restructuring process feels chaotic, yet in many ways is simple and orderly. Multiple layers of internal and external activities go in myriad directions, yet the results are the identification of a new career identity that combines internal meaning with external opportunities, and a reality-based action plan for achieving this new career.

On one level, the career changer is moving through the more formalized four steps of the career change process: 1) Self-Assessment; 2) Career Exploration; 3) Future Directions and Focus; and 4) Strategic Action Plan, to be described in detail in the remaining chapters. On another level, those in career change are traveling up a steep self-learning curve to establish their new identity, spurred on by the pain of the old identity. They acquire the tools for building self-esteem, psychological success, and career maturity, the factors needed for permanent personal power. This is quite an order for someone in midlife, but the trip is worth it: It keeps us youthful!

Adults acquire the tools of their personal power by gaining new insights into themselves and the work environment; making creative decisions on their future by integrating these external and internal insights; and taking planned, focused action. Facing the necessity for a career change, moving from the fear and pain, beyond the self-defeating powerlessness of Falling Apart, and beginning the renewing process, finally feeling personal power, is a strong course in building self-esteem. Along the way, you develop the tools and resources to know that you are a creative survivor and thriver. Indeed, though life may be painful and chaotic, you can exert a measure of control in shaping your own destiny.

In accepting full personal responsibility we free ourselves from dependency on our former established system of one career or one company to give us what we want. To hang on in fear, if indeed that is an option, is to be imprisoned. When we can emotionally detach, we are then free to become who we really are, to be whole, to succeed or fail based on our own abilities. Again, we may not choose to act on our options, but we should know we have them.

Darkness can be a great liberator in facing adversity and fear. To face freedom and options awakens us from a life of mindlessness and limitation. After going through great external and internal turmoil and chaos, after journeying through a dark night, and then reaching the other side, we are free from fear. To creatively thrive in our changing workplace, we must no longer fear our freedom and our own personal power.

Although we want to be free, we may irrationally feel that if we do not have our responsibilities and burdens, we might be so free that we would disappear, simply fly away. We sometimes think we need the chains to ground us in reality. Convoluted thinking it may be, but frequently we fear our freedom. A client once said to me, "If I turned loose of blaming my family for my problems, who would I be? Who would I become? I have been so angry at them for years, if I dropped it, there wouldn't be anything in that big space." So we cling to our fears, because they are known.

In this client's case, we found that she closely fit the profile of someone working in the interactive multimedia field. She is now picking up this training, teaching in a computer lab, and taking on an internship in animation with a company. She has filled the space well and the bag of grief is dwindling.

THE POWER OF CHANGE

Moving From Pain to Personal Power

Overview of the Career Change Process

11

"In order that people may be happy in their work, these three things are needed: They must be fit for it, they must not do too much of it, and they must have a sense of success in it."

—John Ruskin

A very important and practical way we can view the successful career change is to see it as a process in the exploration and search for answers to four key questions. These four simple but potentially powerful questions are critical to a successful career change process. Actively asking these questions and discovering the answers to them requires both internal and external insight, reality-based information, and purposeful, results-oriented action.

What does our world need today and in the future?

These are the critical first questions. Frequently, the answer to what the world needs is based on those very needs that we, or people we know, have already had. It can be a need we've satisfied or are currently seeking to fulfill. It can also be an emerging need identified by current or coming trends in our society.

Examples of future needs could relate to alternative education, holistic medicine, stronger communication skills, stronger communities—the list is endless, as are our personal needs and interests. Trends include community, education, art, science, medicine, technology, lifestyle, business, enterprise, law, and politics. Specifically, coming needs relate to accepting diversity, viewing aging differently, improving public education, expanding distance learning, recognizing coffee houses as a social gathering alternative to bars, improving daycare, living longer, providing home buying services, saving time, eliminating poverty, "privatizing," outsourcing support services, franchising, providing housing for the elderly, providing financing for small businesses, expanding personnel and temporary services, globalizing consumer products, consulting, and alternative dispute resolution. This list of current and coming needs (compiled by Pathfinders for the Future, a group of my current and former clients) seems endless. As we move out of the Industrial Age, while much is dying, new needs are developing rapidly.

Do I have the necessary skills and competencies to meet these needs, or could I acquire them?

This step requires that we understand clearly our skills and aptitudes: what we do instinctively and uniquely well, coupled with our learned technical skills. The learned skills can be acquired usually without too much difficulty if they are based on our basic aptitudes, what we have a "knack" for. However, it's amazing what learned skills we can acquire if we are strongly motivated and have the basic underlying aptitude and instinct for the skill.

Would I value doing that?

Would meeting this need, solving these problems, provide meaning and purpose, a sense of mission for me? Does it fit my future image, my self-concept of me in the future? This is an absolutely basic, fundamental question in changing careers. If the connection with the need doesn't excite you, if you don't know deeply that you can feel real commitment, connection, and a sense of mission in meeting that need, you are probably going in the wrong direction, regardless of the coming need and regardless of your skills and ability in meeting it. Discovering what has meaning for us as individuals has no rote formula; it varies from individual to individual. However, knowing and honoring this is the heart of a successful career change.

Can I make a living meeting this need?

This is an essential question since practical realities dictate that we pay attention to our financial needs.

In considering a career change, it is important to ask these questions in this order and over time throughout the redirection process. If the answers are very strong regarding the first three questions—on the need, the compatibility of skills, and value or meaning—we frequently can be very resourceful in finding a way to make a living at it. Also, some individuals initially begin the career change process with extremely high financial expectations, which they are willing to relax as they discover a career focus that has strong meaning for them.

In essence, this career change process is discovering what you want based on your heart and your head—both meaning and money must be considered. In this process, you are discovering, naming, and matching your internal needs and natural, instinctive skills with external reality opportunities in the environment, discovering the most appropriate career path for integrating self and the work world, and developing a definite but flexible action plan for achieving your career goals.

This time of facing the career issues and problems begins the very creative but loosely structured four-step learning, deciding, and doing process of taking creative career control:

1. *Self-Assessment*—gaining in-depth self-awareness and insight into our success criteria, our unique DNA fingerprint

2. *Career Exploration*—researching current workplace realities and tracking future trends for career and environmental awareness and information

3. *Future Directions and Focus*—evaluating, determining, and understanding our options, meaning, and mission, a long-term career focus and direction

4. *Strategic Action Plan*—developing and implementing definite strategies, steps to achieve our future image, our career direction and mission.

Individuals experiencing a comprehensive career change process examine themselves and emerge with new depths of motivation based on their uniqueness and trust in their instincts, a sharper sense of career direction, and a more vital awareness of how they want to live on the job. Growth in this sense is personalized and vital. It is the heart of any change and learning. Real change must begin internally, gut level, not peripheral. These changes are most frequently changes in perceptions, attitudes, and understanding, as well as changes in knowledge, experience, skills, or work environment.

The career change process can be conducted on your own, with the help of career self-help books, or you may decide to get the help of a professional advisor. The process is generally the same four basic steps, a progressive process involving learning, deciding, and doing. Each step emphasizes a distinct activity and results, but all can overlap. Table 3 outlines the key questions asked, the follow-up activity, and intended results.

TABLE 3   FOUR-STEP MODEL: PROCESS OF CAREER CHANGE

Critical Questions Asked	Activity	Results
1. Who am I? What can I do?	Self-Assessment	Self-Awareness, Skills, Success criteria for your future
2. Where can I do it? What's out there?	Career Exploration	Work environment awareness, Information on opportunity and future trends
3. What do I really want?	Future Direction How do I see myself?	Creative match of self and work for long-term meaning and career direction
4. How do I get there? What are my options?	Strategic Action Plan	Focused plan to reach future image

Self-Assessment   12

"Listen to your stomach, not your head. Your head will rationalize you right into a job that you shouldn't have."

—Ray Bradbury

In the career change process, this first major step, *self-assessment,* focuses on understanding yourself from all directions, as if putting yourself in a house of mirrors where the mirrors are only facing you. In the second step of the career change process, *career exploration,* the mirrors are directed outward to scan and research the environment, and then these two views are creatively synthesized into a conscious and intentional decision on *future image,* the third step of the process. You catch inner and outer glimpses and reflections of yourself and the work environment from all directions and from every corner. The fourth step is the *strategic action plan,* and tactics for achieving it.

The self-assessment process has no instant solution; there are no automatic paint-by-number steps. The difficulty involved in this step has been stressed by two of our most successful contemporaries, John Gardner, who said, "I must find out who I am," and Peter Drucker, who in an article in *Psychology Today* said, "Here I am 56 years old and I still don't know what I want to do when I grow up" (Hall, 1982, pp. 60–67).

It typically requires a minimum of three to four months, but can take much longer, to make lasting progress in this self-assessment process. Actually, it is ongoing throughout our lives, but here I'm referring to the formal step. It can take longer if your time and energy are limited by a pressured or stressful work schedule. Also, the time involved depends very much on your starting point. Some individuals in career change have negative or self-defeating issues to plow through before they can become effective in their career self-assessment. This may involve work with a psychiatrist or psychologist.

There are four major groups of activities involved in the self-assessment process and all are aimed at generating your highly individualized list of success criteria. Activities include:

1. *Completing a variety of untimed career assessment tools*

2. *Conducting "career conversations"*

3. *Remembering and surfacing the puzzle pieces*

4. *Identifying skills and success criteria*

    Recalling and analyzing past achievements

    Developing a sense of community

    Developing an individualized success criteria list

    Selecting career options

CAREER ASSESSMENT TOOLS

This activity involves a series of well-researched, validated assessment inventories to provide clues for identifying interests, values, motivation, skills, personality traits, temperament, communication, and workplace style. These formal but untimed tests provide clues and validation later in the assessment process but comprise only about 15 percent of the career self-assessment step. I strongly stress that any paper and pencil type career tests are tools only and may perhaps provide critical pieces but can have limited value, especially with some adults. For experienced adults, this personal phase of planning a career is too critical and too complex to rely on external (paper and pencil) resources only. Such resources are useful primarily in validating thinking about self and career issues after becoming really involved in the career thought process.

The inventories are the first stage, but results of these are not presented until much later, at the end of a personalized in-depth group skills assessment process. If given these test results early on, many adults, overly eager to find the answer immediately, tend to stop thinking for themselves. They read the results but never really own or fully absorb the information. Later they seldom remember the results, having never fully understood them nor taken action using them. To visualize and integrate the results, it is important for you to own the information and then judge its reliability for you so that you can take the actions and make the decisions yourself based on what you know.

This formal testing can be helpful to expand career options, to validate a career decision, or as a second opinion after insight is gained through other methods of self-assessment, including career conversations and autobiographical exercises. All assessment tools should be accompanied by a full explanation of the results and the basic underlying theory. In the case of testing, "a little learning can be a dangerous thing" if the results alone are used to refocus a career.

Jungian personality theories and John Holland's vocational theories are used in this assessment process. Each of the assessment tools, for interests, skills, personality temperament, values, workstyle, and personal motives, point out specific information that we tie directly to career and occupational fields. These tools and theories are helpful indicators, not final decision makers for those reestablishing career identities. Career change is a "hands on" process, its purpose not merely to gain information but to use information thoughtfully and to accept and reject it discriminately. The idea is to arrive at reliable and focused self-information, not to move from one closed box into another. Your personal career meaning and direction must ultimately come from you after careful assessment and research.

CONDUCTING CAREER CONVERSATIONS

After you complete the untimed paper and pencil inventories, engage in a number of individual career conversations as well as a number of autobiographical exercises designed to get you to think about yourself and your past. This activity is important. Your current thoughts may be quite chaotic as a result of long-term career unrest and dissatisfaction, so we need to change your thought processes. Not all those who successfully change careers are coming from this position of extreme stress and burnout, but the adults with whom I work often are. If they could have solved the career problem, they would have already done so since most of them are very bright and motivated.

In the career self-assessment step, we are tapping into a center, a core of being that is uniquely your own. This is your bedrock at the very basis, the foundation of your career needs, like a DNA fingerprint containing the coding for your innate and natural interests, personality, traits, skills, and motivation. These success criteria, a listing of all the factors one requires to feel successful, are collected and written during the scheduled sessions. Think of your success criteria as the foundation of a house. If the piers of the foundation rest on solid bedrock, they may shift somewhat in changing soil conditions; however, the foundation does not crack and degenerate and the house remains solid. So it is with adults in career collision. With careers well centered on their own unique bedrock, they may not escape the career chaos but they can maneuver through it with a firm foundation and focus.

In career self-assessment, you are on a passionate pursuit to uncover, discover, piece together your high individualized and unique success criteria and the elements that will provide you with that special career meaning you are seeking. It is through our differences—even our eccentricities—that we may build the foundation of our career. Once surfaced, identified, and accepted, the task is to find the environment, the special niche where you can be your best self and be paid for it.

REMEMBERING AND SURFACING THE PUZZLE PIECES

In career self-assessment, we are creating a remembering process by asking ourselves countless questions. This is the basis for building a personal collage, a composite portrait from snapshots from all ages, stages, roles, and jobs: from your very youngest memories as a child, throughout kindergarten, elementary, high school, college, and all work and volunteer experience. It represents all your shadings, skills, interests, and motivations (needs and payoff). In this activity, you can begin to write your success criteria, those things that you know are deeply critical for you to feel successful. They will surface as you work through this process; this list is your prescription for your future and it is the heart of the career change process.

Also at this time you are identifying your functional skills, what you do naturally and instinctively well, perhaps so easily that you are unaware of it. What are you doing when you forget about time because you are so connected and engrossed? What are you doing when you feel best about yourself? What is your safety release valve to relieve stress? Your goal is to get all skills, interests, and needs surfaced so you can look at them from different angles. In this activity of the self-assessment process, we identify, assemble, and evaluate all the scattered pieces of your personal work patterns and history and then decide which pieces are important for you to keep, to take with you into your future, or to leave behind. Actually, you are in a pattern-making process, but first it is imperative to get all the essential pieces identified.

You want to know: Who were your favorite teachers and classmates? What were your favorite thoughts, activities, and interests? How do you remember yourself as a child and as a junior high, high school, and college student? When were you happiest, most productive, saddest? What did you think and dream about as a child? What do you daydream about now? What games did you play and what did you fantasize about? Who were important people in your life, real and imaginary? What are key thoughts and feelings you remember? Tapping these memories is important because those experiences that we remember may well have significance in our present and future.

What do you remember about your family: parents, grandparents, siblings, and others who have influenced your life? Sketch the positive and negative key events in your life as you see them. What are your current family relationships? What does it mean today to come from your family? What were the messages you received from family, school, and community? What was the best and the worst advice your parents ever gave you? What significant teachings do you remember about how you were to be, about how to handle your world, both positive and negative? What messages did you learn as a child and continue to use today? Do you see them as valid? Why? Why not?

What do you actively do with time off the job? What do you read, think about, talk about, watch on T.V.? How involved are you in the community? What key relationship do you have now? Who are your friends? How do you solve problems with your friends? What are your spiritual needs? Think in depth about every job you have ever had, both paid and volunteer, since you were very young, not just those listed on your current résumé. What are your preferred lifestyle needs now and in the future, including how and where you want to live?

At this point very early in the self-assessment, don't be concerned with how all these pieces fit together or whether they are important enough to be used in your current or future pattern. Simply uncover all the pieces, large and small, even those that may not seem significant, since they could be a key piece to the future fit. You may discard some later, but initially simply catch all of them. What you are doing with all the exercises and questioning is creating a remembering environment to bring all critical parts of yourself to the surface, releasing bits and pieces from the subconscious that you may never have realized, much less verbalized. Once these surface you will think, How obvious! Why haven't I seen that before? It is only after we have the vocabulary, the words for a trait, skill, or need, that we can take ownership of it and use it in an effective way. We can't direct or own what is in our subconscious until we become aware, put words to it, and connect it with our present time and place.

Another very critical reason for going through an in-depth past remembering process is because we were much more creative, spontaneous, and natural when we were younger. This was before we discovered so many rules, the ways we should or ought to be, before we were schooled in the right way to handle our lives, and later our careers, as dictated by the workplace, culture, family, and school systems. For years, research has indicated that by the time children are in the third grade, 60 percent of their creative imagination has disappeared. Recognizing our potential for creativity and recovering at least a small part of it is an essential part of self-assessment. These glimpses of our younger and later years, both off the job and on, are the snapshots we use to piece together what in time can be a rich, full-length, colorful lifetime portrait for our future.

I have found that many individuals who have been in ill-fitting careers or jobs, for whatever reason, have lowered self-esteem; important parts of themselves are stashed away and almost forgotten. These pieces of your pattern must be brought to a fully conscious level and accepted or rejected before you can even begin to make decisions about moving forward in any solid career decision making: They must be identified and perhaps strengthened before you gain enough self-esteem and enough information to make a sound career decision. This growth and development cannot be accomplished in a structured, linear process only. Try carrying a small pad of paper on which to write randomly occurring thoughts that surface while involved in another activity. These random thoughts often provide important clues.

IDENTIFYING SKILLS AND SUCCESS CRITERIA

Following the testing tools, the early individual career conversations, and the autobiographical exercises, an important part of the self-assessment step for changing careers is to identify your skills, temperament, personality traits, interests, motives, payoff, and ultimately to refine your success criteria list as discussed earlier. Another important part of the skills assessment process is the weekly two or three hour workshops approximately six to ten clients meet in for ten to thirteen weeks.

One client, a very successful and articulate public relations specialist, described the value of interacting in the small group:

• The interaction was confirming. This process is unsettling because everything you are, or thought you were, goes on the table for examination.

- I was honored by the group's willingness to help me with honest, tactful feedback.

- No one made me feel like a flake or a fool when I expressed my real feelings and ideas.

- I learned about myself by watching the others struggle with their own issues and questions.

- I learned a great deal by watching Helen interact with others: how she pushed sometimes, questioned others, and kept us all moving.

- It allowed me to examine my feelings or preconceptions and decide if they were still accurate or useful.

- Good motivation—I found myself becoming more committed to the process so as not to hold the group back. I don't always have the same discipline by myself.

Recalling and Analyzing Past Achievements

An important assignment made early on in these small skills groups is an individual "achievement analysis." You recall in detail and write specific accomplishments or activities that meet the following three criteria: You did it well, enjoyed doing it, and felt proud of it. You go back to your very earliest memories and list three of these accomplishments for each four-year period of your life.

Initially this exercise can be very difficult if you have been or are still in therapy recalling painful, negative, destructive incidents. As a result, you may feel that indeed you have no accomplishments, nothing that fits these criteria. Also, if you have been or are currently in a negative, ill-fitting work environment and are burned out and turned off, you may not have recently thought in terms of positive accomplishments. A few have never thought about positive accomplishments at any time in their lives.

According to Masterson (1988, p. 24), when we manage an activity or relationship well, i.e., we believe we did it well, we enjoyed doing it and felt proud, using our own unique style, this experience is integrated to reinforce our self-image, so that we remember it and it builds up our self-esteem. Viscott (1976, p. 27) reminds us that the defenses that block unpleasant memories also block pleasurable ones. The inability to remember what is positive robs us of energy and joy and prevents us from forming an optimistic attitude.

Some in this process have further to go and simply need more time and thought, and they are encouraged to go through a workshop series a second time if we feel they were not thinking clearly during the first series. The goal is to do what it takes to help them gain the insight into themselves that they need, and this process does not necessarily work on a time clock. It simply takes longer for some than others and patience is critical here.

On the other hand, many clients, articulate and confident, and after some thought, can work through and list these accomplishments rather easily. However, I watch for the quick, glib answers that are surface only. This is an important part of the remembering process and it is essential for some of the participants in creating a more positive self-view. For others, it may be simply taking the necessary time for serious reflection, which they haven't done before. It is critical for you to remember and discuss these past achievements and receive feedback on them from the others in the group.

Each member of the group selects five or more accomplishments to narrate in detail to the group, who record on individual small cards all the varying skills they hear from the speaker. While we have discussed and completed exercises on the different skills, I do not give specific instructions on what participants are to write. You need freedom of expression, since I learn much about you by the feedback you give the speaker. After each participant relates his or her accomplishment, each listener reads aloud the skills he or she listed for the speaker. These skills cards go into an envelope labeled with the description of the accomplishment and given to the speaker, who later sorts through these to remember what the others listed as the major skills employed by them in their accomplishments.

While we keep this moving somewhat briskly, it is amazing how the clients respond, especially those who may have earlier appeared shy and reticent. After a session of these exercises, those who may have had real problems remembering their accomplishments can frequently open up with a stream of them, as sometimes the descriptions of the other participants pique their memory. This exercise is additionally successful because participants learn to listen for and verbalize the skills of others; they acquire a vocabulary for consciously naming skills as well as the ability to identify them.

There's something quite reassuring to have strangers listen and write out a list of your skills. Also, since the participants come from a diversity of personal and professional backgrounds, they bring a different perspective and vocabulary to the skills identification. Many are extremely good at hearing and naming skills for others in the group but at first may have a problem applying this process to themselves and their own career. I've frequently noticed that getting a response on their skills from other members of the group can be perhaps even more validating than what I say. As a professional, they expect me to recognize and name their specific skills. However, they think, Well, if several almost total strangers identify these as my skills, I must really have them!

One of the main factors we identify as the participants talk of their accomplishments is their consistent, unique payoff. This is their primary thrust, their motive, a special drive that dominates their voluntary behavior and surfaces when we talk about our accomplishments. Anytime you do something that gives great satisfaction and a sense of accomplishment, this payoff is involved. You absolutely must be able to identify and name it so you can systematically, not randomly, duplicate it in your next career move. These payoffs are unique but could include for example, meeting challenges, gaining recognition, having impact, being on a constant learning curve, overcoming obstacles, creating something new, dealing with a tangible product, displaying leadership and independence. To be in creative control of your career, you must discover and name the unique thread or motive that is universally and consistently important to you, as tracked from these accomplishments.

It is not unusual for participants, who may be very successful financially, to never mention any accomplishment related to their job or career field. Also, the particular span of years they remember as having the most accomplishments can be significant. Conversely, some years can yield few if any accomplishments.

In the meantime, using our house of mirrors metaphor, the workshop participants examine, prioritize, and record skills from numerous other methods assigned in the workshop. These skills are all prioritized once again and listed together. Though different exercises and methods are used to surface these skills and needs, there will be an obvious similarity, a top three or five skills that will emerge for you though the specific words or vocabulary for each assessment process may differ somewhat.

Developing a Sense of Community

These small groups function as learning sessions, not group therapy. However, you will get much support and specific workplace information from each other, and there is always very active and spirited participation and connecting in these groups. These groups are also valuable for a number of other reasons. You interact with other bright and experienced people dealing with similar career problems, giving you a sense of community so that you don't feel isolated or different. You also gain and share community and organization contacts, and broaden your knowledge and insight into the varying career fields and work environments of others. Another important benefit of the skills sessions is that you are provided with an early opportunity to verbalize and to become more articulate and assertive about your career skills, needs, and issues. You become more aware of your background and the information you will need to make your next career move.

This group time of the self-assessment step is an extremely important part of the career change process. Much activity and many critical subjects related to change, the changing environment, chaos theory, etc., are covered during these workshops. Special films, handouts, and material designed for a particular group are used as needed.

Developing an Individualized Success Criteria List

The continuing identification and naming of each person's individual and unique list of career success criteria, begun in the earlier conversations, is a most critical part of the group. Each time you identify a factor essential in your work life, write it down. You may also volunteer observations or information that relates to others in the group. This cumulative list is designed so that all insights can be recorded easily. I also ask participants to give an example so that their criteria can be measured. For example, if you list "professional environment" as an essential success criteria, I ask you to describe what you mean by that. One client who listed this as one of her criteria said that it meant "getting dressed in a business suit, driving downtown, and going to the top floor of a fourteen-story building." On the other hand, another individual in the same group listed "casual environment," as measured by never having to wear panty hose! And casual dress has remained a very important item on her list of success criteria.

As these criteria are discovered and added, reworded, and revised throughout the process of career change, you will begin to get critical pieces of your career pattern filled in. However, at this point there may be no coherent pattern of what your "big picture" will be.

Selecting Career Options

As we begin to wind up the skills workshops, I teach the participants Dr. Holland's Hexagon Theory for fitting people to careers to serve as a structure and provide a vocabulary for understanding both themselves and careers. My concern here is that you perceive how the theory matches people and careers so you can continue to build on the information. We also use the work of Carl G. Jung, focusing on the *Myers-Briggs Type Indicator.*

At this time, I collect all the information that we have on you—all testing, exercises, and work papers—and create a career design profile, which brings together and summarizes all the information about you from varied directions. These profiles are returned to you and at that time we go through the profile, covering each assessment tool and the results. I carefully interpret what was assessed and ask each client to write out specific careers that evolved from each tool covering their interests, skills, values, temperament, work style, and internal needs.

From all these, you will record on an Occupational Summary sheet the specific careers that have evolved as a possible match for you from the varying sources. This is important because you can then compare the occupations that have surfaced from the various assessment tools, the workshop, and also our individual conversations. At that time, we may add other occupations and other career options relating more specifically to you and your work situation. We also add related special niche careers that have not been named directly from the assessment but that we sense could be a fit.

Sometimes all the career fields have a strong connection, such as teaching, social service, or religious activities, or they have the common thread of science, health, and medical service, or perhaps they all group under business, accounting, and finance. Sometimes, however, careers will surface from all of these areas, seemingly a hodgepodge. Sometimes they will relate to your current career field, but other times the careers will have little relationship on the surface to what you have ever done in your life.

At this time, near the end of the formal self-assessment step, you will select your three best-fitting career options or directions that you would like to research in more detail in the next step of the career change process. This concludes the formalized first step, self-assessment, but I do caution that these patterns accompany us throughout all the additional career change steps—indeed, it will remain fairly constant throughout our lives.

You now should have a strong sense of yourself but as yet have not determined a specific career field. However, while you have sound, quality information about yourself and we may well understand your career issues, you may have not solved your entire career problem. While we have data on alternative career fits, in some cases we can't see how the pieces go into any coherent pattern—there is yet important work to do so that you continue to move forward to the *career exploration* phase.

Figuring out this new career identity can be a most complex process. It would be easy to push it on instant automatic, but this process provides those of you exploring career change the opportunity to get all of your career pattern pieces brought to the surface and evaluated. We seek nothing less than genuine self-awareness. What you are learning will not dramatically shift even as the world changes; it will be just as true for you in the future as in the present, though you will certainly continue to add to the self-knowledge. Because you know what you are all about, you can shift and adjust your career in the future but maintain your basic foundation. The knowing of your identity is your one real security in our chaotic, upside-down work world. Genuine career self-knowledge is our key to thrive and to maintain creative control over our careers in a chaotic age!

When we reach real insight, a knowing on a deeper level, we can move beyond our old ways—away from our old fears, insecurities, the maybe's and "yes, but's." When we know that we can hide no longer from ourselves, we must move forward, trust our instincts, and stop fearing the system and the future. This is freedom to thrive creatively. Indeed, freedom is knowing our options, whether we choose among them or not.

Career Exploration   **13**

What is needed in our world today? What are our future needs? What is available? What is happening in our environment, in our culture, and in the work world? What is the reality of current and emerging opportunities? What specifically fits my success criteria? You will seek answers to these questions in *career exploration,* the second major step in the process of changing careers. This is the development of a keen awareness and insight into coming trends, into the realities of the environment, and into the specific career fields that the self-assessment step has indicated as a possible career match. You move out of the familiar career box and begin an active search for information, insight, and connections in the environment, specifically in different career areas that could be a match for your success criteria.

DISCOVERING WHAT'S OUT THERE

This exploration and gathering of knowledge is comparable to getting a Ph.D. in field research in "What's happening in our world?" You are developing the Proteus Principle of foresight, searching to determine your present needs or your emerging needs. This exploration involves becoming tuned in and acutely aware of the external environment, listening with what I call our "third ear" to what is being said and happening all around us. It is questioning, searching, exploring, and connecting with others in the community and the workplace and tracking current and future trends as they relate to issues that hold an interest for you. Even more important, it is deliberately moving out from your routine space and seeking to meet and connect with people in industries or career fields that have an appeal. You deliberately develop a deep and genuine curiosity about what others do in their work life. You learn and practice the "art of inquiry"—asking questions, seeking information and insight from others. You engage in creative brainstorming and active listening to gain information and perceive possible opportunities. You genuinely become the curious seeker at this time.

PRACTICING GRAIL SPEECH

Peter Drucker, who has spent his career focusing on careers and leadership, says that one lesson has become very clear to him: "Above all, regardless of their almost limitless diversity of style, the effective leaders know how to ask questions—the right questions. They start out asking, 'What needs to be done?' Then they ask, 'What can I do to make a difference?'" (Hesselbein, 1996, p. xiii).

In stressing the necessity for asking questions as we search for a path through our chaotic Age of Information, I tell the story of Percival, one of the most famous knights of the Round Table involved in the quest for the Grail. His mother, after losing her husband and two realms, fled with Percival to hide in the forest. She shielded him from all worldly knowledge of knighthood and battle, teaching him to be a passive onlooker and never to ask questions. Percival then accidentally got into the Grail castle and saw wondrous things. He met the Fisher King who was in despair and suffering from deep wounds. The prophecy was that the King could only be healed if an "innocent fool" visited the castle and asked questions.

Percival was the innocent fool, and though deeply curious, he asked no questions about the wondrous Grail castle, and so he missed his opportunity for greatness and fame through saving the kingdom. He did eventually get to King Arthur's court, where he was called a simple goose and shamed publicly for failing to free the Fisher King. It took him a lifetime to find his way back to the Grail castle.

Linda Sussman, who retells this story in her book, *Speech of the Grail,* interprets the spoken word as an act of heroism. Grail speech "transmits meaning and inspires change or movement by opening a space in which its recipients experience the freedom to choose, the freedom to create; no intention of coercion, manipulation, or persuasion—overt or subtle—cloud this speaking" (1995, p. 7).

Our failure to give ourselves permission to ask simple questions, to make inquiries, to practice Grail speech, will be a major self-defeating behavior as we move toward taking creative control of our careers. This story also demonstrates the necessity to discard some of the teachings of our parents and culture. Percival left home but still carried the unexamined mother lode of messages that created problems for him in a different world. Jane Healey (1992) urges parents to encourage creative questioning from children. It's amazing how similar this is to what I teach my adult clients!

This stage initiates a breaking apart of our old routines and patterns, and we realize that we must give ourselves permission to ask questions of others and of self. This is an extremely active and creative part of the career change process, for it involves taking our written success criteria, bits and pieces of seemingly disjointed information gained from the self-assessment step, discovering information in the environment that seems to fit, and then beginning to assemble a coherent picture of a future career. This career exploration step can be quite difficult, since it directly involves asking for what we want and need—information. Surprisingly, those who would help anyone, anytime, are frequently the most reluctant to ask for information they need. They are the ones who "don't want to bother someone."

The previous step of self-assessment has indicated potential career matches, and, based on the success criteria, unique needs, values, skills, and interests, and the thousands of career fields have been narrowed down to three or so choices for a possible fit. Without this initial self-information and a degree of career focus, it would be an overwhelming job to sort through the mass of career and vocational information to determine what is valid and what is fiction and decide upon a targeted match. Some internal focus is necessary before this targeted external environmental search begins.

RESEARCHING CAREER REALITIES

It is important to remember that seeking career information from others is absolutely not job seeking or job networking in disguise. Don't go out with a résumé in hand, pretending to seek career change information. This step is exploring career fields to gain information and advice, and not a specific job at this point. Unfortunately, too frequently the information interview has been used as a guise for trying to get a job from the interviewee. While most people are open to providing information on their career field, they naturally resent being the target of a misrepresentation. Quality, reality-based career information is a premium product today, and effectively and efficiently capturing and updating this information is a serious responsibility for professionals who provide career resources for adults.

However, talking with people either employed in a career field or very familiar with it is really the only effective way to learn what a career field is all about. Career fields are changing so rapidly that by the time someone researches and writes a book on a specific field and gets it published and into bookstores, the field may well have dried up. Banking, real estate, college teaching, law, computer hardware, indeed, almost all fields have changed dramatically in a very short time span; what was reality five years ago may well be passé today.

You can still enter a field that you discern to be on a downswing, but you should understand the reality of the pleasure and the pain *before* entering it and have ideas on how you could deal with its problems. If you really feel that it is an appropriate match, you may be motivated and creative enough to find a way to make it work well. However, if you were to slide or back into the career, or merely heard it to be a secure job field, you would not be likely to care enough for what you are doing, when the field hits a downturn, to make the sustained effort necessary to make it continue to work for you.

The more you talk with people about a career field, the more you will learn. It is most unwise to consider a career change into a field without sound information and advice from at least six to eight people working in that field. This also requires some wisdom and creativity in sorting the wheat from the chaff.

RETURNING TO THE ACADEMIC WOMB

I encounter many who try to solve a career problem by immediately returning to the "academic womb," by obtaining another advanced college degree, though they still have no idea what a career in their academic field is all about, what the opportunities are, and how to break into these. By adding another degree we may merely delay the career crisis. If in a career crisis, do not simply rush back for a degree unless you really know what you want to do with it and how it fits into your career picture.

Recently I visited with a young woman who is a new entry to the paralegal field. For years she had been a word processor in a major law firm. She left her job, spent five thousand dollars on paralegal training, and has discovered she doesn't like the paralegal field at all. With her solid work history and experience and with some help, if not on her own, she could have picked up some additional technical skills in the evening and moved directly into a paralegal position without such expensive formal training, perhaps in the very law firm for which she worked. Even more important, she should have been much more aware of her preferred skills, as well as those required in the paralegal field, before taking a year off from work and borrowing the tuition. She could have asked extensive questions of the paralegals in her office, which she did not do, and through her own experience found that her original expectations were not based on reality. She doesn't like paralegal work any better than word processing, and indeed the two are very similar in many workplaces, though perhaps they should not be. There is absolutely no substitute for knowing yourself, your success criteria, and the reality of a career field before entering it.

Not only will you seek specific career information at this point but you will also begin a very active and creative process of building your foresight and skills in identifying and tracking current and future trends affecting our society and the career fields being considered. This involves research, questioning, and creatively integrating the findings with their career success criteria.

It is absolutely critical for you to be the active seeker in this career research. This is a major step in achieving a sense of your own personal power, a sense of knowing that you are a creative thriver in a chaotic age. This realization is a major goal of the career change process; as a consequence, fear of change begins to diminish.

This career exploration step not only results in focused career information, it also builds additional important skills. For many adults, actively and assertively researching and asking for the information they need to understand a career field is in itself a giant growth step. It is clearly an important step forward in the process of building assertion skills, self-esteem, and a sense of personal power. You will learn to ask others for what you need and realize that most others will respond positively. These exchanges begin to build a sense of connection and community. It is affirming, and part of the realization that we are not so isolated in solving all our problems; there are resources responsive to our needs if we ask for help.

ASKING FOR CAREER INFORMATION

Asking for information and insight from others is absolutely necessary but can be formidable. Reluctance to ask can be based partly on:

1. Being taught to wait passively for what we want and need and not bother people or waste their time. For multiple reasons, many of us have learned to wait silently, respectfully, and patiently, like expectant children whose parents or other adults are to anticipate and meet our needs. We carry this same expectation to school, to our workplace, and to our personal relations.

2. Not knowing what we wanted and deserved, and even when we did, often failing to give ourselves permission to ask for it. Of course, we tend to become frustrated, eventually angry, and passive-aggressive for not having our needs met automatically by our boss, friends, spouse, family. We can't name our needs except in free-floating terms such as "I want something different" or "I want to be appreciated."

3. The fear of rejection, of looking silly, or feeling embarrassed because we don't have all the answers. Your role is to ask questions and get information on the career field, professional organizations, materials to read, and others with whom you can discuss the field.

GAINING POWER THROUGH INFORMATION

When you begin to take action, to ask for information, to research the environment and discover that people respond, you will feel a surge, a sense of strength and trust that perhaps had never before surfaced, or had been impaired by earlier triggering event loss. This is a powerful experience, for it is indeed amazing the opportunities and information that an active, interested career exploration can reveal. In coming out of your isolated career/job box, you will realize what else is going in our world and also what additional options exist.

While you may not go into one of the original fields of interest researched by talking with others, you may discover a special niche that becomes an even better match. A person who knows the career field very well will frequently say something like, "You really ought to check out so and so! I see it as a good match for you." They are, in effect, using their creativity to help you solve your career problem. Smaller niche careers are becoming more common, but we can't know they are evolving unless we are searching and someone brings them up, for these niche careers haven't even hit the mainstream yet.

In our Age of Information, we suffer from information starvation and at the same time information overload. A system to work through both of these is crucial for changing careers. We must have some strong initial focus on the specific information we need, or we could search forever without advancing!

People on the verge of career change, who often have personal problems as well as career problems, improve dramatically when they begin to get insight into themselves and see how to construct a system to take action and move through those problems. They see the proverbial light at the end of the tunnel and feel confident that it isn't an oncoming freight train. Interaction with others who have actually changed careers successfully is affirming and a major asset to those who are still in the process.

Most important, however, are the actions and activity that you as part of this career change research step must personally begin to take. With resources, direction, contacts, and guidance, actively search and ask for the career information you need. Take focused action and as a result you will learn. Investigative and analytical thinking may be necessary for some introverted types who need more "looking inward" than others who are more action-oriented. However, after a time this may ultimately be nonproductive; it becomes time to move through the active research and exploration of career options.

Future Direction and Focus

14

"Vision is a picture of the future that you really care about. It is an expression of your core values, your sense of purpose . . . the future you want to create . . . vision brings something from within and says, 'I really want to put my life energy into creating this.'"

—Peter Senge

Dreams can become realities. So think and talk honestly about your dreams! Ask yourself, What do I really want and value? How do I see myself in the future? These are the key questions we answer in this third step of the career change process. Holland, a seasoned career researcher, says he is increasingly convinced that our daydream jobs can have much validity in helping us select a career, and he has formalized a system for tracking them.

Changing careers successfully is a highly creative process for discovering and deciding your purpose, your vision of yourself in the future, and what has lasting meaning for you. It involves knowing and naming your purpose based on a vision of yourself in the future. It means turning to your authentic self with our list of success criteria developed in Step I, self-assessment; and then in Step II, career exploration, exploring, researching, and connecting with the realities of current and emerging needs in the environment. You then creatively integrate these opportunities and external needs with your inner needs and skills into a vision, a future image you can actually see in your mind's eye. This third step, future directions and focus, the integration into a clearly focused *future image,* is a pilot function that guides all else and one of the greatest and most creative challenges you will ever face. Lack of this image based on an appropriate, well-defined purpose or mission in your life and career is a major cause of career dissatisfaction and failure.

Csikszentmihalyi (1990, p. 214) stresses that as long as enjoyment follows piecemeal from activities not linked to one another in a meaningful way, one is still vulnerable to the vagaries of chaos. Even the most successful careers, the most rewarding family relationships, eventually run down. People die and we retire. We must harmonize life and career goals, making separate pieces fit. Each activity will thus make sense in the present, as well as in view of the past and the future. In such a way we give meaning to our entire life.

Many talented people feel guilty because they are searching for meaningful work. They have been programmed for "success" according to the external definition but now know that definition is falling far short. Am I expecting too much? they wonder. Am I being too childlike, deluded by a fantasy, to want to want to wake up each morning and be totally enthused about getting into my day? Is our search, our drive for work with meaning a futile effort designed to be met with disappointment? This is the fear of the millions of Americans who have resorted to cynicism and pessimism as a response to the chaos and the problems facing our work and personal lives. But the seeking, not the absolute possession, is what gives us a meaningful life. A career with meaning always takes us beyond ourselves, giving us a sense of direction.

In the past, we have made great effort against overwhelming odds to create a sense of purpose for ourselves and our descendants. We can now refuse to accept that life is meaningless. It doesn't matter what our ultimate goal is—provided it is compelling enough for a lifetime's worth of psychic energy. Congruence between inner and outer ultimately leads to that strength and serenity we admire in people who seem to have come to terms with themselves and their world.

When we are young and making our initial career decision, we have not experimented and tested ourselves enough to have many real clues as to what we can do well and what will give us meaning. Our basic aptitudes are there but are not connected to career fields. Neither do we have much sound information on career fields themselves. Frequently our perceptions are off target, or the field experiences major changes before we get into it. So our selections are often long shots with little insight into the reality of the career field, our career potential, or ourselves—our skills, values, and interests.

By early midlife, we have accumulated family and work responsibilities and also harbor a great fear of change, as well as concern for what others would think if we even considered moving from an already established career path to another one. Barriers set by society, such as the myths discussed in Part II especially, that "one life equals one career," are very strong here. Later in midlife, we've acquired another myth, the mind-set that the "best is behind us." So we settle into day-to-day inertia and entropy takes over. At times we agonize about "what could have been" and fret over countless "if only's," which become a sad refrain.

Individuals who successfully change careers actively engage in a creative struggle to find spirit, meaning, and identity in their work life at whatever age or stage. This is why they undertake this career change process. For them, work is an important vehicle for commitment and transformation since so much of our time and energy is expended working and, through work, we are engaged in life.

This third step of the career change process is the discovery and naming of our compelling passion—our meaningful purpose. In this step, we creatively match our success criteria and our career options, learned during in-depth self-assessment, with the current or emerging opportunities in the workplace and society, discovered during career exploration.

Capturing our future image is the creative synthesis of these major pieces of our career pattern. In our mind, we can visualize into the years ahead and see ourselves as active in a certain career role. We know that strong, successful people have one major characteristic in common: They see themselves fulfilling a destiny. This is a magnet that draws focus and directs us. We have engaged in active research and self-assessment until we are confident that this future image fits us and we actually feel its pieces coming together for us. What a feeling of personal power and direction this creates! For many, this is the first time they have a feeling of being connected to a real power source. This connection releases a great surge of confidence and creativity. They are no longer blocked by uncertainty and bewilderment. A word of caution: This does not mean that all things fall into place easily or quickly, as in fairy tales. It does mean, however, that you have insight, focus, and direction to make something definite happen.

SEEING WHO YOU WANT TO BECOME

As you go through the earlier career exploration step, you meet and talk with people in fields related to those you have identified as a possible fit from intuitive judgments and the formal assessment and testing process. Juggling all the pieces of your success criteria career pattern, about 85 percent of the time you will talk with someone or read about someone in a career who is doing something that reveals to you a small but critical missing piece. At this point, the major pieces of the pattern can begin to fall into place. For example, maybe after talking with someone who is designing and producing interactive multimedia for educational science programs, who explained that they use their writing, computer systems, and design skills in a small team project, you realize that you can see yourself integrating skills in a similar way. You are discovering your future image, one that will provide real meaning. Most important, this is built not only on aspirations but, since you have personally investigated it, also on the reality of opportunities in a particular career field. You know and see how you can fit all the pieces together and make it work.

It is amazing how quickly and actively people can move at this point, almost as if they are propelled. You usually won't have a problem getting what you want once you know what it is. At this point, you can turn on your creativity to close the gap between your future image vision and your current reality to generate the energy for making the change necessary. By this time, you will have focus and be able to see how most of the pieces can be brought together and implemented in your life—and you are off and running to make it happen!

This is an "aha" experience, a glimpse of the obvious. More than a peak experience, which may not last, this is more like a conversion. For some individuals, more ground-based and analytic, it is strong hope. They see the pieces coming together in a logical fashion. They haven't made it happen yet, but they see what it is and how they can bring it about.

Having a clearly focused future image gives a great sense of personal power. You have cut through the jungle of chaos, taken control of the information starvation, information overload, and your own self-defeating behavior. Earlier fears can be set aside more easily now that there's a definite direction to follow. This future image based on internal and external realities provides your own unique way of reaching for your future and taking responsibility to discover it with contacts and help from others.

Visualizing our future image—getting it through to the subconscious—is a critical part of what happens in this stage of the career change process. Psychologists have said for years that the subconscious mind cannot tell the difference between an actual experience and a vividly imagined one. Thus the visual image experience begins working to make the actual experience come true in our lives. Making a clear choice based on the reality of ourselves and the environment is the key to making a successful career change. Our subconscious can now become our ally and not remain mere unpacked baggage we drag about but fail to use.

Visualization begins with mental images—important successful pictures in the mind's eye. This isn't casual daydreaming but active imagination. Such imagined events are recorded by the brain and are not distinguished from actual physical experiences. Our conscious mind and actions plant the particular seeds for our future image. Our unconscious is then the soil that grows them. What we plant in our unconscious thrives there whatever it is, positive or negative. Visualizations without the reality of our carefully discovered success criteria to use as a foundation may well be untrustworthy.

ROLE OF EARLY ASPIRATIONS AND DAYDREAMS

When we can't daydream, fantasize about the future and an ideal situation, then the career change process will be difficult for us. It is important to remember that our daydreams or aspirations are not random; they have great validity and predictability as to our future occupations, according to Dr. Holland. The writer David Henry Thoreau in *Walden* said, "Build castles in the air. That's where they belong. Then get busy and put foundations under them" (1854, p. 287). With many individuals in misfitting careers, we can frequently trace back and find that earlier they started to go into the right career field but were discouraged by family or "reality".

One client, a chief financial officer with a Harvard M.B.A., fired from two major national banks, saw himself as the suave businessman. However, in reality, his skills, needs, and interests fit the loafers and the rumpled tweed jacket of a psychologist or college professor, and that's the career he would have fit. Later, when he became a math teacher in a private school and felt comfortable for the first time in his work life, it was an awakening from his self-imposed distortions of reality.

Individuals who are in a career field that is a mismatch often initially started off in the right career direction but side-tracked themselves. They may have perceived that financial or status rewards would be missing. They could have listened to the conventional wisdom of parents or friends and moved from their original choice, or they may have dropped their first choice from fear of failure. One young woman, an advertising media buyer, became nauseated daily on her way to work. As she said, working with the "artsy, zany" people didn't fit her personality. All her self-assessment pointed to the more technical fields, and she became a successful industrial engineer after completing a master's degree. But she remembered, after we had zeroed in on a radical career change, that she had planned an engineering major early in college. However, since she was only one of a very few women in her classes, with all male instructors, she felt uneasy. Add a fear of math and engineering, experienced by many young women, and it was overwhelming. She dropped out and submerged the entire experience.

Dan, a serious young corporate financial planner, was in a fast-track career that kept him on a hot seat almost hourly, as his corporation made countless rapid changes to survive. Dan said he always felt that he was running in place but was just not as quick with the numbers as his colleagues. He was also in constant emotional pain, feeling that he had to "step over dead bodies" to move ahead in his corporation. Dan was definitely operating from his weakness with his highly specialized financial business training. He had no role models except the super-charged business warrior. With no background in the humanities, it is little wonder he felt so alone.

Through much difficulty and change, and after much research, Dan discovered that what he really wanted to do was become an organizational psychologist. Psychology had in fact been his first college major but he had switched to business finance when his father told him there was no future in the study of psychology. This was also the heyday for financial majors, which has since cooled dramatically. He is now taking the classes to move more into organizational development and eventually psychology. Originally Dan was an uptight perfectionist, constantly guarding against letting others see that he was not a rapid-fire financial wizard. Now that he has accepted himself—that his strengths are understanding people and how to help them perform better in an organization—he has become more relaxed in his financial responsibilities.

During the earlier self-assessment step, you brought out your earliest occupational and personal dreams, saw whether they were still intact. If so, now you must explore a way to set them or a version of them into reality. All may not fall perfectly into place, but you must begin to recognize and perhaps to validate them—to give them space in your life.

ACHIEVING PERSONAL POWER THROUGH FUTURE IMAGE

Achieving personal power, moving from a passive, powerless mentality, regardless of material rewards, requires both conscious and subconscious activities; it also requires a future image, a vision of who we want to be in the future and what we want to do. This is based on our personal truths, our internal reflection combined with a connection and awareness of what is going on around us in the outside world. This image ties together and justifies all the things we do. It's a magnetic field that attracts, and all our lesser goals are tied to this. It defines the challenges we are to face and conquer. It energizes us and leaves us stronger.

This personal vision forms the cornerstone of personal power. This means living our lives creatively and continually clarifying what is important to us—reminding ourselves of the path and learning to see reality more clearly as we move toward our future image.

Whether we call this discovery and knowledge our commitment or vocation, it is our continuing mission and purpose, what we are especially called upon to undertake. To feel successful, to develop our higher character, our career must fit a purpose in life rather than simply function as a means to pay the bills. Discovering and naming the source of our motivation is critical—the meaning in life counteracts the fear of nothingness. It must be tied to more than self-fulfillment, though; it must address the larger issues in society as well as the interior needs of our soul. Marilyn Ferguson writes in her *Brain/Mind Newsletter* that an intentional purpose brings forth "genius and talents." "Vision is a mode of remembering the future, moving toward some target that the culture has not yet articulated but that can be sensed by the sensitive . . . and vision becomes a state of mind, perhaps eventually a state of grace" (1995, p. 6). It alerts us to a particular purpose, an imagined goal that organizes our intelligence and lights our fire. Vision sees beyond the norm and beyond the present, anticipating needs and possibilities. Ferguson writes that vision is radical common sense in action. It goes beyond the common sense ability to see and avoid the hole in the road or to pluck the riper fruit from the branch. Vision is the ability to grasp the larger picture—the world beyond this particular road, this piece of fruit.

The goal of our future image is not to reach an unchanging static objective to be held onto, but to focus on growth, evolution, and change. It is in the process of acting, of acquiring knowledge, that human thinking evolves. The purpose of learning is growing and changing oneself, not the mere acquisition of knowledge. Again, it is the process of actively seeking the Grail, not owning it, that matters to us so greatly.

Ferguson continues to stress the value of vision: "As we discover work to be done, needs to be met, and visions to manifest, we discover a sense of direction. Here is something to work for, a contribution to make, a commitment to keep. Failures are now seen as the raw material, the essential ingredients for our personal art" (1995, p. 6). We can accept the unknown, and let it guide us.

Strategic
Action Plan

15

"Hell is to drift, Heaven is to steer."

—George Bernard Shaw

Setting it all into motion and movement, creating a step-by-step strategic action plan based on our success criteria and future image, is the fourth step in taking creative career control. First we *see* it—and then we *do* it. This step covers the details, strategy, planning, and doing to activate our future image. It could include some or all of the following:

- Learning and building new skills and strengths on our own—on the job or in a classroom.

- Modifying self-defeating behavior: learning to become what we are, not what we think we ought to be.

- Communicating, connecting, and making contacts. If moving into a job in a new career field, it could be developing job leads, executive letters, job proposals, creating résumés and cover letters to take us where we want to go, not just where we have been.

- Researching companies, learning interview techniques, and learning to negotiate.

The result of all this is directed toward gaining the job, work, or skills to move you toward your future image goal of Step III. You may choose one of the following options:

- New job, same field

- Refocus, same field

- Radical career change

- Independence as an entrepreneur, contractor, freelancer

- Other options

Changing careers successfully involves a deeper emotional shift than the single act of moving oneself from one career field to another. It combines the *knowing* from the self-assessment step and the future image vision developed during the future directions and focus step and the *doing* of the career exploration and strategic action plan steps. It is the process of synthesis, the integration of our internal emotional and psychological needs with external visible and tangible results for now and for the future. New insights, new ways of seeing into both ourselves and our environment are necessary for making this successful career change. However, while these new insights and perceptions are essential for getting to our own unique DNA pattern, they will be barren if not coupled with deliberate intention, action, and application. Awareness and insight without action can cause depression and paralysis. Knowing, seeing, and doing are tightly joined in making a successful career change. This is your strategic action plan.

Wanting to be committed, or understanding the importance of commitment in itself, is not enough. We must develop and initiate our plan and keep working on it. After we know what has meaning for us and what feeds our soul, we are almost compelled to act on it—no more excuses, alibis, or other self-defeating behavior.

At this point in the career change process, the road to failure is paved with ideas and commitments *not* acted upon. All the self-knowledge, listening, thinking, researching, connecting, visualizing, and even talent and potential, will get you nowhere without planned action to achieve the goal. Here's where you bring together your dreaming and doing.

You can be successful in your work if you persistently create these conditions: a clear goal; a match between the job and your skills; frequent feedback to measure progress; directed focus; and control over actions. If you approach even the most mundane things as goals, your sense of purpose increases, you see more clearly, your inner intelligence begins operating more powerfully. Social scientists have found that people who have suffered calamitous illness or accident often have more confidence and joy in their lives after than before because their goals and challenges are now clear, focused, and important to them.

So the critical questions to be answered in this fourth step of a career change are, What is my plan? How do I get to where I want to be? What actions do I begin to take *now*? How do I make this meaning, this future image real for me? How do I accomplish this commitment? I know my direction, my destination, so how do I begin the journey? What are the key stops along the way?

With the vision of a future image as a guide, you begin to see and understand where you want to go and grow, and you begin the fourth major step in the career change process. This is to translate your future image into a concrete, immediate, and long-term strategic action plan with steps and goals that you can achieve through your own efforts and with the help of others. The important point is that you, with support and information, are setting these action goals yourself from your own internal and external needs and realities and you bring the motivation to act on them. Owning the decision is a critical step toward achieving your goals.

John Gardner says, "We are just beginning to understand that free men must set their own difficult goals and be their own task masters. There is no one to tell them what to do; they must do it themselves" (1963, p. 160). On one level, this realization can be frightening. I call it the "no one is coming to rescue us" scenario. Taking refuge in the Cinderella complex is not an option here if we are motivated to succeed in our life mission. By this time in the process, people in career change are beginning to realize their own personal power, to fully understand, to know that they can make it happen.

A future image that has this much appeal for us demands our careful and thoughtful attention and the concentrated effort that will lead to this targeted action. This is the time to put together the plan and strategy to move toward the goal, which may not be so very difficult when we have a focused picture of what is involved in moving toward our image. This strategic action plan step is actively tied to the exploration step.

Our strategic action plan follows our strong sense of vision and purpose. Without such a working plan, success can only occur by luck, random behavior, sheer inspiration, or accident. While these events are always welcome, and do happen occasionally, they are not the major tools of the directed person with a mission or commitment; rather they are the approach of a novice.

Those in career change are involved deeply in designing their plan and writing specific activities based on their goals and research. The career change process teaches us that we can learn to act with purpose and succeed. Achieving our goals can become a habit; we can plan it and expect it. We factor in setbacks and failures along the way, because they are simply part of the process. We get closer to what we expect if we are attentive, focused, and willing to experiment and keep moving throughout the change process. Our vision, our future image, provides the real motive for the successful design and consistent implementation of a strategic action plan.

Whatever the plan to achieve the long-term goal, the actions you take to arrive should be mostly enjoyable. For example, if extensive computer training is a major need for meeting your ultimate career goal, then it should be an enjoyable learning process for you, although not necessarily easy. If your future image seems clear, but there is great distaste and dread in experiencing the necessary steps to get it going, then there could be a problem with the future image itself; it may not be a true picture for you. Not all learning is fun and games, but the process should not only move you toward a worthy goal but also provide pleasure along the way. If you determine that your future is as a communications specialist, then you should, for the most part, enjoy the course work, the learning activities, and the experiences that you need to get there. Learn what you love. Be sure that what you dislike is not a major part of the career you plan to enter.

In taking this strategic action step, you will stay on a sharp learning curve both internally and externally. This can be a very exciting time. Action steps can include self-directed learning, attending meetings of professional organizations and conventions to interact with others already working in a targeted field, reading professional journals and newsletters, returning to structured learning situations for credit and to gain specialized certification, or attending local informal continuing education courses. You may need to learn the jargon and specific or technical skills such as finance, accounting, marketing, technical writing, interactive multimedia, and public relations to be successful.

The learning curve of a strategic action plan could also include internal work to understand and replace self-defeating behavior, e.g., nonassertion, perfectionism, procrastination, anxiety, fear of failure, or success, etc. You may need to build new self-management skills: self-esteem, assertion, decision making, communication, negotiation, time and stress management. If you see that this learning curve is an important part of your long-range plan, you will be motivated to move beyond your comfort zone.

However, it frequently is not the amount of action we take but the consistency of action and purpose that gets us where we finally want to be. All of us would like to make a grand leap and arrive quickly, but the skills of consistency, patience, involvement, good decision making, and purposeful action take time to hone. As you move toward your goal, watch for new opportunities but at the same time remain cautious so that, like Ulysses, you don't get sidetracked and heed the sirens singing sweetly from another shore.

Eventually, there is a sense of timelessness in achieving your future image. In other words, as you move toward the goal almost unaware, you know that your "I" is consistent with your purpose and that you will achieve it, if not today or next week, perhaps next month or next year. This goal is a major "glass ball," not to be dropped, and you honor it by moving consistently and creatively when faced with adversity or setbacks, rather than beating yourself up. This special sense of knowing that you are arriving is a high that can't be duplicated.

Another important and paradoxical point is that you do not go about taking the action steps to achieve your future image by yourself: You must be independent and take the responsibility for your own career, yet to succeed you must also connect with others. Count on yourself, but ask for help as needed from others. A key factor in building self-esteem is to be able to ask for help and know that you can gain it. So ask yourself who can help you in achieving your strategic action plan, and then ask those people for what you need; don't expect help from others unless you ask for it.

When you achieve your goals, stop and acknowledge your success. This is critical, since many people have a tendency to gloss over their achievements and never give themselves positive strokes for what they accomplish. Say to yourself, I accomplished this! I had the courage to ask and they helped me. You must take the time to feel and internalize your success and to celebrate your achievement. If you fail to do so, your achievement will not build your self-esteem. Don't think, Oh well, I had help so what I did doesn't really count, or, If so and so hadn't accidentally happened, I wouldn't have done it. I was just lucky. No big deal!

Instead, you need to say, Hey, I set this train in motion and made some important things happen. I asked for help and look what I accomplished with it. This recognition creates a sense of achievement and gives you the self-esteem necessary for you to take another step. This needed recognition is psychological success and self-esteem building in action.

In summary, the four-step career change process is as follows:

1. Step I: *Self-Assessment.* Know your unique success criteria and target three potentially matching career options.

2. Step II: *Career Exploration.* Research and explore the realities of your targeted career options.

3. Step III: *Future Directions and Focus.* Picture yourself there—see your future image in your mind's eye and decide on long-term focus and meaning.

4. Step IV: *Strategic Action Plan.* Take action: Develop specific strategic plans, take steps to achieve your future image.

Before we leave this section on the strategic action plan step, I want to mention a psychological impasse many clients experience: the "Valley of Despair."

Sometimes, after making a strong and vital career decision and when they are just beginning to move forward, some clients hit the bottom emotionally for a last brief time due to negative habits and fears not easily released. I caution clients that this can happen after they see the future image and then realize the challenging action steps necessary for them to arrive there. They have been on a high, seeing themselves succeeding in what really matters to them. From this honeymoon stage they suddenly perceive the volume of what they must do, the research and learning, how far they must go. They may become trapped in the Valley of Despair: This is the reality and I have made a mistake! I can't work through it all.

I explain that this seemingly deep hole is not in fact the reality of their choice. Momentarily, self-defeating behavior is trying to get one last grip on us. In addition, at this time, we have as yet experienced no tangible rewards. This is not the way the career itself will ultimately be. We are at the bottom of the learning curve.

The actual reality of where you're going may not be as high as the honeymoon stage felt at the beginning, but it is certainly not the valley you feel now; it is 80 percent up from where you are now. This merely means that you have selected a challenging but worthy goal and now you must begin all the career action steps to make it succeed. Never confuse this stage with your eventual reality. Our future image is not a state of perfection, but it is a stage of a more mature process. Accepting the reality as less than the honeymoon is not selling your future image out as being second rate but is an accepting of yourself.

Initially, you want to climb out of the Valley of Despair and jump up to the honeymoon stage again. But you cannot. You must maintain consistency of your "I" and your action toward your future image.

At this point, we introduce a Type CC Chaos Chaser thriver technique—creative rate of recovery. This means that when you hit a troubled state and know you're headed for the valley, you immediately activate your safety valve—what you know is healthy and will slow the downward slide and help you move back to your normal level.

It is imperative that you know what your safely valve is, what relieves stress and pressure without adding more problems. Sometimes, this is physical exercise, good music, playing with your children or grandchildren, meeting a friend for a movie, reading a book, volunteering, working in the greenhouse, taking pictures, things that you know feed your soul and provide you with internal strength to recover and move on creatively with your life and work.

Approach the problem like cutting up a huge roll of salami—one thin slice at a time. Before you know it, you're up there again, in charge.

You now know your future image and you realize all you must do to gain that image. Mission gives you the motivation to work on all these things.

Keep that future image, but take action steps according to a time line that works for you. You don't have to do things according to a specific schedule. If it's right, it will get done.

Develop a sense of order and time. Outline your steps and keep moving toward your goal. Establish deadlines but allow yourself to be flexible. Deadlines can be changed. A sense of timing is important.

Peak Psychological Points for Change

16

"There is nothing enlightening about shrinking so that other people won't feel unsure around you. . . . As we let our own Light shine, we unconsciously give other people permission to do the same. As we are liberated from our own fear, our presence automatically liberates others."

—Nelson Mandela

As we go through the four-step process of a successful career change, we also begin to develop new skills, both personal and career skills, for working and living more creatively now and in the future.

Knowing your safety valve to help deal with difficult situations is important for maintaining resilience. When problems and difficulties hit, Type CCs first activate their safety valve, their individual positive resource that revives and restores them. Second, they pull out their success criteria list. Third, they identify their large and small "glass balls," those things that are absolutely first priority since they shatter and can't be mended. The "rubber balls" can be dropped until later, or maybe even forever. Fourth, they connect with another who has empathy and who understands their pain. Asking for help from those who can provide it when needed shows strength, not weakness, and makes people strong enough to give back to others.

Making a successful career change is a continuing process, not a one-time event with a clearly defined beginning and ending. It is highly creative, integrating common sense, aspirations, and our individualized success criteria with current and emerging opportunities and needs in our external environment.

Clients changing careers successfully go far beyond the simple "how to" steps and get involved on a deeper level, going past surface data and obvious information about themselves from testing and researching obvious career opportunities. Ferguson (1980) used this analogy in a Dallas workshop: The difference between transformation by accident and transformation by a planned system is like the difference between lightning and a lamp. Both give illumination, but one can be unavailable, unreliable, even dangerous. The other is relatively safe, directed, and available. Deliberately planning and completing the process of a career change gives us continuing access to our own personal power. We also realize that personal power is not "power over" but "power for."

Surface realignment is easy—a few simple adjustments and little fear of real change—but ultimately risky. However, unless this process creates an "aha" moment, a perceived shift, there is no insight and thus no lasting internal wisdom or real growth.

This final chapter illustrates these power points in two ways: First is an unedited description of a career change written by one of my clients. Her story demonstrates that freedom is knowing your options, and that being in charge of your career is a continuing learning, growing process. Second is a list summarizing the peak psychological points and insights that I experienced—and are common to many of my clients—moving from pain to personal power. These are the "aha's" of insight discovered as we custom design our careers for taking creative control in a chaotic age. I recommend that you keep a list of yours as you move through the steps of taking creative control of your career.

SARAH'S STORY

How many times had I driven to Helen's home and eagerly listened to yet another "career change" success story? Without exception, the scenario was always the same. A diverse group of men and women would congregate around the huge table. At one end was the video camera perched upon the tripod. The completed videotape would not provide a slick, professional rendition of the session, but it would record for posterity the words of wisdom generously offered by the speaker. The speakers were always poised, self-assured individuals who portrayed an aura of success and affluence. They had followed Helen's guidance and as a result had attained professional success.

I was no different from the other bewildered souls trying to find a niche in the workplace. Yes, I could always find employment, but that was no longer the issue. I had already progressed past the erroneous belief that I was only suited for the job that I was currently doing and would therefore never find another position. I had come to realize that my skills were transferable; regardless of which path I ultimately chose, my skills would go with me, they were a part of who I was. Now, my expectations had expanded. Not only did I want to make a career change, I also wanted more money, recognition, and fulfillment in my work. I was eager to learn how others had achieved their goal.

One burning question always surfaced at these presentations. I asked it once, then quickly learned that, if I didn't pose the question, someone else would. Invariably, the speaker would be confronted with, "How long did it take you to reach your objective?" The responses usually seemed vague and not applicable to our individual situations. I never had a clear vision of how long it would take me to grasp the golden ring of success.

Finally my day had arrived. Tomorrow would be my turn to be in the spotlight. As the guest speaker, I would share knowledge regarding my new career, computer-based training. I would describe how I had created my plan, divulging any secrets that would facilitate the course for others. To ease any anxieties about speaking before an audience, advance preparation seemed like a reasonable strategy.

I retraced my association with Helen, recalling the overwhelming depression that had prompted enlisting the aid of a career counselor. I had been employed by a nonprofit arts organization for eight years. While I enjoyed my work, ongoing sexual harassment and office politics had taken a toll. I exhibited stress-related physical symptoms, and any remnants of self-confidence I might have manifested were merely the portrayal of a faint memory. The work environment became intolerable. I realized that before long I would either be fired, or I would succumb to a life-threatening illness. From my perspective, I had reached a dead end and could see no way out. In truth, I was blind to the many alternatives that are always available to all of us.

After taking numerous tests to evaluate my interests, aptitudes, skills, and personality traits, I opted to pursue an MBA in international management. Initially, the choice seemed clear-cut. I liked to travel, spoke several languages, had experienced different cultures, and was more than eager to earn an excellent salary.

I barely made the grades on the GMAT entrance examination, but once admitted, I did quite well. There was only one problem: I detested all the courses. After one year, Helen asked, "What is the pay-off?" I could not answer. There was no pay-off. The world of business and high finance held no appeal whatsoever. I remember Helen's exact words: "Sarah, sometimes there is wisdom in knowing when to quit." As always, she was right. International management was not my path.

I discovered that I truly wished to enhance my education by obtaining a master's degree. Given my interest in health care, I enrolled in a two-year graduate program at the local medical school. I thoroughly enjoyed the experience. My M.A. degree is in biomedical communications with emphasis in instructional design. Amazingly, many of the skills from my previous occupation transferred to the new discipline.

Graduation was followed by the ruthless task of job hunting. While I had special interest in medicine, I had always known that I did not possess the credentials to easily be accepted in that field. I decided to keep my options opens.

The job search led to a position with a consulting firm. I utilized my newly acquired instructional design endorsement to specialize in multimedia computer-based training. There was much that appealed to me: writing, autonomy, creativity, variety of subject matter, a casual dress code, and a good salary.

After having mentally reviewed my work history, I concluded there was little need for preparation after all. As I delivered my presentation, I was thoroughly relaxed and truly enjoyed sharing my knowledge and experiences. Predictably, I was addressed with the dreaded question, "How long did it take you to arrive where you are now?" I answered with the truth.

Our career or vocational path begins when we are born and ends only upon death. Preparation for a career starts very early in life, when we first discover what we like to do and what it is that we do well. As we add layers of knowledge and experience, our work grows with us. Career development is part of life's journey and not an end in itself. Helen often describes career growth as a process rather than a goal. Like the facets of a gemstone, what we do is a reflection of who we are.

A little over a year has passed since my guest appearance at Helen's home. I shared openly, and in so doing, hopefully helped others in their search for self-understanding.

As I sit before the computer writing my personal account, it is once again the eve of a career change. In a couple of days, I will begin summer school. After taking the required courses for teacher certification, I will be assigned a classroom where I intend to undertake the challenge of being a bilingual elementary teacher. I was very happy with my previous work, but as I grew and expanded, my requirements changed. Money is less important now. Instead, I am driven by the need to make the world a better place. I want to experience greater fulfillment in my life's work. I also desire more free time for personal growth and travel.

Had I chosen to pursue teaching earlier in life, would I have made a wiser choice? I think not. As a result of my experiences and previous career selections, I will bring to teaching a richness and an understanding that I did not previously possess.

Ironically, after having made the commitment to teach and receive substantially reduced earnings, I was informed of the potential for receiving an excellent salary as an education administrator. By selecting this new path, once again I have opened a multitude of possibilities.

I am no longer afraid of changing jobs or careers. Helen has taught me that the impermanence of our occupations is a part of our evolution as a culture and as human beings. Life itself is change. Career divergences are merely stepping-stones in the journey.

PEAK POWER POINTS FOR CHANGE

From the successful completion of the career change process, we learn to take creative career control and live a life for embracing change. You will encounter many peak psychological points as you move from your pain to personal power. These are points that I have learned:

- Career change is highly achievable and rewarding, but perhaps painful: $CC = P > F$.

- The Type CC Chaos Chaser is the new personality for the future that understands well that commitment, meaning, and connection with a community all provide food for the soul, an essential ingredient for a successful career.

- Freedom is knowing your options. If you believe that you have none, you are a slave. You can choose not to take the options, but you should know you have them.

- Your success criteria, your unique DNA fingerprint, your bedrock— this is your own definition of success.

- The reality you are using must be yours, not someone else's. What's real and what's false for you?

- Conventional wisdom shortcuts your instincts.

- Become an entrepreneur with your career. Have a vision and a plan of action for taking creative control of your work life.

- Consciously become like Proteus, the god with the gift of foresight and prophecy and the power to change.

- Become a pattern-maker, a paradigm shifter, an educated risktaker, a Type CC Chaos Chaser.

- Move out of closed boxes and go beyond your former boundaries.

- If you specify the real source of your career unrest, you will solve the right problems successfully.

- Changing careers is an art and a science—a creative, somewhat structured but continuing process, not a single, linear, short-term, one-time event.

- Internal and external needs such as meaning and money require balance and integration.

- Creative, intuitive, and logical analytic problem solving is used to change careers.

- Identify the consistent "I" in your past, present, and future and integrate it with a need in the work world.

- What you do naturally and instinctively well can be researched and you can discover where you can do what you're good at and get paid for it.

- A career is based on your highest strengths—shoring up weaknesses will not guarantee success.

- Self-defeating behavior can be controlled.

- Outdated myths, self-defeating behavior, and false assumptions severely limit career success, and these tend to surface under pressure. Change what you can, but don't focus all your attention on these negatives.

- Career and personal lifestyles form a seamless coat and can't be completely separated without an ill fit.

- Change is a growth and transition process—a moving across. The old dies, we accept and release it and move toward the new, with a "dark night" of chaos bridging the two.

- The change process is similar to the death and loss grief process.

- Openness, ideas, people, and our own unconscious resources can sometimes be threatening.

- Our age is the chaotic, transitional bridge between the old, valuing muscle and money, and the new, valuing mind and information.

- Significant inner change is change to what you are, not what you think you "ought" to be.

- You can learn to adapt and thrive creatively on change. Get comfortable traveling with an incomplete map.

- There's a time to turn loose, cut your losses, and walk away (maybe even run).

- Our weaknesses are an overextension of our strengths—too much of a good thing.

- You can have it all, but not all at one time. Learn to say no without guilt.

- You can creatively rethink your boundaries: Replace "either/or" with "both/and."

- A career contingency plan, a back-up plan in case the present career disappears is important.

- Leaving behind formerly valued familiarities, "things," or even people is painful but frequently freeing.

- The "golden handcuffs" and the "success image" are the invisible chains holding you back from real growth.

- Self-esteem is developed by valuing, accepting, being kind, encouraging, and being nonjudgmental about yourself.

- Wisdom is knowing when to turn loose of perfectionism.

- You can learn to feel free and open. When in doubt, be authentic, honest, genuine.

- If you know what you want, ask for it, act to gain it, and know you deserve it, you have high self-esteem.

- The search for purpose, meaning, passion, commitment, personal power in your work is ongoing.

- Your foresight and vision, if developed and trusted, will detect and synthesize patterns in your environment.

- Certain forces—such as your own self-defeating behavior and the changing forces in your environment—have potential to create problems.

- A calculated, educated risktaker uses failures as stepping stones.

- Create an inquiring mind: Ask questions and be curious about yourself, others, and your current and coming environment.

- The power of positive uncertainty allows extra room for new ideas.

- Be mindful, not mindless.

- Seek, recognize, value, accept, and cultivate your options.

- Reinvent and redefine yourself; design a new model, a new order—a different pattern.

- To understand major change, see both the forest and the trees.
- Freedom can seem foreign and frightening.
- It requires courage, freedom, and self-insight to recreate yourself.
- Transcendence is the power to be born anew, to make a fresh start, a conversion.
- Set priorities—identify "glass balls" that can't be dropped and "rubber balls" that can be picked up later.
- You can step out of your comfort zone and get comfortable embracing ambiguity and positive uncertainty.
- Follow the path of least resistance in building a new self-concept. Know and trust what is natural and instinctive.
- Develop and maintain the ability to wish, dream, plan, act, change, grow, learn, and be happy.
- Hold fast to dreams and know your future image, your desired destiny, and see yourself fulfilling it.
- Rediscover your heroes/heroines.
- One with great strength will also have great weaknesses.
- Connection and community thrives through relationships.
- Identifying and using your safety valve shortens the rate of recovery between "down" times.
- Consistency of behavior means focusing on one small step at a time over time.
- Know what potential employers need and are searching for.
- The majority is always wrong: Growth happens on the edge.
- Courage and freedom are required to create ourselves.
- It helps to hang on to something comfortable: Don't throw away everything.
- If you can't change a situation, change your response!
- A learning curve is a lifetime endeavor: Learn, unlearn, relearn: Learn how to learn.
- What you don't know can hurt you.
- Ultimately, you are your greatest source of wisdom.
- Needs change, but adults do not change easily: It hurts!
- For a successful career choice, activate your third eye and third ear, ask questions for feedback and information. You would not drive

your car blindfolded even if the street is straight and the car turned in the right direction.

- Identifying and solving your career unrest can be a course in creativity development.

- You have multiple options: the challenge is in discovering them.

- Long tenure in an organization can be detrimental, as you become less independent and concerned about growth.

- If you don't make mistakes, you don't make anything.

- Your racial and family heritage provide clues about you.

- Family, friends, co-workers, neighbors, and authorities who put you down will stop you from moving beyond them.

- Contrary to conventional wisdom, the past may not be a reliable indicator of the future.

- "If only's" are the saddest words in our language!

- It is important to be aware of: 1) what you are doing when you feel so good that you forget time and place; and 2) your "pull phenomenon," the instinctive drawing toward something.

- Fear of failure builds avoidance, not success! Failure can be the first step to growth.

- Don't mistake data for information, information for knowledge, or knowledge for wisdom.

- Be a visionary of means rather than a mere dreamer of ends.

- Security today is in brainware, so it is worthwhile to advance your skills, not just your college degrees.

- Your courses should excite you but be part of an overall plan.

- Little attention or recognition is focused on the human side of change.

- We live in times of change, uncertainty, insecurity, ambiguity, and contradictions but have been taught to value status, stability, and above all, security.

- Cherished past rules are being broken, so we are impelled to rewrite our own.

- Ironically the world engages in developing complex technology when many of us can't even program the VCR.

- Timing is critical—if you change too early, you feel like a loner; if you change too late, you play catch up constantly.

- The edge of your rut is not your horizon. The distance between your rut and your grave is about one foot.

- The opposite of work may not be free time but disorder and chaos; work provides form, order, control, and structure.

- Our sense of dignity and self-worth depends on being recognized by others through our work. We need to work. It helps us practice commitment.

- Whether work is inherently noble or ignoble is not the issue. The simple fact is that most of us work, and work has economic, psychological, and social functions.

- Work is the primary way that most adults identify themselves, regardless of sex, age, or occupation, and it is a central organizing principle of our lives.

SUMMARY FOR UNDERSTANDING CHAOS OF CHANGE

Know this to live successfully in the age of change:

- Change will accelerate: It can create depression and stress.

- We have less to give to others when we are changing.

- Change is frightening if we feel it isn't in our control.

- Crisis is opportunity blowing on a dangerous wind.

- Change is the only guarantee in life: Major failure today is failure to change.

- An unpredictable event or sudden insight can trigger massive change.

- A transcendental conversion or change can seem agonizingly slow.

- To develop new patterns, deliberately think about old situations in multiple new ways.

- Change can occur internally or externally. Outward change happens to us; inner change is self-directed.

- Change does not occur in a straight line nor on a time-line.

- We impede change by denying that it is happening.

- Planning for change provides a measure of security and some sense of control, but it's difficult to plan for the emotions that accompany change.

- Changing careers is no easy victory but can be well worth the cost of the battle.

- Overcoming our fear and resistance to change is the first step to positive change.

- We live in an age of chaos, constant change, and contradiction but are taught to value stability, order, and certainty, realities from another age.

- We know the old rules don't work, but we don't know the new ones.

- We need new personal and professional skills for our changing age but only dimly see what these are.

- The change process has predictable stages.

- Learning to embrace change, to thrive creatively during chaos, will move us from paralysis and pain to our personal power.

- In summary, career change is a process of answering these four questions:

  1. What does the world need now and in the future?

  2. Could I meet that need? Do I have the skills?

  3. Would I value doing this? Would it provide meaning for me?

  4. Can I make a living at it? Can I support my needs doing this?

References

American Association of University Professors. 1995. "The Status of Non-Tenured-Track Faculty," data from 1988 U.S. Department of Education, National Center for Education Statistics: National Survey of Post-Secondary Faculty. Washington, D.C.

American Women's Economic Development Conference. 1993. *Harvard Review* (Sept/Oct).

Assagioli, Roberto. 1965. *Psychosynthesis.* New York: Viking Compass.

Associated Press. 1995. "Emotional Support May Lower Blood Pressure." *The Dallas Morning News* (November 26).

Barger, Nancy J., and Linda K. Kirby. 1995. *The Challenge of Change in Organizations: Helping Employees Thrive in the New Frontier.* Palo Alto, CA: Davies-Black Publishing.

Barron, Frank. 1963. "Personal Soundness in University Graduate Students." In *Creativity and Psychological Health.* D. Van Nostrand Company.

Beil, Laura. 1995. "Think Your Job is Killing You? Take Heart—You May Be Right." *The Dallas Morning News* (January 23).

Beil, Laura. 1995. "Heart Failure Statistics Give Reason for Optimism, Caution." *The Dallas Morning News* (November 16).

Bly, Robert. 1988. *A Little Book on the Human Shadow,* ed. by W. Booth. San Francisco: Harper & Row.

Borysenko, Joan. 1993. *Fire in the Soul: A New Psychology of Spiritual Optimism.* New York: Warner Books, Inc.

Braus, Patricia. 1992. "What Workers Want." *American Demographics* (Vol. 14, No. 8, August).

Brown, Jonathan, and Shelly Taylor. 1994. "Positive Relations and Wellness." *The Psychological Bulletin,* Volume 116 (Winter).

Burns, David. 1980. *Feeling Good.* New York: NAL Dutton.

Cambell, Joseph, with Bill Moyers. 1988. *The Power of Myth.* New York: Doubleday.

Camus, Albert. 1959. *Myth of Sisyphus and Other Essays.* New York: Random House.

Capra, Fritjof. 1982. *The Turning Point.* Toronto: Bantam Books.

Cetron, Marvin. 1994. "An American Renaissance in the Year 2000." *The Futurist* (March-April).

Csikszentmihalyi, Mihaly. 1990. *Flow: The Psychology of Optimal Experience.* New York: Harper & Row.

Csikszentmihalyi, Mihaly. 1993. *The Evolving Self: A Psychology for the Third Millennium.* New York: HarperCollins Publishers.

Durning, Alan T. 1993. "Are We Happy Yet?" *The Futurist* (January-February).

Eliot, T. S. 1954. *The Confidential Clerk.* London: Faber & Faber, Ltd.

Ferguson, Marilyn. 1980. *The Aquarian Conspiracy: Personal and Social Transformation in the 1980s.* Los Angeles: J. P. Tarcher, Inc.

Ferguson, Marilyn. 1994. "Prigogine Solves Time Paradox: A Very Brief History of Certainty." *Brain/Mind Newsletter* (Vol. 19 No. 8, May).

Ferguson, Marilyn. 1995. Commentary: "Vision: Still a Scarce Commodity." *Brain/Mind Newsletter* (August).

Flach, Frederic F. 1974. *The Secret Strength of Depression.* Philadelphia: J. B. Lippincott Company.

Flach, Frederic F. 1977. *Choices: Coping Creatively with Personal Change.* Philadelphia: J. B. Lippincott Company.

Flach, Frederick F. 1988. *Resilience: Discovering a New Strength At Times of Stress.* New York: Fawcett Columbine.

Frankl, Viktor E. 1992. *Man's Search for Meaning: An Introduction to Logotherapy.* Boston: Beacon Press.

Freedman, A. M. and H. I. Kaplan, eds. 1975. *Psychiatry and Dentistry: Comprehensive Textbook of Psychiatry II, Volume 2.* Baltimore: Williams and Milkins Co.

Freeman, Arthur, and Marge Lurie. 1994. *Depression: A Cognitive Therapy Approach.* (Viewers Guide with Video) New York: Newbridge Professional Programs.

Gardner, John W. 1963. *Self-Renewal: The Individual and Innovative Society.* New York: Harper & Row.

Gardner, John W. 1984. *Personal and Organizational Renewal.* Austin, Texas: University of Texas, Hogg Foundation for Mental Health.

Gardner, John. 1990. "Leadership in the Future." *The Futurist* (May-June).

Greiner, Mary. 1996. "What About Me?" *Texas Bar Journal* (September).

Goldberg, Philip. 1983. *The Intuitive Edge: Understanding Intuition and Applying It in Everyday Life.* Los Angeles: Jeremy P. Tarcher, Inc.

Hall, Elizabeth. 1982. "A Conversation with Peter F. Drucker." *Psychology Today* (December).

Halper, Jan. 1988. *Quiet Desperation: The Truth About Successful Men.* New York: Warner Books.

Handy, Charles. 1989. *Age of Unreason.* Boston: Harvard Business School Press.

Harkness, Helen Leslie. 1988. "Discovering Career Options: Introduction to the Self-Directed Search™," Dallas: Videotape, Career Design Associates, Inc.

Hayflick, Leonard. 1994. *How and Why We Age.* New York: Ballantine Books.

Healey, Jane M. 1992. *Is Your Bed Still There When You Close the Door? . . . And Other Playful Ponderings.* New York: Doubleday.

Hendlin, Steven J. 1992. *When Good Enough Is Never Good Enough: Escaping the Perfectionist Trap.* New York: A Jeremy P. Tarcher/Putnam, G.P. Putnam, New York.

Hesselbein, Frances, Marshall Goldsmith, and Richard Beckhard, eds. 1996. *Leader of the Future.* Foreward by Peter Drucker. San Francisco: Jossey-Bass.

Hill, Napoleon. 1987. *Think & Grow Rich.* New York: Fawcett Book Group.

Hillman, James, and Michael Ventura. 1991. *We've Had a Hundred Years of Psychotherapy and the World's Getting Worse.* San Francisco: Harper & Row.

Hillman, James. 1996. *The Soul's Code.* New York: Random House, Inc.

Holland, John L. 1973. *Making Vocational Choices: A Theory of Careers.* Englewood Cliffs, New Jersey: Prentice-Hall, Inc.

House, J. S. 1972. "The Relationship of Intrinsic and Extrinsic Work Motivations to Occupational Stress and Coronary Heart Disease Risk." University of Michigan: Unpublished Ph.D. Thesis.

Howe, Neil, and Bill Strauss. 1993. *13th Generation.* New York: Vintage Books.

Huey, John. 1993. "Managing in the Midst of Chaos." *Fortune* (April 5).

Isachsen, Olaf. 1996. *Joining the Entrepreneurial Elite: Four Styles to Business Success.* Palo Alto, CA: Davies-Black Publishing.

Jaffe, Dennis T., Cynthia D. Scott, and Glenn R. Tobe. 1994. *Rekindling Commitment.* San Francisco: Jossey-Bass.

Jahoda, Marie. 1958. *Current Concepts of Mental Health.* New York: Basic Books, Inc.

Jung, Carl G. 1957. *The Undiscovered Self.* New York: Little, Brown and Company.

Jung, Carl. G. 1963. *Memories, Dreams, Reflections,* recorded by Aniela Jaffe, translated by R. Winston and C. Winston. New York: Pantheon.

Jung, Carl G. 1976. *The Portable Jung,* ed. J. Campbell. New York: Penguin Books.

Jung, Carl. G. 1994. *Modern Man in Search of a Soul.* New York: A Harvest Book, Harcourt Brace & Company.

Kanter, Donald and Philip H. Mirvis. 1989. *Cynical Americans: Living and Working in An Age of Discontent and Disillusion.* San Francisco: Jossey-Bass.

Kanter, Rosabeth Moss. 1991. "Transcending Business Boundaries: 12,000 World Managers View Change." *Harvard Business Review* (69:3, May-June).

Kanter, Rosabeth Moss. 1994. "Collaborative Advantage: The Art of Alliances." *Harvard Business Review* (July/Aug).

Karpinski, Gloria D. 1990. *Where Two Worlds Touch: Spiritual Rites of Passage.* New York: Ballantine Books.

Korman, Abraham K. 1980. *Career Success/Personal Failure.* Englewood Cliffs, New Jersey: Prentice-Hall, Inc.

Kornhauser, Arthur. 1965. *Mental Health of the Industrial Worker.* New York: Wiley.

Kuhn, Thomas. 1970. *The Structure of Scientific Revolutions.* Chicago: University of Chicago Press.

Kunde, Diana. 1993. "Workers Stressed Out." *Dallas Morning News* (September 3).

Lehman, Harvey C. 1953. *Age and Achievement.* Princeton, NJ: Princeton University Press for the American Philosophical Society, (Ann Arbor, MI: University Microfilms).

Levinson, Harry. 1969. "Emotional Toxicity of the Work Environment." *Archives of Environmental Health* (Vol. 19, August).

Marmot, Michael, and Paul Elliott, eds. 1992. *Coronary Heart Disease Epidemiology: From Aetiology to Public Health.* Oxford: Oxford University Press.

Masterson, James F. 1988. *Search for the Real Self: Unmasking the Personality Disorders of Our Age.* New York: The Free Press.

May, Rollo. 1953. *Man's Search for Himself.* New York: W. W. Norton & Company, Inc.

May, Rollo. 1975. *Courage to Create.* New York: Bantam Books.

May, Rollo. 1977. *The Meaning of Anxiety.* New York: W.W. Norton & Company, Inc.

May, Rollo. 1991. *The Cry for Myth.* New York: W.W. Norton & Company, Inc.

Miller, Eric. 1994. "The Context of Trends: The Reshaping of America." *Research Alert Newsletter.*

Mills, Roger C. 1995. *Realizing Mental Health: Toward a New Psychology of Resiliency.* New York: Sulzburger & Graham Publishing, Ltd.

Mircea, Eliade. 1958. *Rites and Symbols of Initiation: The Mysteries of Birth and Rebirth.* New York: Harper Torchbooks.

Moore, Thomas. 1992. *Care of the Soul: A Guide for Cultivating Depth and Sacredness in Everyday Life.* New York: HarperCollins Publishers, Inc.

Mother Teresa. 1983. *Words to Love By.* Notre Dame, Indiana: Ave Maria Press.

Mother Teresa, compiled by Lucinda Vardey. 1995. *A Simple Path.* New York: Ballantine Books.

Myers, David. 1993. *The Pursuit of Happiness.* New York: Avon.

Nasbitt, John. *John Naisbitt's Trend Letter.* 1992. "Increasing Job Stress Costs Businesses Millions." (May).

Nasbitt, John. *John Naisbitt's Trend Letter.* 1992. "Employers Smell the Smoke, Extinguish Burnout." (November).

Nasbitt, John. *John Naisbitt's Trend Letter.* 1993. "Visionary Companies Reset Sights on New Age Tool." (January).

Nasbitt, John. *John Naisbitt's Trend Letter.* 1993. "Franchising Abroad." (July).

Nasbitt, John. *John Naisbitt's Trend Letter.* 1994. "Downsizing." (March).

Nasbitt, John. *John Naisbitt's Trend Letter.* 1994. "Collaborative Spirit Fosters Unlikely Alliance." (July).

Nasbitt, John. *John Naisbitt's Trend Letter.* 1994. "From Immediacy to Foresight." (October).

Nasbitt, John. *John Naisbitt's Trend Letter.* 1994. "Entrepreneurism." (November).

Naisbitt, John, and Patricia Aburdene. 1985. *Re-Inventing the Corporation.* New York: Warner Books, Inc.

Novak, Michael. 1970. *The Experience of Nothingness.* New York: Harper Colophon Books.

Oliver, Robert. 1981. *Career Unrest: A Source of Creativity.* New York: Columbia Graduate School of Business, Center for Research in Career Development.

O'Toole, James. 1973. *Work in America: Report of a Special Task Force to the Secretary of Health, Education and Welfare.* Cambridge, Massachusetts: MIT Press.

O'Toole, James. 1977. *Work, Learning and the American Future.* San Francisco: Jossey-Bass.

O'Toole, James. 1995. *Leading Change: Overcoming the Ideology of Comfort and the Tyranny of Custom.* San Francisco: Jossey-Bass.

O'Toole, James, Jane L. Scheiber and Linda C. Wood, eds. 1981. *Working, Changes and Choices.* New York: Human Science Press. *Gerontology* (Winter).

Palmore, Erdman. 1969. "Predicting Longevity: A Follow Up Controlling For Age."

Perkins, Donald S. 1987. "What Can CEO's Do for Displaced Workers?" *Harvard Business Review* (Nov./Dec.).

Peters, Thomas J. 1982. *In Search of Excellence.* New York: Harper & Row.

Peters, Tom. 1987. *Thriving on Chaos: Handbook for a Management Revolution.* New York: Alfred A. Knopf.

Peters, Tom. 1992. *Liberation Management: Necessary Disorganization for the Nanosecond Nineties.* New York: Fawcett Columbine.

Peters, Tom. 1993. "Thriving In Chaos." *Working Woman* (September).

Peters, Tom. 1994. "Crazy Times Call for Crazy Organizations," from *The Tom Peters Seminar Success* (July/August).

Plato. *The Republic.* Translated by Allan Bloom. New York: Basic Books, Inc., 1968.

Prigogine, Ilya. 1980. *From Being to Becoming.* San Francisco: W.H. Freeman.

Prigogine, Ilya, and Isabelle Stenger. 1984. *Order Out of Chaos.* New York: Bantam Books.

Reinhold, Barbara Bailey. 1996. *Toxic Work: How to Overcome Stress, Overload, and Burnout and Revitalize Your Career.* New York: A Dutton Book.

Roethke, Theodore. Quoted by Keck, L. Robert, in *Sacred Eyes.* Indianapolis, Indiana: Knowledge Systems, 1992.

Ropaille, G. Clotaire. 1976. *The Creative Communication.* Paris: Dialogues.

Sampson, Edward E. 1975. *Ego at the Threshold.* New York: Delacorte Press.

Sarason, Seymour B. 1977. *Work, Again, and Social Change.* New York: Free Press.

Sardello, Robert. 1992. *Facing the World with Soul: The Reimagination of Modern Life.* Hudson, New York: Lindisfarne.

Saturday Review/World. 1974. "An Inventory of Hope." Fiftieth Anniversary Year Special (December 14).

Schaef, Anne Wilson, and Diane Fassel. 1990. *The Addictive Organization.* San Francisco: Harper & Row.

Scheele, Adele M. 1979. *Skills for Success: A Guide to the Top.* New York: William Morrow & Company.

Scheinin, Richard. 1995. Interview with John Gardner, "The Greater Society." Living Section, *San Jose Mercury News* (Saturday, January 21).

Schor, Juliet B. 1991. *The Overworked American: The Unexpected Decline of Leisure.* USA: Basic Books.

Siegel, Bernie S. 1986. *Love, Medicine & Miracles.* New York: Harper & Row.

Smith, Emily T. 1985. "Are You Creative?" *Business Week* (September 20).

St. John of the Cross. 1577-78. Peers, E. Allison, translator, ed. *St. John of the Cross: Dark Night of the Soul.* Garden City: Doubleday, Image Books, 1959.

Sussman, Linda. 1995. *The Speech of the Grail: A Journey Toward Speaking That Heals and Tranforms.* Hudson, New York: Lindisfarne Press.

Terkel, Studs. 1972. *Working.* New York: Pantheon.

Texas Bar Association. 1991. "The State of the Legal Profession." *Barrister* (Fall).

Texas Medical Association Study. 1993. *The Dallas Morning News* (March 11).

The Futurist. 1992. "Outlook '93." (November-December).

Thoreau, Henry D. 1854. *Walden,* ed. Sandy Lesberg. New York: The Peebles Class Library.

Thoreau, Henry D. 1993. *Faith in a Seed,* ed. B. P. Dean. Washington, D.C.: Island Press, Shearwater Books.

Tiger, Lionel. 1979. "Optimism: The Biological Roots of Hope." *Psychology Today* (January).

Toffler, Alvin. 1970. *Future Shock.* New York: Random House.

Toffler, Alvin, ed. 1974. *Learning for Tomorrow: The Role of the Future in Education.* New York: Vintage Books.

Toffler, Alvin. 1975. *The Eco-Spasm Report.* New York: Bantam Books.

Toffler, Alvin. 1980. *The Third Wave.* New York: William Morrow.

Toffler, Alvin. 1983. *Previews and Premises.* New York: William Morrow and Company, Inc.

Toffler, Alvin. 1990. *Power Shift.* New York: Bantam Books.

Toynbee, Arnold. 1972. *A Study of History.* New York: Oxford University Press.

Troyat, H. 1967. *Tolstoy.* (*Leo Tolstoy in letter to Valerya Arensenyev*, November 9, 1856.) New York: Doubleday.

U.S. Department of Education. 1993-94. "Schools and Staffing Survey," National Center for Education Statistics. Washington, D.C.

Vaillant, George E. 1977. *Adaptation to Life.* Boston/Toronto: Little, Brown & Company.

Viscott, David. 1976. *The Language of Feelings.* New York: Pocket Books.

Waterman, Robert H., Jr., Judith Waterman, and Betsy Collard. 1994. "Toward a Career-Resilient Workforce." *Harvard Business Review* (July/August).

Watts, Alan. 1951. *The Wisdom of Insecurity: A Message for an Age of Anxiety.* New York: Pantheon Books.

Williams, Redford B. 1989. *The Trusting Heart.* New York: Times Books, A Division of Random House.

Wilson, Joan Oliver. 1980. *After Affluence: Economics to Meet Human Needs.* New York: Harper & Row.

Worsham, James. 1996. "The Flip Side of Downsizing." *Nation's Business* (October).

Yankelovich, Daniel. 1981. *New Rules: Searching for Self-Fulfillment in a World Turned Upside Down.* New York: Random House.

Zuckerman, Marilyn R., and Lewis J. Hatala. 1992. *Incredibly American: Releasing the Heart of Quality.* Milwaukee, Wisconsin: ASQC Quality Press.

About the Author

Helen Harkness, Ph.D., who founded Career Design Associates, Inc. (CDA) in 1978 is a creative, resourceful strategist and catalyst in teaching adults how to work and thrive in an age of change and chaos. She is a futurist, a successful entrepreneur in business and investments, an experienced educator and administrator, and a pioneer in the development and implementation of career management programs and resources to assist individuals facing worklife transitions. Her work through Career Design reflects and integrates her own multidimensional career. She is a former academic dean/provost, college professor, and director of continuing education, as well as a director of human services in city government.

Index

absenteeism, and job dissatisfaction, 61
academe, as a retreat, 125, 176–77
achievement analysis, 167–69
age
    and career change, 100–105
    myths about, 116–17
alcohol, problems with, 71
anger, change and, 141
anxiety, change and, 142
archetypes, universal, 50
aspiration, early, and career choice, 185–86
attorneys, career unrest among, 58–59

balls, glass, as priorities, 129, 193, 197
behavior, self-defeating, to eradicate, 192
brainware, 31
burnout, 65

career
    age and, 100–105
    changing. *See* career change
    choice, myths about, 126–27
    creative strategy for, 27
    defining, 98–99
    environment, changing, 108
    explorations of, 153, 159, *160*, 161,
        173–79, 193
    field research on, 173–74, 177–78
    focus and, 153, 159, *160*, 181–87, 193
    myths about, 111–32
    new paradigm for, 150–54
    options, identifying, 109–10, 170–71, 189
    path, changing, 109–10
    planning, myths about, 121–22
    refocusing, 106
    restructuring, 106
    society and, 15–17, 18–19
    specialtization in, 107–108

career change, 3
    barriers to, 114–15
    chaos theory and, 52–54
    first-hand account of, 198–201
    levels of, 105–10
    process of, 157–59, *160*
    radical, 105–106
    steps in, 159–*60*
career content unrest, 71, *72*, 79–82
    exercise to identify, 79
career conversation, 162, 163–64, 175–76
career self unrest, 71, *72*, 83–92
    exercise for identifying, 83
career shock, 4–6, 8–10.
    See also syndrome, career shock
career unrest, 55, 57–60
    effects of, 60–67
    levels of, 71–94
    sources of, 69–71
        exercises for identifying, 73, 76, 79,
        83, 92
challenge, and success, 30
change
    archetypes of, 50–52
    decisions provoked by, 146–50
    and falling apart, 141–42
    fear of, 45, 46–50, 138
    myth about, 113–14
    peak power points for, 198, 201–206
    resistance to, 45–46
    responses to, 28–30
    risk and, 152
    social, 16
    stages of, 134–43
    understanding, 206–207
change-making, success and, 30
chaos
    and change, 134–43, 206–207

chaos *(continued)*
  organizational and industrial, 71, *72,*
    75–78
      exercise to identify, 76
    theory of, 52–54, 138–39
choice, and change, 138–39, 145–46
civilization, crisis in, 17–18
class, and education, 124
collage, personal, 164–65
commitment, 38–41, 84–86, 187
common sense, 32–33
community, sense of, 169–70, 193, 197
compartmentalization, effects of, 86–88
competency, 30–32
complexity, change and, 49–50
confidence, 33–34
control
  and creativity, 25
  lack of, and the fear of change, 47–48
  as a personality trait, 23–24
conversation
  career, 162, 163–64, 175–76
  negative internal, 48
conversion, visualization of future image
  as, 184
cooperation, 41–42
coping
  necessity for, 19
  skills for, 89–92, 93
costs, medical, and career unrest, 61
counterculture, and the fear of change, 48
courage, 34–35
creativity
  and career unrest, 60
  and control, 25
  as a personality trait, 24–28, 166
crisis, midlife, 29
curiosity, 36–38

death, as a triggering event, 139
denial, change and, 141
dentists, career unrest among, 60
depression
  and change, 142
  indicators of, 91
despair, change and, 142, 194
disbelief, change and, 141
disintegration, psychological, and change,
  141–42
disorder, personality, and career unrest, 93
divorce, as a triggering event, 139
doctors, career unrest among, 59
downsizing, effects of, 77, 104–105
dreams, and career choice, 181
drugs, problems with, 71

education

education *(continued)*
  myths about, 123–26
  and status, 64
  value of, 125
enjoyment, importance of, 192
entrepreneurship, as a career change,
    108–109
event, triggering, 138–39
expectations, false, 117–19

facing and solving, as a reaction to change,
    150
failure, road to, 190
family
  environment, and job unrest, 74
  work and, 98, 129–30
fear, and change, 142
fight, as a reaction to change, 146, 147–48
flexibility, 28
flight, as a reaction to change, 146, 148
foresight, 26–27
forgetting, as a reaction to change, 146, 149
formula, for career change, 4, 201
freeze (or fret), as a reaction to change,
    146, 149
fretting, as a reaction to change, 146, 149
frustration, change and, 142
function
  job, and skills for, 80–81, *81*
  overlaid, 79
future image, and career choice, 153, 159,
    160, 161, 181–87, 191, 193
  activating. *See* plan, strategic action

generation, thirteenth, 7
government, as a resource, 57
Grail speech, 174–75
grief, pocket of, 93

health
  and job dissatisfaction, 62–67
  mental, 22–23, 66–67, 94.
    See also problems, personal
heart disease, and job stress, 62–66
help
  asking for, 37, 175, 177–78, 193, 197
  sources of, 57
Holland, John, 163, 170
hope, 34, 35
hostility, and heart disease, 66
hypertension, and feeling of victimization,
    62

identity
  familiar, and change, 135–38
  loss of, 140–41
  work and, 97, 98

identity *(continued)*
income, and career choice, 158
independence. *See* control
industry, changes in, 78
inquiry, as an art, 37
insight, 26
intelligence, 26–27
interview, informational. *See* career conversation
intuition, 25–26
inventory, assessment, 162–63

job
    ambiguity in, 77
    loss of, as a triggering event, 139
    requirements in, 74–75
    sources of, 105, 118, 124–25
job market, and career choice, 127
job unrest, 71, *72*
    defined, 74
    exercise to identify, 73
Jung, Carl G., 3, 163, 171

language, and archetypes, 50
learning, lifelong, 31, 125
life expectancy, 63
lifestyle, balance in, 89, 119
    myths about, 129–30
limbo, change as, 142

meaning
    defined, 85
    and the practice of law, 58–59
    search for, 38–41, 56, 84–86, 158, 182–83
men, roles of, 7, 98
messages, mixed, 40
    and the fear of change, 46–47
middle class, expectations of, 118
midlife
    and career unrest, 87, 102, 182
    crisis, 139
mindset, "either/or," 130–32
money, and meaning, 40, 119–20
motivation, 75, 120–21
myth
    contemporary, about careers, 111–32, 182–83
    Sisyphus, 11–12

needs
    and career choices, 157–58
    inner, and career self unrest, 83
newcomers, career options for, 101

organizations
    change in, 47–48

organizations *(continued)*
    as resources, 57

pain, meaning of, 140–41
paradigm, both/and, 132
paralysis, and change, 142
payoff, identifying, 169
perfectionism
    myths about, 127–29
    as a trap, 90–91
personality
    Type A, 22, 64, 66, 89–90
    Type B, 22
    Type CC Chaos Chaser, 22–23
        personality profile of, 23–42
        thriver technique, 194, 197
plan, strategic action, for career change, 153, 159, *160*, 161, 189–95
policemen, career unrest among, 59–60
population, aging of, 103–104
postponement, as a reaction to change, 148
power
    information as a source of, 178
    personal, 186–87
    points, 198, 201–206
powerlessness, and change, 142
priorities, as glass balls, 129
problems
    handling, 197
    personal
        and career unrest, 71, *72*, 92–94, 179
        exercise for identifying, 92
productivity, and career unrest, 61
Proteus Principles, 12–13, 17, 173
psychology, shift in, as a triggering event, 139
psychosynthesis, 132
puzzle pieces, remembering and surfacing, 162, 164–66

quality, as a notion, 51
questions
    about career change, 157–58, *160*, 207
    about career choice, 127
    about career unrest, 70–71
    asking, 174–75, 177–78
    and the search for meaning, 56
    for the strategic action plan, 190
quick fix, and the fear of change, 48–49

reappraisal, age of, and career options, 101–102
recovery, safety valve for, 194–95
resilience, 34, 35–36
responsibility
    and job unrest, 77
    personal, 153

retirees, and career options, 102–103
retirement, traditional, 103–104
revenge, change and, 141
reward, myths about, 122–23
risk, and change, 152
rites of passage, 134
running, and change, 142–43

safety valve, 194–95, 197
savings, and retirement, 104
self
    autotelic, 29
    false, 93–94, 144
self-assessment, and career change, 153,
        159, *160*, 161–72, 175, 190, 193
self-concept, work and, 97, 98, 115
self-destruction, as a reaction to change,
        143
self-esteem
    building, 193
    and career choice, 166
    and heart disease, 64
self-management (adaptation), skills in,
81–82, *82*
self-renewal, and change, 53
shock, change and, 141.
        See also career shock
Sisyphus. *See* syndrome
skills
    acquiring new, 21
    adaptive, 21–22, 81–82, *82*, 123
    and career choice, 79–82, 158
    functional, 164
    identifying, 162, 164, 166–72
    technical, 123
soul
    dark night of the, 17, 40, 132, 133–44,
        146
    values and, 38
specialization
    changing, 107–108
    effects of, 88, 131
spirit, hardiness of, 33–34
spirituality, 38
stability, and heart disease, 64
status, and education, 124
status quo, 135–38
stress, occupational, and heart disease,
        64–66
students, college, career options for, 101
success
    acknowledging, 193
    conditions for, 190
    costs of, 23
    defining, 120
    expectations for, 6–7, 99
    formula for, 7–8

success *(continued)*
    identifying criteria for, 162, 163, 166,
        170, 197
    myths about, 119–21
suicide, 60
survivor, creative, 29
syndrome
    career shock, 8–10
    Sisyphus, 11–12, 17, 55, 66
    survivor's, 77

teamwork, collaborative, 41–42
technology
    and change, 8
    and human interaction, 39
    skills for, 80
Theory, Dr. Holland's Hexagon, 170
time, required for self-assessment, 161–62
tool
    acquiring, 153
    career assessment, 162–63
trait, personality, and success, 23–24
transcendence, 29
transfer, lateral, 82
transformation, change as, 51–52
type. *See* personality

unconscious, the cultural, 51
unemployment, and self–image, 98

values, changing, 113
victim, mentality of, 55, 62
visualization
    and career choice, 183–85
    failure of, 49
vocation. *See* commitment

weakness, myths about, 126
wholeness, pursuit of, and career unrest,
        86–89
women, roles of, 7, 98
work
    dissatisfaction with, 58–60
        and heart disease, 62–66
    functions of, 97–98
    meaning of, 40, 95–98, 158, 182
workaholism, 89–90
workshop, for skills assessment, 166–67